Aleph Isn't Enough

HEBREW FOR ADULTS
Book II

LINDA MOTZKIN

HARA PERSON, SERIES EDITOR

Hebrew Literacy Task Force

Co-Chairs

Jan Katzew

Lawrence Raphael

Rick Abrams

Andrew Davids

Sharon Forman

Dan Freelander

Dru Greenwood

Deborah Joselow

Hara Person

Jamie Rosenberg

Peter Schaktman

Linda Thal

Josée Wolff

Eric Yoffie

Acknowledgments

Aleph Isn't Enough, Book II is the second book in the new UAHC adult Hebrew series. Along with the first book, *Aleph Isn't Tough, Book I*, it owes its existence to the vision of Rabbi Eric Yoffie, President of the UAHC, who inaugurated an historic campaign in 1996 to revive Hebrew literacy throughout the Reform Movement. The UAHC Hebrew Literacy Task Force, co-chaired by Rabbis Jan Katzew and Lawrence Raphael, was convened to respond to this challenge and provided direction and input in the development of this series.

Many rabbis and educators in the field of Hebrew-language instruction were consulted regarding the development of this series. The following individuals graciously shared their perspectives and provided suggestions regarding adult Hebrew learning. While all their views may not have been incorporated into this book, their willingness to contribute their ideas was greatly appreciated: Sylvia Abrams, Deborah Eisenbach-Budner, Susie Cook, Sarah Gluck, Rabbi Paula Feldstein, Rabbi Doug Kohn, Shlomit Lipton, Dina Maiben, and Iris Petroff.

Some of the individuals named above also piloted this text in adult classes in their communities. I am grateful to all the students and teachers in the following congregations for their feedback, which was critical to the final shaping of the book: Temple Beth Israel, Altoona, PA; Congregation Achduth Vesholom, Fort Wayne, IN; Temple Shaaray Tefila, New York, NY; Temple Beth-El, Hillsborough, NJ; Central Synagogue, New York, NY; Beth Tikvah Congregation, Hoffman Estates, IL; Beth Torah Temple, Philadelphia, PA; Central Reform Congregation, St. Louis, MO; Temple Society of Concord, Syracuse, NY; The Scarsdale Synagogue–Tremont Temple, Scarsdale, NY; Temple Emanuel, Worcester, MA; Temple Sinai, Toronto, ONT; Temple Anshe Amunim, Pittsfield, MA; Congregation Kol Haverim, Glastonbury, CT; Kehillat Israel, Pacific Palisades, CA; Temple Brith Achim, King of Prussia, PA; and Central Synagogue, Rockville Centre, NY.

I had the good fortune of piloting this text in my own congregation, Temple Sinai of Saratoga Springs, NY, with a wonderful group of outstanding and dedicated students. My thanks to each of the following for their feedback and enthusiasm and for allowing me to share my love of Hebrew: Lollie Abramson Stark, Catherine Golden, Dianna Goodwin, Ingrid Gordon, Johnna Maiorella, Michael Maiorella, Naomi Meyer, Trudi Renwick, Art Ruben, Ellen Sheets, Robyn Silverman, and Patti Steinberger.

At the UAHC Press, a number of people assisted in the publication of this book. First and foremost, my heartfelt thanks go to Rabbi Hara Person, editor of the UAHC Press, whose input was as essential and invaluable for this second book as for the first. Those who assisted in all the various aspects of the production of this book include Ken Gesser, Stuart Benick, Debra Hirsch Corman, Liane Broido, Helaine Denenberg, Eric Eisenkramer, Rick Abrams, and Itzhack Shelomi.

On a personal level, I am grateful beyond words for being blessed with a wonderful husband and life-partner, Rabbi Jonathan Rubenstein, who provided support and assistance to this project at all hours of the day and night. For his love and patience, and for that of our three children, Rachel, Ari, and Shira, I am deeply thankful.

The author gratefully acknowledges the following for permission to reprint previously published material:

BLOCH PUBLISHING COMPANY: Excerpts from *The Authorized Daily Prayer Book* by Joseph H. Hertz, published by Bloch Publishing Co., copyright © 1948. Used by permission of Bloch Publishing Company.

CENTRAL CONFERENCE OF AMERICAN RABBIS: Excerpts from *Gates of Prayer for Shabbat and Weekdays: A Gender Sensitive Prayerbook*, edited by Chaim Stern, copyright © 1994 by Central Conference of American Rabbis and are reproduced by permission; excerpts from *On the Doorposts of Your House*, edited by Chaim Stern, copyright © 1994 by Central Conference of American Rabbis and are reproduced by permission; excerpts from *Gates of Prayer*, edited by Chaim Stern, copyright © 1975 by Central Conference of American Rabbis and are reproduced by permission; excerpt from *The Open Door*, edited by Sue Levi Elwell, copyright © 2001 by Central Conference of American Rabbis and is reproduced by permission.

HEBREW PUBLISHING COMPANY: Excerpts from *Daily Prayer Book*, transl. Philip Birnbaum 1949, Hebrew Publishing Co., Spencertown, NY. Used by permission of Hebrew Publishing Company; excerpt from The Passover Haggadah, transl. Philip Birnbaum 1953, Hebrew Publishing Co., Spencertown, NY. Used by permission of Hebrew Publishing Company.

KTAV PUBLISHING HOUSE, INC.: Excerpt from *On Wings of Freedom: The Hillel Haggadah for the Nights of Passover*, by Richard N. Levy, copyright © 1989. Used by permission of KTAV Publishing House, Inc.

RECONSTRUCTIONIST PRESS: Excerpts from *Kol Haneshamah: Shabbat Vehagim* © 1994. Used by permission of the Reconstructionist Press; excerpts from *Kol Haneshamah: Shirim Uvrahot* © 1998. Used by permission of the Reconstructionist Press.

THE RABBINICAL ASSEMBLY: Reprinted from *Siddur Sim Shalom*, edited by Rabbi Jules Harlow. Copyright by The Rabbinical Assembly, 1985. Reprinted by permission of The Rabbinical Assembly. Reprinted from *Feast of Freedom*, ed. Rachel Anne Rabinowicz, 1982, Rabbinical Assembly. Reprinted with permission. *Sabbath and Festival Prayerbook*, p. 304. Copyright by The Rabbinical Assembly, 1946. Reprinted by permission of The Rabbinical Assembly.

A Note on the Translations

The translations provided in this book for all the Reading Practice selections are as close to literal as possible, so that you can easily compare them with the original language. In some instances, a word or phrase is followed by another possible translation that is included in brackets {like this}. A different style of brackets [like this] occasionally appears in this book and is used to indicate words not included in the Hebrew that have been inserted for clarity in the English translation.

The terms "Eternal One," "the Eternal One," or "the Eternal" are used throughout this book as the translations for the symbol יְיָ and the four letters יהוה. The Hebrew pronouns used in the Bible and in the prayer book to refer to God can be translated literally as either "He" or "Him" or "His" (or as "It" or "Its"). In this book, we have chosen to translate such pronouns as "God" and "God's" followed by brackets {like this} indicating the literal masculine translation. (A fuller explanation of gender issues in translation is included in Chapter 2, in Extra Credit.)

Table of Contents

Welcome

בְּרוּכִים הַבָּאִים

Each chapter of this book begins with a section of Hebrew reading practice, consisting of excerpts from the prayer book, Bible, or other Jewish texts, or common Hebrew expressions. Many of these excerpts include the symbol יְיָ, used as a substitute for the unpronounceable four-letter name of God, יהוה. When encountering the symbol יְיָ or the four letters יהוה, the most common practice is to pronounce each of them as *Adonai* (a form of the Hebrew word meaning "Lord"). The traditional practice is to say *Adonai* only when actually engaged in prayer, otherwise substituting the word *HaShem* (which means "the Name"). In our day, some suggest using alternatives to the masculine term *Adonai* such as *Yah* (the first two letters of the four-letter name of God) or the feminine term *Shechinah* ("Divine Presence"). As you read aloud, choose the word you prefer as a substitution for the symbol יְיָ. Feel free to experiment.

Reading Practice

Blessing Formula

בָּרוּךְ אַתָּה יְיָ

Blessed are You, Eternal One

Bar'chu

בָּרְכוּ אֶת יְיָ הַמְבֹרָךְ.
בָּרוּךְ יְיָ הַמְבֹרָךְ לְעוֹלָם וָעֶד.

Bless the Eternal One, the blessed One.
Blessed is the Eternal One, the blessed One, forever and ever.

Shema and **Baruch Shem**

שְׁמַע יִשְׂרָאֵל, יְיָ אֱלֹהֵינוּ, יְיָ אֶחָד:
בָּרוּךְ שֵׁם כְּבוֹד מַלְכוּתוֹ לְעוֹלָם וָעֶד.

Hear, Israel: the Eternal is our God, the Eternal is One.
Blessed is the name of the glory of God's {His} sovereignty forever and ever.

Expressions

בָּרוּךְ הַשֵּׁם

Thank God! {Literally: Blessed is the Name.}

בְּרוּכִים הַבָּאִים

Welcome! {Literally: Blessed are the ones who come.}

Psalm 118:26 (included in circumcision and marriage ceremonies)

בָּרוּךְ הַבָּא בְּשֵׁם יְיָ

Blessed is the one who comes in the name of the Eternal.

From the Introduction to *Birkat HaMazon*—The Blessing after Meals

בָּרוּךְ הוּא וּבָרוּךְ שְׁמוֹ

Blessed is God {He} and blessed is God's {His} name.

Vocabulary

Each chapter contains a list of seven or eight basic vocabulary words to be learned. These words have been chosen because they appear frequently in Hebrew texts or are often used in Jewish life. Try to locate each of these words in the Reading Practice selections above.

blessed *m*	—	בָּרוּךְ
you *m*	—	אַתָּה
he, it *m*	—	הוּא
Israel *m*	—	יִשְׂרָאֵל
name *m*	—	שֵׁם
universe, eternity, world *m*	—	עוֹלָם
forever and ever	—	לְעוֹלָם וָעֶד

Note:

1. Sometimes a Hebrew word can have more than one meaning in English. For example, the word עוֹלָם can refer to both vast time, "eternity," and vast space, "universe." It can also be used to mean "world." It is usually clear from the context which is the best translation.

2. Most Hebrew words are grammatically either masculine or feminine, and this is indicated in the vocabulary of each chapter with the abbreviation *m* or *f*. A fuller explanation of grammatical gender is provided in Chapter 2.

Hebrew Roots

Most Hebrew words are built around a combination of three letters called a root. Many different words can be formed from the same root by changing the vowels or attaching prefixes or suffixes. Words that share the same root are generally related.

Knowledge of basic roots makes it possible to recognize the core meaning of many different Hebrew words. Each chapter of this book will present two basic Hebrew roots, both of which appear in the Reading Practice at the beginning of the chapter.

בּ־ר־ךּ

The root בּ־ר־ךּ has the basic meaning of "bless." The following words from the Reading Practice selections of this chapter are derived from this root:

blessed	—	בָּרוּךְ
bless (command form)	—	בָּרְכוּ
the blessed one	—	הַמְבֹרָךְ
blessed	—	בְּרוּכִים

The word בְּרָכָה, a "blessing," is also derived from this root.

שׁ־מ־ע

The root שׁ־מ־ע has the basic meaning of "hear," "listen," or "obey." It is the root of the word *Shema*: שְׁמַע, which is the only word from this root appearing in the Reading Practice selections of this chapter. The following are other Hebrew words derived from this root:

announcement, proclamation	—	שְׁמוּעַ
rumor, report	—	שְׁמוּעָה
audible	—	שָׁמִיעַ
hearing	—	שְׁמִיעָה
audibility	—	שְׁמִיעוּת
auditory, aural	—	שְׁמִיעָתִי
announcing, proclaiming	—	הַשְׁמָעָה
obedient	—	מְמֻשְׁמָע
obedience	—	מִשְׁמַעַת

CHAPTER 1

Building Blocks

Attached Letters: The Prefix הַ

Many words that are expressed in English as independent words are formed in Hebrew by attaching additional letters as prefixes or suffixes onto other words. For example, the English word "the" is expressed in Hebrew by attaching the letter הַ, usually with the vowel ⬚ but occasionally with the vowels ⬚ or ⬚, to the beginning of a word. Most of the following examples appear in this chapter's Reading Practice selections.

name	—	שֵׁם
the name	—	הַשֵּׁם
universe	—	עוֹלָם
the universe	—	הָעוֹלָם
blessed one	—	מְבֹרָךְ
the blessed one	—	הַמְבֹרָךְ
comes, one who comes	—	בָּא
the one who comes	—	הַבָּא
come, ones who come	—	בָּאִים
the ones who come	—	הַבָּאִים

"A" or "An" in Hebrew

There is no word in Hebrew for the English word "a" or "an." Rather, depending on the context, it is implied. For example, the Hebrew word שֵׁם could be translated as either "name" or "a name." The word עוֹלָם could be translated as "eternity" or "an eternity," or "universe" or "a universe," or "world" or "a world," depending on the context.

The Simple Sentence

In English, the simplest noun sentence consists of three words: *Sam is big.* In Hebrew, a simple sentence can be formed with just two words, without using any verb at all. This is because there is no present tense form of the verb "to be" in Hebrew. There is no word in Hebrew for the English words "is," "am," or "are." They must be inserted in the English translation, as in the following examples:

He *is* Israel. or It *is* Israel.	—	הוּא יִשְׂרָאֵל.
You *are* blessed.	—	אַתָּה בָּרוּךְ.

The following examples of simple sentences are taken from the Reading Practice at the beginning of this chapter:

Blessed *are* you.	—	בָּרוּךְ אַתָּה.
Blessed *is* the Eternal One.	—	בָּרוּךְ יְיָ.
The Eternal *is* our God.	—	יְיָ אֱלֹהֵינוּ.
The Eternal *is* One.	—	יְיָ אֶחָד.
Blessed *is* the name.	—	בָּרוּךְ הַשֵּׁם.
Blessed *are* the ones who come.	—	בְּרוּכִים הַבָּאִים.
Blessed *is* the one who comes.	—	בָּרוּךְ הַבָּא.
Blessed *is* he. *or* Blessed *is* it.	—	בָּרוּךְ הוּא.

Note that it can take as many as five or six English words to translate two Hebrew words. Often it is possible to translate a Hebrew phrase in more than one way. A good example of this is provided by the *Shema*:

$$\text{שְׁמַע יִשְׂרָאֵל, יְיָ אֱלֹהֵינוּ, יְיָ אֶחָד:}$$

Hear, Israel: the Eternal is our God, the Eternal is One.

The following are translations of the *Shema* from different prayer books. The name of God is variously rendered in English as "*Adonai*," "the Lord," "the Eternal One," and "the Eternal." The word שְׁמַע is translated as "Listen" and as "Hear." More significant, however, are the differences in meaning resulting from the translation of the last four words. The placement of the word "is" subtly changes the meaning of the entire statement. The *Shema* could primarily be an assertion of the oneness of God, as in the translation "the Lord our God, the Lord is One!" Or it could be two separate assertions, as in the translation "the Lord is our God, the Lord is One!" Or it could be an assertion that the Eternal is our God, as opposed to any other gods. In such translations, the English word "is" appears only once, and the Hebrew word אֶחָד is translated figuratively, not literally, as "alone": "the Eternal One is our God, the Eternal One alone!"

Hear, O Israel: the Eternal One is our God, the Eternal God alone!

GATES OF PRAYER FOR SHABBAT AND WEEKDAYS: A GENDER SENSITIVE PRAYERBOOK, ED. CHAIM STERN. NEW YORK: CCAR PRESS, 1994.

Hear, O Israel: the Lord is our God, the Lord is One.

DAILY PRAYER BOOK, TRANS. PHILLIP BIRNBAUM. NEW YORK: HEBREW PUBLISHING CO., 1949. (THE SAME TRANSLATION ALSO APPEARS IN GATES OF PRAYER: THE NEW UNION PRAYERBOOK, ED. CHAIM STERN. NEW YORK: CCAR PRESS, 1975.)

Hear, O Israel: the Lord our God, the Lord is One!

SABBATH AND FESTIVAL PRAYER BOOK, ED. MORRIS SILVERMAN. THE RABBINICAL ASSEMBLY OF AMERICA AND THE UNITED SYNAGOGUE OF AMERICA, 1946.

Listen, Israel: The Eternal is our God, the Eternal One alone!

KOL HANESHAMAH: SHABBAT VEHAGIM. WYNCOTE, PA.: THE RECONSTRUCTIONIST PRESS, 1994.

Hear, O Israel: Adonai is our God, Adonai alone.

SIDDUR SIM SHALOM FOR SHABBAT AND FESTIVALS. NEW YORK: THE RABBINICAL ASSEMBLY, 1998.

GRAMMAR Enrichment

Pronouns

The vocabulary list for this chapter includes two Hebrew pronouns: הוּא, which means "he" or "it," and אַתָּה, which means "you." These two were included because they are the pronouns that appear most frequently in the Bible and the prayer book.

A full chart of all the subject pronouns in Hebrew is included here for your general information. It is not necessary to memorize all these pronouns in order to do the readings and exercises in this book.

	Plural		Singular		
we	אֲנַחְנוּ, אָנוּ	I	אֲנִי, אָנֹכִי	*first person*
you *(masculine)*	אַתֶּם	you *(masculine)*	אַתָּה	*second person*
you *(feminine)*	אַתֶּן	you *(feminine)*	אַתְּ	
they *(masculine)*	הֵם, הֵמָּה	he, it *(masculine)*	הוּא	*third person*
they *(feminine)*	הֵן, הֵנָּה	she, it *(feminine)*	הִיא	

Note that there are more subject pronouns in Hebrew than in English, which has only seven: I, you, he, she, it, we, they. In part, this is due to the fact that all Hebrew pronouns, except the first-person "I" and "we" forms, have grammatical gender: masculine or feminine. For example, there are four different ways in Hebrew to say the subject pronoun "you," depending upon whether one is addressing a single male, a single female, a group of males, or a group of females. A fuller explanation of grammatical gender in Hebrew will be provided in the next chapter.

FROM OUR TEXTS

Blessings

The act of saying a blessing, a בְּרָכָה, when eating or drinking or seeing a rainbow or enjoying some other aspect of Creation is an acknowledgment that all that exists belongs to God. In a sense, we earn the privilege of enjoying our blessings through our expressed awareness that they are divine gifts.

In the following talmudic passage, two seemingly contradictory verses from the Bible are linked to reflect this view:

אָמַר רַב יְהוּדָה אָמַר שְׁמוּאֵל: כָּל הַנֶּהֱנֶה מִן הָעוֹלָם הַזֶּה בְּלֹא
בְּרָכָה כְּאִילוּ נֶהֱנָה מִקָּדְשֵׁי שָׁמַיִם, שֶׁנֶּאֱמַר: "לַה' הָאָרֶץ וּמְלוֹאָהּ."
ר' לֵוִי רְמֵי כְּתִיב "לַה' הָאָרֶץ וּמְלוֹאָהּ" וּכְתִיב "הַשָּׁמַיִם שָׁמַיִם לַיהוָה
וְהָאָרֶץ נָתַן לִבְנֵי־אָדָם." לֹא קַשְׁיָא כָּאן קוֹדֶם בְּרָכָה כָּאן לְאַחַר בְּרָכָה.

Rav Judah said that Rav Shmuel said: One who enjoys something from this world without a blessing is like one who makes personal use of things consecrated to heaven, as it is said: "The earth belongs to the Eternal One, and all its fullness" (Psalm 24:1). R. Levi noted the following contradiction: It is written (in Psalm 24:1) that "The earth belongs to the Eternal One, and all its fullness," but it is written (in Psalm 115:16) that "The heavens are the heavens of the Eternal One, but the earth was given to human beings." There is no contradiction between these verses. The first verse (Psalm 24:1) describes reality before a blessing is said and the second verse (Psalm 115:16) after a blessing is said.

BERACHOT 35A–B

Exercises

1. Draw a line connecting each Hebrew word to its English translation. For some words, there can be more than one correct English translation.

1) blessed	5) לְעוֹלָם וָעֶד
2) universe	1) בָּרוּךְ
3) he	4) יִשְׂרָאֵל
4) Israel	8) אַתָּה
5) forever and ever	2), 9) עוֹלָם
6) name	6) שֵׁם
7) it	3), 7) הוּא
8) you	
9) eternity	

2. Read and translate the following sentences.

a. בָּרוּךְ אַתָּה. _____

b. בָּרוּךְ הוּא. _____

c. בָּרוּךְ יִשְׂרָאֵל. _____

d. בָּרוּךְ הַשֵּׁם. _____

e. בָּרוּךְ הָעוֹלָם. _____

f. הוּא יִשְׂרָאֵל. _____

g. אַתָּה יִשְׂרָאֵל. _____

h. אַתָּה בָּרוּךְ. _____

i. הוּא הַשֵּׁם. _____

j. הוּא הָעוֹלָם. _____

k. הָעוֹלָם בָּרוּךְ לְעוֹלָם וָעֶד. _____

l. בָּרוּךְ הַשֵּׁם לְעוֹלָם וָעֶד. _____

3. Circle the words in the following prayer book excerpt that are derived from the root בּ-ר-ךּ.

The End of *Birkat Shalom* (*Shalom Rav* and *Sim Shalom*)

וְטוֹב בְּעֵינֶיךָ לְבָרֵךְ אֶת עַמְּךָ יִשְׂרָאֵל בְּכָל עֵת וּבְכָל שָׁעָה
בִּשְׁלוֹמֶךָ. בָּרוּךְ אַתָּה יְיָ, הַמְבָרֵךְ אֶת עַמּוֹ יִשְׂרָאֵל בַּשָּׁלוֹם.

And it is good in Your eyes to bless Your people Israel at every time and in every hour with Your peace. Blessed are You, Eternal One, the One who blesses God's {His} people Israel with peace.

4. Circle the words in the following prayer book excerpt that are derived from the root שׁ-מ-ע.

From the Weekday *Amidah*

שְׁמַע קוֹלֵנוּ, יְיָ אֱלֹהֵינוּ, חוּס וְרַחֵם עָלֵינוּ, וְקַבֵּל בְּרַחֲמִים
וּבְרָצוֹן אֶת תְּפִלָּתֵנוּ, כִּי אֵל שׁוֹמֵעַ תְּפִלּוֹת וְתַחֲנוּנִים
אָתָּה. בָּרוּךְ אַתָּה יְיָ, שׁוֹמֵעַ תְּפִלָּה.

Hear our voice, Eternal our God, have mercy and compassion upon us, and receive with compassion and with favor our prayer, for a God who hears prayers and supplications are You. Blessed are You, Eternal One, hearer of prayer.

5. Translate the following biblical excerpts, using the extra vocabulary words provided in addition to the words introduced in this chapter. Check your translations against the English translations that follow.

a. **From I Samuel 25:32**

the Eternal One (*the unpronounceable four-letter name of God*) —	יְהֹוָה
God of —	אֱלֹהֵי

בָּרוּךְ יְהֹוָה אֱלֹהֵי יִשְׂרָאֵל...

b. From I Chronicles 29:10

the Eternal One *(the unpronounceable four-letter name of God)*	—	יְהוָֹה
God of	—	אֱלֹהֵי
our father	—	אָבִינוּ
from *(attached prefix)*	—	מֵ־
and unto	—	וְעַד

...בָּרוּךְ אַתָּה יְהוָֹה אֱלֹהֵי יִשְׂרָאֵל אָבִינוּ מֵעוֹלָם וְעַד־עוֹלָם:

c. Deuteronomy 28:3, 6

in the city	—	בָּעִיר
and *(attached prefix)*	—	וּ־
in the field	—	בַשָׂדֶה
in your coming {when you come}	—	בְּבֹאֶךָ
in your leaving {when you leave}	—	בְּצֵאתֶךָ

בָּרוּךְ אַתָּה בָּעִיר וּבָרוּךְ אַתָּה בַּשָׂדֶה: בָּרוּךְ אַתָּה בְּבֹאֶךָ
וּבָרוּךְ אַתָּה בְּצֵאתֶךָ:

Translations:
a. From I Samuel 25:32—Blessed is the Eternal One, God of Israel...

b. From I Chronicles 29:10—...blessed are You, Eternal One, God of Israel, our Father, from eternity and unto eternity.

c. Deuteronomy 28:3, 6—Blessed are you in the city and blessed are you in the field. Blessed are you in your coming {when you come} and blessed are you in your leaving {when you leave}.

EXTRA CREDIT

Individual and Communal Prayer

One need not be in a synagogue or be part of a community service in order to open one's heart in prayer. Nonetheless, the Jewish tradition regards communal prayer as optimal. In the Talmud (*Berachot 6a*), it is written:

How do you know that if ten people pray together the Divine Presence is with them? For it is said: "God stands in the congregation of God." [אֱלֹהִים נִצָּב בַּעֲדַת־אֵל] *(Psalm 82:1)*

This view is also reflected in the following Chasidic story:

Once in a tropical country, a certain splendid bird, more colorful than any that had ever been seen, was sighted at the top of the tallest tree. The bird's plumage contained within it all the colors of the world. But the bird was perched so high that no single person could ever hope to reach it. When news of the bird reached the ears of the king, he ordered that a number of men try to bring the bird to him. They were to stand on one another's shoulders until the highest man could reach the bird and bring it to the king. The men assembled near the tree, but while they were standing, balanced on one another's shoulders, some of those near the bottom decided to wander off. As soon as the first man moved, the entire chain collapsed, injuring several of the men. Still the bird remained uncaptured.

The men had doubly failed the king. For even greater than his desire to see the bird was his wish to see his people so closely joined to one another. [Or Ha-Hokhmah 4:31b–32a]

FROM *YOUR WORD IS FIRE: THE HASIDIC MASTERS ON CONTEMPLATIVE PRAYER*, ED. ARTHUR GREEN AND BARRY W. HOLTZ. WOODSTOCK, VT.: JEWISH LIGHTS PUBLISHING, 1993.

Communal prayer establishes a connection not only between ourselves and the Most High, but between ourselves and our community. Most of the prayers in our prayer book are worded in the plural, reflecting that when we engage in communal prayer, we pray not by ourselves nor for ourselves alone, but within and for a larger community. The members of a community can assist one another in lifting up their prayers higher than any might reach alone, just as voices joined in song produce a stronger sound and beautiful harmonies that a single voice cannot accomplish.

Certain prayers are traditionally said only in the context of community, which for the purpose of prayer is defined as ten adult Jews (age thirteen or older). Such a prayer quorum is called a minyan. Reform and other liberal Jewish communities include women along with men in the minyan.

The Reading Practice selections at the beginning of this chapter include both individual prayers and prayers requiring a minyan. An example of a communal prayer is the *Bar'chu*, sometimes termed "the Call to Worship." It consists of a line said by the prayer leader followed by a congregational response, and it signals the beginning of community prayer in the evening and morning services. On the other hand, most blessings that begin with the words בָּרוּךְ אַתָּה יְיָ are individual prayers. An obvious exception are the blessings said before and after the reading of the Torah, which always occurs in a communal context.

Review

In Chapter 1, six vocabulary words and one Hebrew phrase were introduced:

שֵׁם הוּא בָּרוּךְ עוֹלָם אַתָּה יִשְׂרָאֵל לְעוֹלָם וָעֶד

Two Hebrew roots were introduced:

ב־ר־ךְ   שׁ־מ־ע

The following Building Blocks were presented:
1. The letter הַ is used as a prefix to mean "the."
2. There is no word in Hebrew for "a" or "an."
3. A simple sentence can be formed without a verb.

Reading Practice

Passover Four Questions

מַה נִּשְׁתַּנָּה הַלַּיְלָה הַזֶּה מִכָּל הַלֵּילוֹת?

שֶׁבְּכָל הַלֵּילוֹת אָנוּ אוֹכְלִין חָמֵץ וּמַצָּה. הַלַּיְלָה הַזֶּה כֻּלּוֹ מַצָּה.

שֶׁבְּכָל הַלֵּילוֹת אָנוּ אוֹכְלִין שְׁאָר יְרָקוֹת הַלַּיְלָה הַזֶּה מָרוֹר.

שֶׁבְּכָל הַלֵּילוֹת אֵין אָנוּ מַטְבִּילִין אֲפִילוּ פַּעַם אֶחָת. הַלַּיְלָה הַזֶּה שְׁתֵּי פְעָמִים.

שֶׁבְּכָל הַלֵּילוֹת אָנוּ אוֹכְלִין בֵּין יוֹשְׁבִין וּבֵין מְסֻבִּין. הַלַּיְלָה הַזֶּה כֻּלָּנוּ מְסֻבִּין.

What differentiates this night from all the [other] nights?

that on all the [other] nights we eat leavened foods and matzah; this night—all of it is matzah.

that on all the [other] nights we eat the rest of vegetables; this night—bitter herb.

that on all the [other] nights we do not dip even one time; this night—two times.

that on all the [other] nights we eat either sitting or reclining; this night—all of us are reclining.

Va-anachnu

וַאֲנַחְנוּ כּוֹרְעִים וּמִשְׁתַּחֲוִים וּמוֹדִים, לִפְנֵי מֶלֶךְ מַלְכֵי
הַמְּלָכִים, הַקָּדוֹשׁ בָּרוּךְ הוּא.

And we bend the knee and bow and give thanks before the Sovereign of sovereigns of sovereigns, the Holy One, blessed is God {He}.

For each of the following Passover seder blessings, two different versions appear. The first is the traditional version, which uses grammatically masculine language to refer to God. The second, an alternate version using grammatically feminine language to refer to God, is from the Reform Movement's haggadah *The Open Door*.

Passover Seder—Blessing over Matzah

בָּרוּךְ אַתָּה יְיָ אֱלֹהֵינוּ מֶלֶךְ הָעוֹלָם, אֲשֶׁר קִדְּשָׁנוּ בְּמִצְוֹתָיו
וְצִוָּנוּ עַל אֲכִילַת מַצָּה.

Blessed are You, Eternal our God, Sovereign of the universe, who makes us holy with God's {His} mitzvot and commands us regarding eating of matzah.

בְּרוּכָה אַתְּ יָהּ אֱלֹהֵינוּ רוּחַ הָעוֹלָם, אֲשֶׁר קִדְּשָׁתְנוּ
בְּמִצְוֹתֶיהָ וְצִוַּתְנוּ עַל אֲכִילַת מַצָּה.

Blessed are You, Yah our God, Soul {Spirit} of the world, who makes us holy with God's {Her} mitzvot and commands us regarding eating of matzah.

Passover Seder—Blessing over Bitter Herb

בָּרוּךְ אַתָּה יְיָ אֱלֹהֵינוּ מֶלֶךְ הָעוֹלָם, אֲשֶׁר קִדְּשָׁנוּ בְּמִצְוֹתָיו
וְצִוָּנוּ עַל אֲכִילַת מָרוֹר.

Blessed are You, Eternal our God, Sovereign of the universe, who makes us holy with God's {His} mitzvot and commands us regarding eating of bitter herb.

בְּרוּכָה אַתְּ יָהּ אֱלֹהֵינוּ רוּחַ הָעוֹלָם, אֲשֶׁר קִדְּשָׁתְנוּ
בְּמִצְוֹתֶיהָ וְצִוַּתְנוּ עַל אֲכִילַת מָרוֹר.

Blessed are You, Yah our God, Soul {Spirit} of the world, who makes us holy with God's {Her} mitzvot and commands us regarding eating of bitter herb.

Passover Seder Blessing over Matzah

Translations

As mentioned previously, the translations provided in this book for the Reading Practice selections are as close to literal as possible, to enable you to easily compare them with the original language. This is also true of other Hebrew excerpts, with the exception of the "From Our Texts" sections. Literal translations, however, often sound awkward in English. Most translations of liturgical Hebrew are not literal, but rather seek to provide language that is appropriate for prayer. As the last chapter demonstrated with the *Shema*, different translations will lend different nuances to a prayer. Each chapter will now include a section providing different translations of one of the chapter's Reading Practice selections.

The first selection below provides the translations of both the feminine and masculine versions of the Passover seder blessing over matzah included in *The Open Door* Haggadah. The remaining selections are translations of the traditional masculine-language version.

Blessed are You, our God, Soul of the world, who sanctifies us with mitzvot and calls upon us to eat matzah.

Blessed are You, our God, Ruler of the world, who sanctifies us with mitzvot and commands us to eat matzah.

THE OPEN DOOR, ED. SUE LEVI ELWELL. NEW YORK: CCAR PRESS, 2001.

You are praised, Adonai our God, Monarch of time and space, who shares Your holiness with us through Your mitzvot, and now bestows upon us the mitzvah of eating matzah.

ON WINGS OF FREEDOM: THE HILLEL HAGGADAH FOR THE NIGHTS OF PASSOVER, ED. RICHARD N. LEVY. HOBOKEN, N.J.: B'NAI B'RITH HILLEL FOUNDATIONS IN ASSOCIATION WITH KTAV PUBLISHING HOUSE, 1989.

Praised are You, Adonai our God, King of the universe, who has sanctified our lives through His commandments, commanding us to partake of matzah.

THE FEAST OF FREEDOM, ED. RACHEL ANNE RABINOWICZ. NEW YORK: THE RABBINICAL ASSEMBLY, 1982.

Blessed art thou, Lord our God, King of the universe, who hast sanctified us with thy commandments, and commanded us concerning the eating of matzah.

THE PASSOVER HAGGADAH, TRANS. PHILLIP BIRNBAUM. NEW YORK: HEBREW PUBLISHING CO., 1953.

Vocabulary

Try to locate each of these words in the Reading Practice selections (Passover Four Questions, *Va-anachnu*, or blessings over matzah and bitter herb). Some of these words appear with pre-fixes and/or suffixes attached.

leavened food *(food not permitted during Passover) m*	—	חָמֵץ
matzah, unleavened bread *f*	—	מַצָּה
bitter herb *m*	—	מָרוֹר
night *m*	—	לַיְלָה
mitzvah, commandment *f*	—	מִצְוָה
sovereign, king, ruler *m*	—	מֶלֶךְ
we *m* or *f*	—	אֲנַחְנוּ, אָנוּ

Note: The words אָנוּ and אֲנַחְנוּ both mean "we" and can be used interchangeably. Both are used for masculine and feminine groups.

Hebrew Roots

א־כ־ל

The basic meaning of the root א־כ־ל is to "eat" or "consume." This root appears in several well-known biblical narratives. The lowly bush where Moses first encountered the Divine Presence in Exodus 3:2 is described as burning with fire but not אֻכָּל, "consumed." The weapon that Abraham brings up the mountain in Genesis 22:6, when he is commanded to offer up his son Isaac as a sacrifice, is a מַאֲכֶלֶת, a "knife," an implement for consuming. In Genesis 41:4, Pharoah tells Joseph his dream in which seven ugly, thin cows וַתֹּאכַלְנָה, "ate," seven fat, healthy cows.

In this chapter's Reading Practice selections, the following examples of the root א־כ־ל appear:

eat	—	אוֹכְלִין
we eat	—	אָנוּ אוֹכְלִין
eating of	—	אֲכִילַת
eating of matzah	—	אֲכִילַת מַצָּה
eating of bitter herb	—	אֲכִילַת מָרוֹר

Other words, biblical and modern, that are derived from the root ל-כ-א include the following:

food	—	אֹכֶל
eating	—	אֲכִילָה
food, meal, a "dish"	—	מַאֲכָל
digested, consumed	—	מְאֻכָּל
feeding	—	הַאֲכָלָה

מ-ל-ך

The root מ-ל-ך has the basic meaning of "rule" or "reign." The word מֶלֶךְ, meaning "king," "sovereign," or "ruler," is derived from this root. In this chapter's Reading Practice selection *Va-anachnu*, we find the following:

sovereign	—	מֶלֶךְ
sovereigns of	—	מַלְכֵי
the sovereigns	—	הַמְּלָכִים

Other words that are derived from the root מ-ל-ך include the following:

sovereignty, reign, kingdom	—	מַלְכוּת
queen, sovereign, ruler *(feminine)*	—	מַלְכָּה
royal, regal	—	מַלְכוּתִי
royalty, kingship	—	מְלוּכָה
dominion, reign	—	מַמְלָכָה

Building Blocks

Attached Letters: The Prefix וֹ

In Chapter 1, we introduced the prefix הַ, meaning "the." The letter וֹ also acts as a prefix in Hebrew. The most common meaning of this prefix is the English word "and." Sometimes the prefix וֹ appears as a vowel וּ and sometimes as a consonant וְ. When it appears as a consonant, it most commonly is accompanied by this vowel: וְ. It can, however, appear with any of the following vowels: וַ, וֶ, וָ, וֵ. Example:

leavened food and matzah — חָמֵץ וּמַצָּה

Grammatical Gender—Masculine and Feminine Nouns

Nouns are words that indicate a person, place, or thing, such as "mother," "town," or "dish." In English, most words have no gender. "Dish" or "town" is not musculine or feminine. Only nouns that refer specifically to a male (such as "he," "father," "king") or to a female (such as "she," "sister," "mother") have gender.

In Hebrew, however, all nouns are either masculine or feminine. The grammatical gender of a Hebrew noun is significant because other words used in relation to that noun must match its gender. For example, in Chapter 1, the masculine pronoun הוּא ("he," "it") was introduced as a vocabulary word. This pronoun can only be used to refer to words that are grammatically masculine in Hebrew. The feminine pronoun הִיא ("she," "it") is used to refer to words that are grammatically feminine in Hebrew.

It is the bitter herb. — הוּא הַמָּרוֹר.

It is the matzah. — הִיא הַמַּצָּה.

The grammatical gender of each noun in the vocabulary of this book is indicated with the abbreviation *m* or *f*.

Plural Endings: ים and וֹת

In English, the plural of a noun is most often indicated by adding the letters "s" or "es":

mother ➞ mothers   town ➞ towns   dish ➞ dishes

In Hebrew, the plural of a noun is formed by adding either the ending ים or וֹת.

שֵׁם ➞ שֵׁמוֹת   עוֹלָם ➞ עוֹלָמִים

Sometimes the vowels of the word change when the ending is attached but the letters remain the same. If, however, the last letter is a silent הָ, this הָ drops out when the plural ending is attached. Examples:

לַיְלָה ← לֵילוֹת   מֶלֶךְ ← מְלָכִים

The ◌ִים ending is most commonly used for masculine nouns, and the וֹת ending is most commonly used for feminine nouns. There are, however, many exceptions to this general rule, and the gender of a noun cannot be determined solely by the plural ending it uses.

The ◌ִים and וֹת Endings on Verbs

Verbs are words that indicate action, such as "jump," "run," or "eat." In English, verbs are gender-neutral, and the same verb can be used with masculine, feminine, and gender-neutral subjects:

He eats. She eats. It eats.
The boys jump. The girls jump. The children jump.

In Hebrew, however, verbs have masculine and feminine, singular and plural forms. More information about verbs will be introduced in Chapters 4 and 10. The one detail about verbs to note here is that the same ◌ִים and וֹת endings that are used to indicate plural nouns in Hebrew are also used to indicate plural verbs. Unlike their usage with nouns, however, the ◌ִים ending always indicates a masculine plural verb and the וֹת ending always indicates a feminine plural verb.

Reading Practice with Building Blocks

Following are the Reading Practice selections for this chapter, reprinted with the new Building Blocks highlighted. Reread these selections, noting each appearance of the prefix וֹ ("and") and the יָם and וֹת plural endings.

Passover Four Questions

מַה נִּשְׁתַּנָּה הַלַּיְלָה הַזֶּה מִכָּל הַלֵּילוֹת?

שֶׁבְּכָל הַלֵּילוֹת אָנוּ אוֹכְלִין חָמֵץ וּמַצָּה. הַלַּיְלָה הַזֶּה כֻּלּוֹ מַצָּה.

שֶׁבְּכָל הַלֵּילוֹת אָנוּ אוֹכְלִין שְׁאָר יְרָקוֹת הַלַּיְלָה הַזֶּה מָרוֹר.

שֶׁבְּכָל הַלֵּילוֹת אֵין אָנוּ מַטְבִּילִין אֲפִילוּ פַּעַם אֶחָת. הַלַּיְלָה הַזֶּה שְׁתֵּי פְעָמִים.

שֶׁבְּכָל הַלֵּילוֹת אָנוּ אוֹכְלִין בֵּין יוֹשְׁבִין וּבֵין מְסֻבִּין. הַלַּיְלָה הַזֶּה כֻּלָּנוּ מְסֻבִּין.

*What differentiates this night from all the [other] **nights**?*
*that on all the [other] **nights** we eat leavened foods **and** matzah; this night—all of it is*
*   matzah.*
*that on all the [other] **nights** we eat the rest of **vegetables**; this night—bitter herb.*
*that on all the [other] **nights** we do not dip even one time; this night—two **times**.*
*that on all the [other] **nights** we eat either sitting or reclining; this night—all of us are*
*   reclining.*

Va-anachnu

וַאֲנַחְנוּ כּוֹרְעִים וּמִשְׁתַּחֲוִים וּמוֹדִים, לִפְנֵי מֶלֶךְ מַלְכֵי הַמְּלָכִים, הַקָּדוֹשׁ בָּרוּךְ הוּא.

***And** we **bend the knee and bow and give thanks** before the Sovereign of sovereigns of*
***sovereigns**, the Holy One, blessed is God {He}.*

Passover Seder—Blessing over Matzah

בָּרוּךְ אַתָּה יְיָ אֱלֹהֵינוּ מֶלֶךְ הָעוֹלָם, אֲשֶׁר קִדְּשָׁנוּ בְּמִצְוֹתָיו וְצִוָּנוּ עַל אֲכִילַת מַצָּה.

Blessed are You, Eternal our God, Sovereign of the universe, who makes us holy with

God's {His} **mitzvot and** *commands us regarding eating of matzah.*

בְּרוּכָה אַתְּ יָהּ אֱלֹהֵינוּ רוּחַ הָעוֹלָם, אֲשֶׁר קִדַּשְׁתָנוּ בְּמִצְוֹתֶיהָ וְצִוַּתְנוּ עַל אֲכִילַת מַצָּה.

Blessed are You, Yah *our God, Soul {Spirit} of the world, who makes us holy with God's {Her}* **mitzvot and** *commands us regarding eating of matzah.*

Passover Seder—Blessing over Bitter Herb

בָּרוּךְ אַתָּה יְיָ אֱלֹהֵינוּ מֶלֶךְ הָעוֹלָם, אֲשֶׁר קִדְּשָׁנוּ בְּמִצְוֹתָיו וְצִוָּנוּ עַל אֲכִילַת מָרוֹר.

Blessed are You, Eternal our God, Sovereign of the universe, who makes us holy with God's {His} **mitzvot and** *commands us regarding eating of bitter herb.*

בְּרוּכָה אַתְּ יָהּ אֱלֹהֵינוּ רוּחַ הָעוֹלָם, אֲשֶׁר קִדַּשְׁתָנוּ בְּמִצְוֹתֶיהָ וְצִוַּתְנוּ עַל אֲכִילַת מָרוֹר.

Blessed are You, Yah *our God, Soul {Spirit} of the world, who makes us holy with God's {Her}* **mitzvot and** *commands us regarding eating of bitter herb.*

Plural Endings for Mixed-Gender Groups

GRAMMAR Enrichment

The feminine plural ending וֹת does not appear with any of the verbs in this chapter's Reading Practice selections. The prayer book excerpt וַאֲנַחְנוּ כּוֹרְעִים וּמִשְׁתַּחֲוִים וּמוֹדִים ("And we bend the knee and bow and give thanks") utilizes only masculine plural verbs, even though both men and women say these words and are included within the word וַאֲנַחְנוּ ("we"). Such masculine plural language appears throughout Hebrew liturgy.

In Hebrew, masculine verbs are used not only for all-male groups, but also for mixed-gender groups. Feminine verbs are used only for all-female groups. If the *Va-anachnu* were written as וַאֲנַחְנוּ כּוֹרְעוֹת וּמִשְׁתַּחֲווֹת וּמוֹדוֹת, the Hebrew would imply that only women were participating. The English translation would still be "And we bend the knee and bow and give thanks," but an important nuance of the Hebrew would be lost in translation.

The same concept applies to nouns. Since there are no gender-neutral nouns in Hebrew, masculine nouns are used both for all-male groups and for groups of mixed gender. Feminine plural nouns are used only for all-female groups. For example, the word בֵּן means "son," but its plural form בָּנִים can mean either "sons" or "children" (male and female). The masculine plural Hebrew phrase בְּנֵי יִשְׂרָאֵל is almost always translated as "Children of Israel," even though it could mean "Sons of Israel." The feminine plural phrase בְּנוֹת יִשְׂרָאֵל can only mean "Daughters of Israel."

מָצּוֹת and מִצְוֹת

The words מִצְוֹת, "mitzvot," and מַצּוֹת, "matzot," are identical when written, as in the Torah, without vowels. From the similarity between these words, the following ethical teaching is derived. (Note the use of verbs derived from the root of חָמֵץ, chametz.)

"וּשְׁמַרְתֶּם אֶת־הַמַּצּוֹת..." רַבִּי יֹאשִׁיָּה אוֹמֵר: אַל תִּקְרָא כֵּן אֶלָּא "וּשְׁמַרְתֶּם אֶת־הַמִּצְוֹת" כְּדֶרֶךְ שֶׁאֵין מַחֲמִיצִין אֶת הַמַּצָּה, כַּךְ לֹא יַחֲמִיצוּ אֶת הַמִּצְוָה, אֶלָּא אִם בָּאָה מִצְוָה לְיָדְךָ, עֲשֵׂה אוֹתָהּ מִיָּד.

"And you will observe the מַצּוֹת [unleavened bread]..." (Exodus 12:17). Rabbi Josiah says: Do not read it thus, but rather "And you will observe the מִצְוֹת [commandments]." Just as one doesn't מַחֲמִיצִין *matzah [allow it to become* chametz/fermented/sour*], so one shouldn't* יַחֲמִיצוּ *a mitzvah [allow it to become* chametz/fermented/sour*]. Rather, if the opportunity to do a mitzvah comes to you, do it immediately! [Note: Matzah becomes* chametz *if more than eighteen minutes elapses from the time that the flour is mixed with water until the baking is completed. Just as one hastens in the preparation of matzah, so one should hasten in the performance of a mitzvah.]*

MECHILTA, PISCHA 9

Exercises

1. Draw a line connecting each Hebrew word to its English translation. For some words, there can be more than one correct translation.

unleavened bread	אָנוּ
king	מָרוֹר
commandment	מֶלֶךְ
bitter herb	לַיְלָה
night	חָמֵץ
sovereign	מִצְוָה
leavened foods	אֲנַחְנוּ
we	מַצָּה

2. The following are the plural forms of nouns introduced as vocabulary thus far in this book. Draw a line connecting each plural noun to its singular form. Translate both into English.

עוֹלָם _____ שֵׁמוֹת _____

מָרוֹר _____ מִצְוֹת _____

שֵׁם _____ חֲמֵצִים _____

מִצְוָה _____ מְלָכִים _____

חָמֵץ _____ מְרוֹרִים _____

לַיְלָה _____ מַצּוֹת _____

מַצָּה _____ עוֹלָמִים _____

מֶלֶךְ _____ לֵילוֹת _____

3. Read and translate the following sentences. The word אוֹכֵל is a verb from the root א-כ-ל. It means "eat" or "eats." Plural forms are created by adding the ים and וֹת endings.

a. אַתָּה אוֹכֵל. _____

b. הוּא אוֹכֵל. _____

c. הַמֶּלֶךְ אוֹכֵל. _____

d. אֲנַחְנוּ אוֹכְלִים. _____

e. אָנוּ אוֹכְלוֹת. _____

f. הַמְּלָכִים אוֹכְלִים חָמֵץ. _____

g. הַמְּלָכוֹת אוֹכְלוֹת חָמֵץ. _____

h. אַתָּה וְיִשְׂרָאֵל אוֹכְלִים חָמֵץ וּמַצָּה. _____

i. אֲנַחְנוּ אוֹכְלוֹת מַצָּה וּמָרוֹר. _____

j. בָּרוּךְ הַלַּיְלָה. _____

k. בָּרוּךְ הַמֶּלֶךְ לְעוֹלָם וָעֶד. _____

l. אָנוּ הַמְּלָכִים לְעוֹלָם וָעֶד. _____

4. Circle the words in the following prayer book excerpt that come from the root מ־ל־ך.

From the Beginning of the Torah Service (a composite of verses from Psalms 86, 145, 10, and 93 and Exodus 15)

אֵין כָּמֽוֹךָ בָאֱלֹהִים, אֲדֹנָי, וְאֵין כְּמַעֲשֶׂיךָ. מַלְכוּתְךָ מַלְכוּת כָּל
עֹלָמִים, וּמֶמְשַׁלְתְּךָ בְּכָל דֹּר וָדֹר. יְהֹוָה מֶֽלֶךְ, יְהֹוָה מָלָךְ, יְהֹוָה
יִמְלֹךְ לְעֹלָם וָעֶד.

There is none like You among the gods, Eternal One, and there are none like Your deeds. Your sovereignty is a sovereignty of all eternities, and Your dominion is in every generation and generation. The Eternal One is Sovereign, the Eternal One was Sovereign, the Eternal One will be Sovereign forever and ever.

5. The following is the introduction to בִּרְכַּת הַמָּזוֹן, the Blessing after Meals. Circle the words that come from the root א־כ־ל. Underline the words that come from the root ב־ר־ך.

From the Introduction to the Blessing after Meals

Leader: חֲבֵרִים וַחֲבֵרוֹת נְבָרֵךְ.

Group: יְהִי שֵׁם יְיָ מְבֹרָךְ מֵעַתָּה וְעַד עוֹלָם.

Leader: יְהִי שֵׁם יְיָ מְבֹרָךְ מֵעַתָּה וְעַד עוֹלָם. בִּרְשׁוּת הַחֶבְרָה,
נְבָרֵךְ אֱלֹהֵֽינוּ שֶׁאָכַֽלְנוּ מִשֶּׁלוֹ.

Group: בָּרוּךְ אֱלֹהֵֽינוּ שֶׁאָכַֽלְנוּ מִשֶּׁלוֹ וּבְטוּבוֹ חָיִֽינוּ.

Leader: בָּרוּךְ אֱלֹהֵֽינוּ שֶׁאָכַֽלְנוּ מִשֶּׁלוֹ וּבְטוּבוֹ חָיִֽינוּ.

Group: בָּרוּךְ הוּא וּבָרוּךְ שְׁמוֹ.

Leader: *Friends [male] and friends [female], let us bless.*
Group: *May the name of the Eternal One be blessed from now and unto eternity.*
Leader: *May the name of the Eternal One be blessed from now and unto eternity. With the permission of the company, let us bless our God that we have eaten from that which is God's {His}, and by God's {His} goodness we live.*
Group: *Blessed is our God that we have eaten from that which is God's {His}, and by God's {His} goodness we live.*

Leader: *Blessed is our God that we have eaten from that which is God's {His}, and by God's {His} goodness we live.*

Group: *Blessed is God {He} and blessed is God's {His} name.*

6. Translate the following biblical excerpts, using the extra vocabulary words listed below in addition to the words introduced in this book. Check your translations against the English translations that follow.

a. Exodus 12:8

and they shall eat	—	וְאָכְלוּ אֵת
meat	—	בָּשָׂר
on that night	—	בַּלַּיְלָה הַזֶּה
roast [with] fire	—	צְלִי־אֵשׁ
on	—	עַל
they will eat it	—	יֹאכְלֻהוּ

וְאָכְלוּ אֶת־הַבָּשָׂר בַּלַּיְלָה הַזֶּה צְלִי־אֵשׁ וּמַצּוֹת עַל־מְרֹרִים יֹאכְלֻהוּ:

---

b. From I Samuel 30:12

he didn't eat	—	לֹא־אָכַל
bread	—	לֶחֶם
he didn't drink	—	לֹא־שָׁתָה
water	—	מַיִם
three	—	שְׁלֹשָׁה
days	—	יָמִים

...לֹא־אָכַל לֶחֶם וְלֹא־שָׁתָה מַיִם שְׁלֹשָׁה יָמִים וּשְׁלֹשָׁה לֵילוֹת:

---

c. From Genesis 2:20

Hint: In Genesis 2:20, the verb appears first, followed by the subject of the sentence. This word order must be reversed when translating into English.

(he) called out	—	וַיִּקְרָא
man, human being	—	אָדָם
for all	—	לְכָל, לְכֹל
cattle	—	בְּהֵמָה
for the birds of the sky	—	לְעוֹף הַשָּׁמַיִם
the animals of the field	—	חַיַּת הַשָּׂדֶה

וַיִּקְרָא הָאָדָם שֵׁמוֹת לְכָל־הַבְּהֵמָה וּלְעוֹף הַשָּׁמַיִם וּלְכֹל חַיַּת הַשָּׂדֶה...

d. From Deuteronomy 6:1

Hint: In Deuteronomy 6:1, the subject of a verb appears directly after the verb, instead of preceding it. This word order must be reversed when translating into English.

this	—	זֹאת
law	—	חֹק
statute	—	מִשְׁפָּט
that	—	אֲשֶׁר
commanded	—	צִוָּה
your God	—	אֱלֹהֵיכֶם

וְזֹאת הַמִּצְוָה הַחֻקִּים וְהַמִּשְׁפָּטִים אֲשֶׁר צִוָּה יְהוָֹה אֱלֹהֵיכֶם...

Translations:

    a. Exodus 12:8—And they shall eat the meat on that night roast with fire, and matzah on bitter herbs they will eat it.

    b. From I Samuel 30:12—...he didn't eat bread and he didn't drink water for three days and three nights.

    c. From Genesis 2:20—The man called out names for all the cattle and for the birds of the sky and for all the animals of the field...

    d. From Deuteronomy 6:1—And this is the commandment, the laws and the statutes that the Eternal your God commanded...

EXTRA CREDIT

Gender Issues in the Prayer Book

Jewish theology holds that God is incorporeal (i.e., has no body) and is, therefore, neither male nor female. There are, however, no gender-neutral nouns and few gender-neutral verb forms in Hebrew. The God-language in the prayer book and Hebrew scriptures is grammatically masculine. A literal translation of such Hebrew must use either "He" or "It" to refer to God. Since "It" in English generally refers to an object or a thing, something that is lesser than, not greater than, a human being, "It" has not been a preferred way of referring to God. Until recent decades, English translations of the prayer book reflected the grammatically masculine language of the Hebrew and referred to God as "He" and "Him."

In recent decades, however, prayer books have been published that reflect the awareness that, while masculine or feminine language in Hebrew may be a grammatical necessity, gender-neutral options, which more accurately reflect what Jews really believe about God, are available in the English translation. For example, the English translations in the Reform Movement's gender-sensitive edition of *Gates of Prayer* use the word "God" instead of "He" or "Him" and "God's" instead of "His." Gender-neutral terms such as "Sovereign" are used in place of masculine terms like "King." This is the practice that has been followed in this book in the translations of the Reading Practice selections and other Hebrew excerpts.

The Hebrew used in prayer is a thornier issue. Some feel that, while English translations can easily provide gender-neutral language, the Hebrew would require too much alteration to accommodate gender concerns and that such alterations would deviate too far from the traditional wording. Others feel that gender concerns must be addressed in the Hebrew as well as the English. The latter approach has been taken in the Reform Movement's Haggadah *The Open Door*, which offers both grammatically masculine and feminine versions of Hebrew blessings, as shown in this chapter's Reading Practice. Another approach to Hebrew blessings included in some prayer books is to provide a gender-neutral construction: נְבָרֵךְ אֶת ("let us bless") instead of, or in addition to, the grammatically masculine בָּרוּךְ אַתָּה ("blessed are You") and the feminine בְּרוּכָה אַתְּ ("blessed are You").

A related issue is the language used in the prayer book to refer to human beings. Since masculine plural nouns and verbs can be used to refer to mixed-gender groups, the language of the prayer book is overwhelmingly masculine. Gender-sensitive versions of Hebrew prayers, composed within the last quarter of the twentieth century, have included feminine plural nouns where they were traditionally omitted. For example, the *Avot* prayer in the traditional liturgy is worded as follows:

בָּרוּךְ אַתָּה יְיָ אֱלֹהֵינוּ וֵאלֹהֵי אֲבוֹתֵינוּ, אֱלֹהֵי אַבְרָהָם, אֱלֹהֵי
יִצְחָק, וֵאלֹהֵי יַעֲקֹב, הָאֵל הַגָּדוֹל הַגִּבּוֹר וְהַנּוֹרָא...

Blessed are You, Eternal One, our God and God of our fathers, God of Abraham, God of
Isaac, and God of Jacob, the great mighty and awesome God...

The word אֲבוֹתֵינוּ, translated above as "our fathers," also could have been translated as "our parents" or, since the context clearly indicates more than a single generation, as "our ancestors." Only male ancestors, however, are mentioned by name in the traditional wording of this prayer. In order to clearly indicate the inclusion of women where they had traditionally been excluded, gender-sensitive versions of this prayer include not only the mention of our female ancestors, but also specifically the word וְאִמּוֹתֵינוּ ("and our mothers") alongside אֲבוֹתֵינוּ:

בָּרוּךְ אַתָּה יְיָ אֱלֹהֵינוּ וֵאלֹהֵי אֲבוֹתֵינוּ וְאִמּוֹתֵינוּ. אֱלֹהֵי אַבְרָהָם,
אֱלֹהֵי יִצְחָק, וֵאלֹהֵי יַעֲקֹב, אֱלֹהֵי שָׂרָה, אֱלֹהֵי רִבְקָה, אֱלֹהֵי לֵאָה,
וֵאלֹהֵי רָחֵל, הָאֵל הַגָּדוֹל הַגִּבּוֹר וְהַנּוֹרָא...

Blessed are You, Eternal One, our God and God of our fathers and our mothers, God of
Abraham, God of Isaac, and God of Jacob, God of Sarah, God of Rebekah, God of Leah, and
God of Rachel, the great mighty and awesome God...

Review

In Chapter 2, eight vocabulary words and two Hebrew roots were introduced:

חָמֵץ מָצָה מָרוֹר לַיְלָה מִצְוָה מֶלֶךְ אֲנַחְנוּ אָנוּ

א-כ-ל מ-ל-ך

The following Building Blocks were presented:

1. The letter וֹ is used as a prefix to mean "and."
2. Hebrew nouns are masculine or feminine, not gender-neutral.
3. יִם and וֹת are plural endings for nouns and verbs. (On verbs, יִם is always a masculine plural ending, and וֹת is always a feminine plural ending.)
4. Masculine plural forms are used for mixed-gender groups. Feminine plural forms are used only for all-female groups.

Reading Practice

***V'shamru* (Exodus 31:16–17)**

וְשָׁמְרוּ בְנֵי יִשְׂרָאֵל אֶת הַשַּׁבָּת, לַעֲשׂוֹת אֶת הַשַּׁבָּת
לְדֹרֹתָם בְּרִית עוֹלָם: בֵּינִי וּבֵין בְּנֵי יִשְׂרָאֵל אוֹת הִיא
לְעוֹלָם, כִּי שֵׁשֶׁת יָמִים עָשָׂה יְיָ אֶת הַשָּׁמַיִם וְאֶת הָאָרֶץ,
וּבַיּוֹם הַשְּׁבִיעִי שָׁבַת וַיִּנָּפַשׁ:

The Children of Israel will keep the Sabbath, to make the Sabbath for their generations a covenant of eternity. Between Me and the Children of Israel it is a sign forever, that [in] six days the Eternal One made the heavens and the earth and on the seventh day [God] rested and was refreshed.

Blessings over Shabbat Candles, Wine, and Bread

בָּרוּךְ אַתָּה יְיָ, אֱלֹהֵינוּ מֶלֶךְ הָעוֹלָם, אֲשֶׁר קִדְּשָׁנוּ בְּמִצְוֹתָיו וְצִוָּנוּ לְהַדְלִיק נֵר שֶׁל שַׁבָּת.

בָּרוּךְ אַתָּה יְיָ, אֱלֹהֵינוּ מֶלֶךְ הָעוֹלָם, בּוֹרֵא פְּרִי הַגָּפֶן.

בָּרוּךְ אַתָּה יְיָ, אֱלֹהֵינוּ מֶלֶךְ הָעוֹלָם, הַמּוֹצִיא לֶחֶם מִן הָאָרֶץ.

Blessed are You, Eternal our God, Sovereign of the universe, who makes us holy with God's {His} mitzvot and commands us to kindle the light of Shabbat.
Blessed are You, Eternal our God, Sovereign of the universe, Creator of the fruit of the vine.
Blessed are You, Eternal our God, Sovereign of the universe, who brings forth bread from the earth.

Havdalah Blessings over Wine, Spices, and Light

בָּרוּךְ אַתָּה יְיָ, אֱלֹהֵינוּ מֶלֶךְ הָעוֹלָם, בּוֹרֵא פְּרִי הַגָּפֶן.

בָּרוּךְ אַתָּה יְיָ, אֱלֹהֵינוּ מֶלֶךְ הָעוֹלָם, בּוֹרֵא מִינֵי בְשָׂמִים.

בָּרוּךְ אַתָּה יְיָ, אֱלֹהֵינוּ מֶלֶךְ הָעוֹלָם, בּוֹרֵא מְאוֹרֵי הָאֵשׁ.

Blessed are You, Eternal our God, Sovereign of the universe, Creator of the fruit of the vine.
Blessed are You, Eternal our God, Sovereign of the universe, Creator of varieties of spices.
Blessed are You, Eternal our God, Sovereign of the universe, Creator of the illumination of the fire.

Blessings over Shabbat Candles, Wine, and Bread

We praise You, Eternal God, Sovereign of the universe: You hallow us with Mitzvot, and command us to kindle the lights of Shabbat.

We praise You, Eternal God, Sovereign of the universe, Creator of the fruit of the vine.

We praise You, Eternal God, Sovereign of the universe, for You cause bread to come forth from the earth.

ON THE DOORPOSTS OF YOUR HOUSE, ED. CHAIM STERN. NEW YORK: CCAR
PRESS, 1994.

Blessed are you, SOURCE OF LIGHT our God, the sovereign of all worlds, who has made us holy with your mitzvot, and commanded us to kindle the Shabbat light.

Blessed are you, THE BOUNDLESS ONE our God, the sovereign of all worlds, who creates the fruit of the vine.

Blessed are you, BOUNTIFUL, the sovereign of all worlds, who brings forth bread from the earth.

KOL HANESHAMAH: SONGS, BLESSINGS, AND RITUALS FOR THE HOME. WYNCOTE,
PA.: THE RECONSTRUCTIONIST PRESS, 1991.

Praised are You, Adonai our God, who rules the universe, instilling in us the holiness of mitzvot by commanding us to kindle the light of Shabbat.

Praised are You, Adonai our God, who rules the universe, creating the fruit of the vine.

Praised are You, Adonai our God, who rules the universe, bringing forth bread from the earth.

SIDDUR SIM SHALOM FOR SHABBAT AND FESTIVALS. NEW YORK: THE RABBINICAL
ASSEMBLY, 1998.

Blessed art thou, O Lord our God, King of the universe, who hast hallowed us by thy commandments, and commanded us to kindle the Sabbath light.

Blessed art thou, O Lord our God, King of the universe, who createst the fruit of the vine.

Blessed art thou, O Lord our God, King of the universe, who bringest forth bread from the earth.

THE AUTHORIZED DAILY PRAYER BOOK, TRANS. JOSEPH HERTZ. NEW YORK: BLOCH
PUBLISHING CO., 1948.

Vocabulary

Try to locate each of these words in the Reading Practice selections (*V'shamru*, Shabbat blessings, or *Havdalah* blessings). Some of these words occur with prefixes and/or suffixes attached. Some appear in word pairs, a grammatical structure that will be explained in this chapter.

son, child *m* (*plural*: sons, children)	—	בֵּן (בָּנִים)
Shabbat, Sabbath *f*	—	שַׁבָּת
covenant *f*	—	בְּרִית
day m (*plural*: days)	—	יוֹם (יָמִים)
heavens, sky *m*	—	שָׁמַיִם
earth, land *f*	—	אֶרֶץ
fruit *m*	—	פְּרִי
bread *m*	—	לֶחֶם

Note: When the prefix הַ, meaning "the," is attached to the word אֶרֶץ, the vowel under the letter א changes: הָאָרֶץ.

Hebrew Roots

בָּ־רָ־א

The basic meaning of the root בָּ־רָ־א is "create." There is an added nuance in the Hebrew that the English translation does not convey: divine creation. This root is used in reference to God's creative acts, as opposed to human acts of creation. The only word from this root that appears in the Reading Practice of this chapter is בּוֹרֵא, which means "Creator." (Because the word itself implies not a human creator, but the Holy One, it is written in this book with a capital letter "C.")

Other words, ancient and modern, derived from the root בָּ־רָ־א include:

creation	—	בְּרִיאָה
creature	—	בָּרוּא *archaic*
creationism	—	בְּרִיאָתָנוּת "ism"

שָׁ־מָ־ר

The root שָׁ־מָ־ר has the basic meaning of "guard," "keep," or "preserve." It is the root of the word *v'shamru*: וְשָׁמְרוּ, which is the only word from this root appearing in the Reading Practice selections of this chapter. This root appears, however, over 400 times in the Bible. In Genesis 2:15, the first human being is placed by God in the Garden of Eden to tend it and לְשָׁמְרָהּ, "to preserve it." In Deuteronomy 5:12, we are commanded: שָׁמוֹר, "Keep" the Sabbath day to make it holy. In Isaiah 62:6, mention is made of שֹׁמְרִים, "guards" or "watchmen," on the walls of Jerusalem.

The following are words, both ancient and modern, that are derived from the root שָׁ־מָ־ר:

guard, keeper	—	שׁוֹמֵר
guarding	—	שְׁמִירָה
watch, shift	—	מִשְׁמֶרֶת
guard, post	—	מִשְׁמָר
conservative, conserving, preservative	—	מְשַׁמֵּר
guarded, reserved, restricted	—	שָׁמוּר

Building Blocks

Word Pairs

 construct

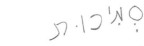

In English, two nouns can be placed together to express a single concept, such as "water fountain" or "seat belt." An analogous construction exists in Hebrew. When two Hebrew nouns are placed together to express a concept, they are called a word pair. The English word "of" generally must be inserted between the Hebrew words of the word pair when translating into English. The following are examples of word pairs:

[the] sovereign of the universe	—	מֶלֶךְ הָעוֹלָם
day of atonement	—	יוֹם כִּפּוּר
a Sabbath of peace {a peaceful Shabbat}	—	שַׁבָּת שָׁלוֹם

Changes Due to Word Pairs

In the examples above, there is no change in the appearance of the individual words when they are joined into word pairs. Often, however, there are changes in the vowels of the first word in a word pair. These changes indicate that the first word is now in "word-pair form," which means that its English translation will generally include the word "of." The last word of a word pair always remains unchanged. Examples:

lord	—	אָדוֹן
lord of eternity {eternal lord}	—	אֲדוֹן עוֹלָם
house	—	בַּיִת
house of God	—	בֵּית אֵל

Though the vowels may change, the letters of the first word do not change in word-pair form unless that word ends with הָ or the plural ending יִם. If the first word ends with הָ, this ending changes to ת in word-pair form. If the first word ends with the plural ending יִם, this ending changes to יֵ. Sometimes there are other vowel changes as well. Examples:

joy, rejoicing	—	שִׂמְחָה
joy of Torah {rejoicing [in the] Torah}	—	שִׂמְחַת תּוֹרָה
reception, receiving	—	קַבָּלָה
receiving of Shabbat	—	קַבָּלַת שַׁבָּת

sons, children	—	בָּנִים
[the] Children of Israel	—	בְּנֵי יִשְׂרָאֵל
blessing	—	בְּרָכָה
[the] blessing of the food *(i.e., the Blessing after Meals)*	—	בִּרְכַּת הַמָּזוֹן
God	—	אֱלֹהִים
[the] God of Abraham	—	אֱלֹהֵי אַבְרָהָם

Adding "the" to Word Pairs

In both English and Hebrew, there are definite and indefinite nouns. Definite nouns are nouns that refer to a definite, specific person, place, or thing, such as "Abraham," "Israel," "my award," or "the book." Examples of indefinite nouns are "a man," "a country," "an award," or "a book." In Hebrew word pairs, if the last word of the word pair is a definite noun, then the entire word pair is definite, and the word "the" may appear in the English translation in front of both words in the word pair. Examples:

the head of the year {the New Year}	—	רֹאשׁ הַשָּׁנָה
the portion of the week {the weekly [Torah] portion}	—	פָּרָשַׁת הַשָּׁבוּעַ
the Land of Israel	—	אֶרֶץ יִשְׂרָאֵל
[the] doorposts of your house	—	מְזוּזוֹת בֵּיתֶךָ

Word-Pair Strings

All of the word pairs examined thus far have consisted of two words. It is possible, however, for more than two words to be joined together in a word-pair string. When this occurs, all of the words in the string, except the last one, appear in "word-pair form" with whatever letter or vowel changes this might entail. The last word remains unchanged. If the last word is definite, the entire word pair string is definite and can be translated with the word "the."

[the] Creator of [the] fruit of the vine	—	בּוֹרֵא פְּרִי הַגָּפֶן
[the] sovereign of [the] sovereigns of [the] sovereigns	—	מֶלֶךְ מַלְכֵי הַמְּלָכִים

Word Order: Subjects and Verbs

You have now learned the Hebrew root שׁ־מ־ר and the word pair בְּנֵי יִשְׂרָאֵל, which begin the *V'shamru* (Exodus 31:16–17), included in this chapter's Reading Practice.

will keep	—	וְשָׁמְרוּ
the Children of Israel	—	בְּנֵי יִשְׂרָאֵל
The Children of Israel will keep [the Sabbath]...	—	וְשָׁמְרוּ בְּנֵי יִשְׂרָאֵל...

The verb וְשָׁמְרוּ appears in the Hebrew before the subject בְּנֵי יִשְׂרָאֵל. It is not uncommon in classical Hebrew for the verb to appear immediately before the subject of a sentence, rather than following it. (Such a word order appeared in Exercise 6 of the last chapter with the translations of Genesis 2:20 and Deuteronomy 6:1.) When translating such a passage from Hebrew into English, the word order of subject and verb must be reversed.

Reading Practice with Building Blocks

Following are the Reading Practice selections for this chapter, reprinted with all the word pairs highlighted. Reread these selections, noting the appearance of each word pair.

V'shamru (Exodus 31:16–17)

וְשָׁמְרוּ **בְּנֵי יִשְׂרָאֵל** אֶת הַשַּׁבָּת, לַעֲשׂוֹת אֶת הַשַּׁבָּת
לְדֹרֹתָם **בְּרִית עוֹלָם**: בֵּינִי וּבֵין **בְּנֵי יִשְׂרָאֵל** אוֹת הִיא
לְעוֹלָם, כִּי שֵׁשֶׁת יָמִים עָשָׂה יְיָ אֶת הַשָּׁמַיִם וְאֶת הָאָרֶץ,
וּבַיוֹם הַשְּׁבִיעִי שָׁבַת וַיִּנָּפַשׁ:

The Children of Israel will keep the Sabbath, to make the Sabbath for their generations a covenant of eternity. Between Me and the Children of Israel it is a sign forever, that [in] six days the Eternal One made the heavens and the earth and on the seventh day [God] rested and was refreshed.

Blessings over Shabbat Candles, Wine, and Bread

בָּרוּךְ אַתָּה יְיָ, אֱלֹהֵינוּ **מֶלֶךְ הָעוֹלָם**, אֲשֶׁר קִדְּשָׁנוּ בְּמִצְוֹתָיו
וְצִוָּנוּ לְהַדְלִיק נֵר שֶׁל שַׁבָּת.
בָּרוּךְ אַתָּה יְיָ, אֱלֹהֵינוּ **מֶלֶךְ הָעוֹלָם**, **בּוֹרֵא פְּרִי הַגָּפֶן.**

בָּרוּךְ אַתָּה יְיָ, אֱלֹהֵינוּ מֶלֶךְ הָעוֹלָם, הַמּוֹצִיא לֶחֶם מִן הָאָרֶץ.

Blessed are You, Eternal our God, **Sovereign of the universe,** *who makes us holy with God's {His} mitzvot and commands us to kindle the light of Shabbat.*
Blessed are You, Eternal our God, **Sovereign of the universe, Creator of the fruit of the vine.**
Blessed are You, Eternal our God, **Sovereign of the universe,** *who brings forth bread from the earth.*

Havdalah Blessings over Wine, Spices, and Light

בָּרוּךְ אַתָּה יְיָ, אֱלֹהֵינוּ מֶלֶךְ הָעוֹלָם, בּוֹרֵא פְּרִי הַגָּפֶן.
בָּרוּךְ אַתָּה יְיָ, אֱלֹהֵינוּ מֶלֶךְ הָעוֹלָם, בּוֹרֵא מִינֵי בְשָׂמִים.
בָּרוּךְ אַתָּה יְיָ, אֱלֹהֵינוּ מֶלֶךְ הָעוֹלָם, בּוֹרֵא מְאוֹרֵי הָאֵשׁ.

Blessed are You, Eternal our God, **Sovereign of the universe, Creator of the fruit of the vine.**
Blessed are You, Eternal our God, **Sovereign of the universe, Creator of varieties of spices.**
Blessed are You, Eternal our God, **Sovereign of the universe, Creator of the illumination of the fire.**

GRAMMAR Enrichment

The Word שֶׁל

The English word "of" is implied in Hebrew word pairs. There is, however, a Hebrew word that means "of"—the word שֶׁל. This word appears in the blessing over Shabbat candles, included in the Reading Practice at the beginning of this chapter.

light	—	נֵר
[the] light of Shabbat	—	נֵר שֶׁל שַׁבָּת

The word שֶׁל appears in a few other contexts in prayer book Hebrew, but in general it appears much less often than word pairs do. This is because the word שֶׁל is a postbiblical Hebrew development. It does not appear in the Bible, nor in prayer book passages that are quotes from the Bible. As the Hebrew language has evolved and changed over time, the word שֶׁל has come into greater usage. It is used quite often in modern conversational Hebrew.

FROM OUR TEXTS Shabbat

Shabbat is described as a foretaste of the world to come, a brief glimpse of paradise. For one day, we act as if the world were already perfected, as if the Messiah had already come. There is a tradition that if only all of us, the entire community of Israel, could make a perfect Shabbat, not once, but two weeks in a row, this sustained communal effort at creating paradise would, in fact, bring it into existence.

The following talmudic passage uses the proximity of two verses from the Book of Isaiah as support for this belief. The plural term שַׁבְּתוֹתַי, "My Sabbaths," in the first verse is understood to refer to the smallest number of Sabbaths that could constitute a plural: two Sabbaths. The idea of the holy mountain in the second verse is a metaphor for redemption.

אָמַר ר' יוֹחָנָן מִשּׁוּם ר' שִׁמְעוֹן בֶּן יוֹחַאי: אִלְמָלֵי מְשַׁמְּרִין יִשְׂרָאֵל

שְׁתֵּי שַׁבָּתוֹת כְּהִלְכָתָן מִיָּד נִגְאָלִין, שֶׁנֶּאֱמַר: "כִּי־כֹה אָמַר יְיָ

לַסָּרִיסִים אֲשֶׁר יִשְׁמְרוּ אֶת־שַׁבְּתוֹתַי," וְנֶאֱמַר אַחֲרָיו: "וַהֲבִיאוֹתִים

אֶל־הַר קָדְשִׁי..."

R. Yochanan said in the name of R. Shimon ben Yochai: If Israel were to keep two Sabbaths as they should be kept, they would be redeemed immediately, for it is said: "Thus said the Eternal of the chamberlains that keep שַׁבְּתוֹתַי [my Sabbaths]" (Isaiah 56:4), and this is followed by: "I will bring them to my holy mountain ..." (Isaiah 56:7).

SHABBAT 118B

Exercises

1. Draw a line connecting each Hebrew word to its English translation below. For some words, there can be more than one correct translation.

land	פְּרִי
day	יָמִים
sky	בֵּן
fruit	שַׁבָּת
sons	בְּרִית
earth	אֶרֶץ
days	לֶחֶם
covenant	שָׁמַיִם
son	יוֹם
children	בָּנִים
bread	
Sabbath	
heavens	

2. The following are the plural forms of nouns introduced as vocabulary in this chapter. Draw a line connecting each plural noun to its singular form. Translate both into English.

_____	אֶרֶץ	יָמִים	_____
_____	שַׁבָּת	פֵּרוֹת	_____
_____	יוֹם	לְחָמִים	_____
_____	בְּרִית	שַׁבָּתוֹת	_____
_____	בֵּן	בְּרִיתוֹת	_____
_____	פְּרִי	אֲרָצוֹת	_____
_____	לֶחֶם	בָּנִים	_____

3. You may be familiar with some of the following phrases from Jewish life or liturgy. All are word pairs. Translate them into English, using the extra vocabulary words listed below in addition to the words introduced in this book.

enjoyment, pleasure	—	עֹנֶג
holiness	—	קֹדֶשׁ
ark, closet	—	אָרוֹן

a. עֹנֶג שַׁבָּת   Shabbat enjoyment

b. שַׁבָּת קֹדֶשׁ   Holiness of Shabbat

c. אֲרוֹן הַקֹּדֶשׁ   The Ark of the Holiness

house, household	—	בַּיִת
assembly	—	כְּנֶסֶת
peace	—	שָׁלוֹם
sukkah, shelter	—	סֻכָּה

vowel change

d. בֵּית כְּנֶסֶת   House of assembly

e. שְׁלוֹם בַּיִת   House of peace

f. סֻכַּת שָׁלוֹם

circumcision	—	מִילָה
daughter	—	בַּת
life	—	חַיִּים
repair	—	תִּקּוּן

g. בְּרִית מִילָה   covenant of circumcision

h. בְּרִית בַּת   covenant of (the) daughter

i. בְּנֵי בְּרִית   children of (the) covenant

j. בְּרִית עוֹלָם   covenant of (the) universe

k. חַיֵּי עוֹלָם   life of (the) universe

l. תִּקּוּן הָעוֹלָם   the repair of the universe (social justice)

nation, people	—	עַם
rock	—	צוּר
Egypt	—	מִצְרַיִם

.m מֶלֶךְ יִשְׂרָאֵל _king of Israel_

.n עַם יִשְׂרָאֵל _people of Israel_

.o צוּר יִשְׂרָאֵל _rock of Israel_

.p אֶרֶץ יִשְׂרָאֵל _land of Israel_

.q אֶרֶץ מִצְרַיִם _land of Egypt_

4. Read and translate the following sentences. The word בּוֹרֵא is a verb from the root
בּ־ר־א. It means "create" or "creates."

.a אַתָּה בּוֹרֵא.

.b הוּא בּוֹרֵא יוֹם וְלַיְלָה.

.c מֶלֶךְ הַמְּלָכִים בּוֹרֵא.

.d הוּא בּוֹרֵא שָׁמַיִם וָאָרֶץ.

.e אַתָּה בּוֹרֵא פְּרִי וְלֶחֶם.

The word אוֹכֵל is a verb from the root א־כ־ל. It means "eat" or "eats." Plural forms
are created by adding the ים and וֹת endings.

.f הַבֵּן אוֹכֵל פְּרִי.

.g בְּנֵי יִשְׂרָאֵל אוֹכְלִים חָמֵץ וּמַצָּה.

.h אָנוּ אוֹכְלוֹת לֶחֶם וּמָרוֹר.

"אַרְצוֹת הַבְּרִית"
"the lands of the covenant/constitution"
"United States"

The word שׁוֹמֵר is a noun from the root שׁ־מ־ר. It means "guardian" or "keeper." It can appear in word pairs in the singular or plural form.

i. הַמֶּלֶךְ שׁוֹמֵר הַשַּׁבָּת. _____

j. אֲנַחְנוּ שׁוֹמְרֵי שַׁבָּת. _____

k. בָּרוּךְ שׁוֹמֵר הַבְּרִית לְעוֹלָם וָעֶד. _____

l. אָנוּ שׁוֹמְרֵי מִצְוֹת לְעוֹלָם וָעֶד. _____

5. The plural of the word שׁוֹמֵר appears in a word pair in the following prayer book excerpt. Translate this word pair. Circle the word that is derived from the root מ־ל־ך.

Yism'chu—from the Shabbat Service

יִשְׂמְחוּ בְמַלְכוּתְךָ שׁוֹמְרֵי שַׁבָּת וְקוֹרְאֵי עֹנֶג.

They will rejoice in Your sovereignty the keepers of Shabbat and proclaimers of enjoyment. [Those who keep Shabbat and proclaim [it] enjoyment will rejoice in Your sovereignty.]

6. Circle the word in the following prayer book excerpt that is derived from the root בּ־ר־א. Underline the word that is derived from the root שׁ־מ־ר. You can also identify the word אַתָּה, which appears four times in this excerpt.

Elohai N'shamah—from the Morning Service

אֱלֹהַי, נְשָׁמָה שֶׁנָּתַתָּ בִּי טְהוֹרָה הִיא. אַתָּה בְרָאתָהּ, אַתָּה יְצַרְתָּהּ, אַתָּה נְפַחְתָּהּ בִּי, וְאַתָּה מְשַׁמְּרָהּ בְּקִרְבִּי.

My God, the soul that You have placed in me is pure. You created it, You formed it, You breathed it into me, and You preserve it within me.

7. The word שֶׁל, meaning "of," appears instead of word pairs in the following excerpt from בִּרְכַּת הַחֹדֶשׁ, the Blessing for the New Month. The first part of the excerpt is translated; the second part is left for you to translate, with the vocabulary words provided below.

...תְּחַדֵּשׁ עָלֵינוּ אֶת הַחֹדֶשׁ הַזֶּה לְטוֹבָה וְלִבְרָכָה, וְתִתֵּן לָנוּ חַיִּים אֲרֻכִּים,

...renew upon us this month for goodness and for blessing, and give to us long life,

life	—	חַיִּים
peace	—	שָׁלוֹם
goodness	—	טוֹבָה
blessing	—	בְּרָכָה
livelihood, economic sustenance	—	פַּרְנָסָה

חַיִּים שֶׁל שָׁלוֹם חַיִּים שֶׁל טוֹבָה, חַיִּים שֶׁל בְּרָכָה, חַיִּים שֶׁל פַּרְנָסָה...

8. Translate the following biblical excerpts, using the extra vocabulary words listed below in addition to the words introduced in this book. Check your translations against the English translations that follow.

   a. From Deuteronomy 6:17

you shall surely keep *(emphatic verb construct from the root* שׁ־מ־ר*)*	—	שָׁמוֹר תִּשְׁמְרוּן
a grammatical particle that does not translate into English (explained in Chapter 4)	—	אֶת
your God	—	אֱלֹהֵיכֶם

שָׁמוֹר תִּשְׁמְרוּן אֶת־מִצְוֹת יְהֹוָה אֱלֹהֵיכֶם...

   b. Isaiah 43:15

I	—	אֲנִי
holy one	—	קָדוֹשׁ
your *(attached suffix)*	—	־כֶם

אֲנִי יְהֹוָה קְדוֹשְׁכֶם בּוֹרֵא יִשְׂרָאֵל מַלְכְּכֶם:

c. From Genesis 2:4

these	—	אֵלֶּה
generations, begettings	—	תּוֹלְדוֹת
when they were created *(from the root ב-ר-א)*	—	בְּהִבָּרְאָם

אֵלֶּה תוֹלְדוֹת הַשָּׁמַיִם וְהָאָרֶץ בְּהִבָּרְאָם...

Translations:

a. From Deuteronomy 6:17—You shall surely keep the commandments of the Eternal One, your God...

b. Isaiah 43:15—I am the Eternal One your Holy One, Creator of Israel, your Sovereign.

c. From Genesis 2:4—These are the generations of the heavens and the earth when they were created...

EXTRA CREDIT

Welcoming and Bidding Farewell to Shabbat

Shabbat is described in our liturgy as מְקוֹר הַבְּרָכָה, the source of blessing, and חֶמְדַּת יָמִים, the most precious of days. It is a day set apart from the six days of the workweek, for appreciating the natural world, for nurturing our relationships with loved ones, and for nourishing our souls. To mark the boundary between this sacred time and the rest of the week, there are beautiful rituals for welcoming Shabbat on Friday evening and for bidding her farewell after nightfall on Saturday. These rituals include the blessings presented at the beginning of this chapter.

Shabbat is welcomed on Friday night with the lighting of candles, a symbol of the divine light or spirit. Two (or more) candles are kindled, representing the two different ways that the commandment to observe Shabbat is worded in the Ten Commandments:

Remember the Sabbath day to make it holy. (Exodus 20:8)	—	זָכוֹר אֶת יוֹם הַשַּׁבָּת לְקַדְּשׁוֹ.
Keep the Sabbath day to make it holy. (Deuteronomy 5:12)	—	שָׁמוֹר אֶת יוֹם הַשַּׁבָּת לְקַדְּשׁוֹ.

The doubling of candles may also symbolize the נְשָׁמָה יְתֵרָה, the extra soul that we are said to acquire on Shabbat.

A blessing to sanctify the Sabbath day is said over a cup of wine, for wine is a symbol of joy and celebration, for as it is said, "wine gladdens the human heart" (Psalm 104:15),

פְּרִי הַגָּפֶן, יַיִן יְשַׂמַּח לְבַב אֱנוֹשׁ. Grape juice may be substituted for wine, as it is also "the fruit of the vine."

The Shabbat meal begins with the blessing said over challah. In some communities, it is customary to have two loaves of challah on Friday evening, as a reminder of the double portion of manna gathered in the wilderness on Fridays in preparation for Shabbat (Exodus 16:22). The challah is covered with a decorative cloth, to beautify the Shabbat table. An ethical lesson is also derived from this: we cover the challah to spare it embarassment at receiving the last blessing. So should we take great pains to regard the feelings of our fellow human beings.

On Saturday evening, we bid farewell to Shabbat with the ritual of הַבְדָּלָה, Havdalah, which means "separation" or "distinction." It marks the separation or distinction between the Sabbath day which is ending and the six days of the workweek. As we greet Shabbat when it begins, so we bid Shabbat farewell with wine or grape juice and with light. The light that is kindled for Havdalah, however, is a single braided candle with multiple wicks, creating a large flame to illumine our path through the coming week. The various strands of the braid symbolize the varied and different elements that together comprise God's Creation: light and darkness, the sacred and the ordinary, Shabbat and workdays, the wondrous variety that enriches our lives.

A box or container filled with sweet-smelling spices is circulated and a blessing said over these spices. We breathe deeply of their sweet scent with the hope that, just as a sweet scent lingers in a room even after its source departs, so may the sweetness of Shabbat linger with us into the workweek.

As the blessing for the illumination of the fire is said over the Havdalah candle, many follow the custom of holding their fingertips out toward the light, curving and extending them to note the interplay of shadow and light. The distinction between darkness and light is specifically mentioned in the Havdalah ritual.

Unlike the candles used in other Jewish rituals, such as Shabbat candles, festival candles, yahrzeit candles, and shivah candles, which are all left to burn down and go out of their own accord, the Havdalah candle is extinguished and can be reused again the following week. Some say the extinguishing of the Havdalah candle marks the departure of the נְשָׁמָה יְתֵרָה, the extra Sabbath soul, which returns to us again with the kindling of the Shabbat candles the following week.

Review

In Chapter 3, eight vocabulary words and two Hebrew roots were introduced:

בֶּן שַׁבָּת בְּרִית יוֹם שָׁמַיִם אֶרֶץ פְּרִי לֶחֶם

ב־ר־א ש־מ־ר

The following Building Blocks were presented:

1. Two or more Hebrew nouns can form a word pair.
2. There are letter and vowel changes that occur in some words in "word-pair form."
3. When the last word of a word pair is a definite noun, the entire word pair is definite.
4. The subject of a verb can come before or after the verb in classical Hebrew.

Reading Practice

Blessing before the Reading of the Torah

בָּרְכוּ אֶת יְיָ הַמְבֹרָךְ.

בָּרוּךְ יְיָ הַמְבֹרָךְ לְעוֹלָם וָעֶד.

בָּרוּךְ אַתָּה יְיָ אֱלֹהֵינוּ מֶלֶךְ הָעוֹלָם, אֲשֶׁר בָּחַר בָּנוּ מִכָּל הָעַמִּים

וְנָתַן לָנוּ אֶת תּוֹרָתוֹ. בָּרוּךְ אַתָּה יְיָ, נוֹתֵן הַתּוֹרָה.

Bless the Eternal One, the blessed One.
Blessed is the Eternal One, the blessed One, forever and ever.
Blessed are You, Eternal our God, Sovereign of the universe, who chose us from all the
peoples and gave to us God's {His} Torah. Blessed are You, Eternal One, Giver of the
Torah.

Blessing after the Reading of the Torah

בָּרוּךְ אַתָּה יְיָ אֱלֹהֵינוּ מֶלֶךְ הָעוֹלָם, אֲשֶׁר נָתַן לָנוּ תּוֹרַת אֱמֶת,
וְחַיֵּי עוֹלָם נָטַע בְּתוֹכֵנוּ. בָּרוּךְ אַתָּה יְיָ, נוֹתֵן הַתּוֹרָה.

Blessed are You, Eternal our God, Sovereign of the universe, who gave to us a Torah of truth, and life of eternity {eternal life} implanted within us. Blessed are You, Eternal One, Giver of the Torah.

Genesis 1:1

בְּרֵאשִׁית בָּרָא אֱלֹהִים אֵת הַשָּׁמַיִם וְאֵת הָאָרֶץ:

In [the] beginning, God created the heavens and the earth.

Blessing before the Haftarah Reading

בָּרוּךְ אַתָּה יְיָ אֱלֹהֵינוּ מֶלֶךְ הָעוֹלָם, אֲשֶׁר בָּחַר בִּנְבִיאִים טוֹבִים,
וְרָצָה בְדִבְרֵיהֶם הַנֶּאֱמָרִים בֶּאֱמֶת, בָּרוּךְ אַתָּה יְיָ, הַבּוֹחֵר
בַּתּוֹרָה וּבְמֹשֶׁה עַבְדּוֹ, וּבְיִשְׂרָאֵל עַמּוֹ, וּבִנְבִיאֵי הָאֱמֶת וָצֶדֶק.

Blessed are You, Eternal our God, Sovereign of the universe, who chose good prophets and found favor in their words spoken in truth. Blessed are You, Eternal One, the [One who] chooses the Torah and Moses, God's {His} servant, and Israel, God's {His} people, and prophets of the truth and righteousness.

Blessing before the Reading of the Torah

Praise the One to whom our praise is due!

Praised be the One to whom our praise is due, now and for ever!

We praise You, Eternal God, Sovereign of the universe: You have called us to Your service by giving us the Torah. We praise You, O God, Giver of the Torah.

GATES OF PRAYER FOR SHABBAT AND WEEKDAYS: A GENDER SENSITIVE PRAYERBOOK, ED. CHAIM STERN. NEW YORK: CCAR PRESS, 1994.

Praise Adonai, the Exalted One.

Praised be Adonai, the Exalted One, throughout all time.

Praised are You Adonai our God, who rules the universe, choosing us from among all peoples by giving us the Torah. Praised are You Adonai, who gives the Torah.

SIDDUR SIM SHALOM FOR SHABBAT AND FESTIVALS. NEW YORK: THE RABBINICAL ASSEMBLY, 1998.

Bless the Lord who is blessed.

Blessed be the Lord who is blessed forever and ever.

Blessed art thou, Lord our God, King of the universe, who hast chosen us from all peoples, and hast given us thy Torah. Blessed art thou, O Lord, Giver of the Torah.

DAILY PRAYER BOOK, TRANS. PHILLIP BIRNBAUM. NEW YORK: HEBREW PUBLISHING CO., 1949.

Vocabulary

Try to locate each of these words in the Reading Practice selections (Genesis 1:1, the Torah blessings, or the Haftarah blessing). Some of these words occur with prefixes and/or suffixes attached. Some appear in word pairs.

people, nation *m* (*plural:* peoples, nations)	—	עַם (עַמִּים)
Torah, teaching, law *f*	—	תּוֹרָה
truth *f*	—	אֱמֶת
life *m*	—	חַיִּים
God *m*	—	אֱלֹהִים
prophet *m*	—	נָבִיא
righteousness, justice *m*	—	צֶדֶק
Moses	—	מֹשֶׁה

Note: Though they translate into English as singular nouns, the words אֱלֹהִים, "God," and חַיִּים, "life," both have the plural ending ים and follow rules for plural nouns in Hebrew. For example, when they are the first word of a word pair, they appear as אֱלֹהֵי and חַיֵּי. Another word of this type appeared in the last chapter: שָׁמַיִם, which can be translated into English as the singular "sky" or the plural "heavens."

Hebrew Roots

נ־ת־ן

The basic meaning of the root נ־ת־ן is "give," though in some contexts it is better understood as "grant" or "permit." In Job 1:21, in the midst of his mourning, Job cries out יְהֹוָה נָתַן וַיהֹוָה לָקָח, "The Eternal One has given and the Eternal One has taken away." In Numbers 21:23, the Amorite king Sichon does not נָתַן, "permit," the Israelites to pass through his territory. In Esther 5:3, King Ahasuerus asks Esther her request, telling her that even to half the kingdom, וְיִנָּתֵן, "it shall be granted" her.

The following examples of the root נ־ת־ן appear in this chapter's Reading Practice in the Torah blessings:

gave	—	נָתַן
and gave	—	וְנָתַן
giver	—	נוֹתֵן

The following are other words from the root נ־ת־ן. When the letter נ is the first letter of a root, it sometimes does not appear in words formed from that root. In some of the examples below, the first נ of the root has dropped out, and only one ת and one נ remain.

present, gift	—	מַתָּנָה
negotiations (give and take)	—	מַשָּׂא וּמַתָּן
given; datum	—	נָתוּן
data	—	נְתוּנִים
given, allowed, permitted	—	נִתָּן
Nathan { [God] gave}	—	נָתָן
Jonathan {יוֹ (the Eternal One) gave}	—	יוֹנָתָן

ב־ח־ר

The root ב־ח־ר has the basic meaning of "choose" or "select." It appears in several prayer book passages that refer to Israel's unique relationship with the Divine, as the people chosen by God. It is also used in reference to choices made by human beings. In Deuteronomy 30:19, the Torah passage read in Reform synagogues on the morning of Yom Kippur, we are urged: וּבָחַרְתָּ בַּחַיִּים, "choose life!"

In the Reading Practice selections at the beginning of this chapter, the root ב־ח־ר appears once in the blessing before the Torah reading and twice in the Haftarah blessing:

chose	—	בָּחַר
the [one who] chooses	—	הַבּוֹחֵר

The following are several words, both ancient and modern, derived from this root. The first word in the list, בָּחוּר, may be familiar to some from the term *yeshiva bocher*, a student in a traditional religious academy. (*Bocher* is the Ashkenazic pronunciation of בָּחוּר, not the Sephardic Hebrew pronunciation that we are using.) A בָּחוּר is a select or choice youngster, in the prime of life.

youth, young man	—	בָּחוּר
young woman, maiden	—	בַּחוּרָה
chosen, select	—	בָּחִיר
choosing, selection, election	—	בְּחִירָה
elections	—	בְּחִירוֹת
choice, selection, elite	—	מִבְחָר

Building Blocks

Participles

In both English and Hebrew, there are verb forms called participles, which can act as a noun or as a verb. An example of an English participle is the word "learning," which appears as a noun and as a verb in the following sentences:

As a noun: *Learning lasts a lifetime.*

As a verb: *I am learning new things all the time.*

An example of a Hebrew participle is the word שׁוֹמֵר, which appeared in Exercise 4 of Chapter 3. Depending upon the context in which a participle appears, it can be translated as a noun or as a verb. Either way, there are several possible translations:

הוּא שׁוֹמֵר.

As a noun:	*As a verb:*
He {it} is **a guard**. He {it} is **one who guards**.	He {it} **is guarding**. He {it} **guards**. He {it} **does guard**.

Forming the Participle

Participles are formed from Hebrew root letters. There are several different participle patterns, but most of the roots introduced in this book follow the pattern shown below. The three ▦s represent the three Hebrew root letters.

▦ ▦וֹ ▦

All of the roots introduced thus far in this book follow this participle pattern, except for the root בּ־ר־ךְ.

Remember that the translation provided beside each root (opposite) is only one of many possible translations for the participle.

אוֹכֵל	א־כ־ל	eat	מוֹלֵךְ	מ־ל־ך	rule
שׁוֹמֵר	ש־מ־ר	guard	נוֹתֵן	נ־ת־ן	give
בּוֹרֵא	ב־ר־א	create	בּוֹחֵר	ב־ח־ר	choose

The root ש־מ־ע follows this pattern, with the addition of a vowel under the final silent ע:

שׁוֹמֵעַ   ש־מ־ע   hear

Every Hebrew participle has four forms: masculine singular, feminine singular, masculine plural, and feminine plural. The following are the four participle forms in the pattern introduced above:

masculine plural	ים ▨ ְ וֹ ▨	*masculine singular*	▨ ֵ וֹ ▨
feminine plural	וֹת ▨ ְ וֹ ▨	*feminine singular*	ת ▨ ֶ וֹ ▨

It is not necessary to memorize the four forms of every participle in order to do the readings and exercises in this book. It is, however, important to be able to recognize the simplest masculine singular form, as it appears frequently in Hebrew prayers. The plural forms are easy to identify once you are familiar with the simple participle form.

Using the Participle Forms

The form of the participle used, masculine or feminine, singular or plural, must match its subject. Examples:

You (*m, sg*) eat bread.	—	אַתָּה אוֹכֵל לֶחֶם.
The nation (*m, sg*) eats bread.	—	הָעָם אוֹכֵל לֶחֶם.
The sons/children (*m, pl*) eat bread.	—	הַבָּנִים אוֹכְלִים לֶחֶם.
The daughters (*f, pl*) eat bread.	—	הַבָּנוֹת אוֹכְלוֹת לֶחֶם.

The masculine plural forms are used whenever the plural group is masculine or of mixed gender, as with the word בָּנִים above. The feminine plural form is used only when the plural group is entirely feminine. For this reason, feminine plural forms very seldom appear in the Bible and prayer book.

Participle Chart

The following chart uses the root נ־ת־ן to illustrate which participle form is used with each of the Hebrew pronouns introduced in the Grammar Enrichment section of Chapter 1. This material is included for your enrichment only. It is not necessary to memorize all these combinations in order to do the readings and exercises in this book.

	Plural		*Singular*		
we give	אֲנַחְנוּ נוֹתְנִים	I give	אֲנִי נוֹתֵן	*first person*	
you give	אַתֶּם נוֹתְנִים	you give	אַתָּה נוֹתֵן	*second person*	*Masculine*
they give	הֵם נוֹתְנִים	he, it gives	הוּא נוֹתֵן	*third person*	
we give	אֲנַחְנוּ נוֹתְנוֹת	I give	אֲנִי נוֹתֶנֶת	*first person*	
you give	אַתֶּן נוֹתְנוֹת	you give	אַתְּ נוֹתֶנֶת	*second person*	*Feminine*
they give	הֵן נוֹתְנוֹת	she, it gives	הִיא נוֹתֶנֶת	*third person*	

Reading Practice with Building Blocks—Participles

Following are some of the Reading Practice selections from this and previous chapters that contain participles. Reread these selections, noting the form of each participle and whether it is acting as a noun or a verb.

Blessings over Wine

בָּרוּךְ אַתָּה יְיָ, אֱלֹהֵינוּ מֶלֶךְ הָעוֹלָם, **בּוֹרֵא** פְּרִי הַגָּפֶן.

*Blessed are You, Eternal our God, Sovereign of the universe, **Creator of** the fruit of the vine.*

Blessing after the Reading of the Torah

בָּרוּךְ אַתָּה יְיָ אֱלֹהֵינוּ מֶלֶךְ הָעוֹלָם, אֲשֶׁר נָתַן לָנוּ תּוֹרַת אֱמֶת,
וְחַיֵּי עוֹלָם נָטַע בְּתוֹכֵנוּ. בָּרוּךְ אַתָּה יְיָ, **נוֹתֵן** הַתּוֹרָה.

*Blessed are You, Eternal our God, Sovereign of the universe, who gave to us a Torah of truth, and life of eternity {eternal life} implanted within us. Blessed are You, Eternal One, **Giver of** the Torah.*

Blessing before the Haftarah Reading

בָּרוּךְ אַתָּה יְיָ אֱלֹהֵינוּ מֶלֶךְ הָעוֹלָם, אֲשֶׁר בָּחַר בִּנְבִיאִים טוֹבִים,
וְרָצָה בְדִבְרֵיהֶם הַנֶּאֱמָרִים בֶּאֱמֶת, בָּרוּךְ אַתָּה יְיָ, **הַבּוֹחֵר**
בַּתּוֹרָה וּבְמֹשֶׁה עַבְדּוֹ, וּבְיִשְׂרָאֵל עַמּוֹ, וּבִנְבִיאֵי הָאֱמֶת וָצֶדֶק.

*Blessed are You, Eternal our God, Sovereign of the universe, who chose good prophets
and found favor in their words spoken in truth. Blessed are You, Eternal One,* **the [One
who] chooses** *the Torah and Moses, God's {His} servant, and Israel, God's {His} people,
and prophets of the truth and righteousness.*

The Word אֶת

A simple sentence can be formed in English or Hebrew with a subject and a verb:

| He eats. | — | הוּא אוֹכֵל. |
| He guards. | — | הוּא שׁוֹמֵר. |

A more complex sentence is formed by indicating *what* he eats or *whom* he guards:

| He eats bread. | — | הוּא אוֹכֵל לֶחֶם. |
| He guards a king. | — | הוּא שׁוֹמֵר מֶלֶךְ. |

In the sentences above, the words לֶחֶם, "bread," and מֶלֶךְ, "king," are the direct objects of
the verbs.

In Hebrew, the word אֶת is used to indicate the direct object of a verb. אֶת does not translate
into English. It appears immediately before the direct object of a verb, but only when the direct
object is a definite noun. As we mentioned in the last chapter, nouns that have the definite
article ה, meaning "the," attached are definite nouns. Possessive words like בֵּיתְךָ, "your
house," and names of people and places are also definite nouns.

He eats the bread.	—	הוּא אוֹכֵל אֶת הַלֶּחֶם.
He guards your house.	—	הוּא שׁוֹמֵר אֶת בֵּיתְךָ.
He guards Moses.	—	הוּא שׁוֹמֵר אֶת מֹשֶׁה.

The Root ב־ח־ר and the Prefix בְּ

In English, the verb "choose" can have a direct object, indicating who or what is chosen:

He chooses a prophet. or *He chooses Moses.*

In Hebrew, verbs formed from the root ב־ח־ר never have a direct object. The word that we would consider the direct object in English is preceded in Hebrew not by the direct object marker אֶת but by the prefix בְּ. This prefix is attached to both indefinite and definite nouns. Examples:

He chooses a prophet.	—	הוּא בּוֹחֵר בְּנָבִיא.
He chooses Moses.	—	הוּא בּוֹחֵר בְּמֹשֶׁה.

The prefix בְּ can appear with different vowels: בִּ, בֵּ, בְּ, בָּ, בַּ. Sometimes the prefix בְּ can also appear without a dot in the middle, as בְ.

Reading Practice with Building Blocks—אֶת and בְּ ב־ח־ר

Following are some of the Reading Practice selections from this and previous chapters that contain the word אֶת and the verb root ב־ח־ר followed by the prefix בְּ. Reread these selections, noting the appearance of each of these Building Blocks. Since the word אֶת and the prefix בְּ following ב־ח־ר do not translate into English, these words are highlighted in the Hebrew together with the following word, which is highlighted in the English translation.

V'shamru (Exodus 31:16–17)

וְשָׁמְרוּ בְנֵי יִשְׂרָאֵל **אֶת הַשַּׁבָּת**, לַעֲשׂוֹת **אֶת הַשַּׁבָּת**
לְדֹרֹתָם בְּרִית עוֹלָם: בֵּינִי וּבֵין בְּנֵי יִשְׂרָאֵל אוֹת הִיא
לְעוֹלָם, כִּי שֵׁשֶׁת יָמִים עָשָׂה יְיָ **אֶת הַשָּׁמַיִם** וְ**אֶת הָאָרֶץ**,
וּבַיּוֹם הַשְּׁבִיעִי שָׁבַת וַיִּנָּפַשׁ:

*The Children of Israel will keep **the Sabbath**, to make **the Sabbath** for their generations a covenant of eternity. Between Me and the Children of Israel it is a sign forever, that [in] six days the Eternal One made **the heavens** and **the earth** and on the seventh day [God] rested and was refreshed.*

Blessing before the Reading of the Torah

בָּרְכוּ **אֶת יְיָ** הַמְבֹרָךְ.

בָּרוּךְ יְיָ הַמְבֹרָךְ לְעוֹלָם וָעֶד.

בָּרוּךְ אַתָּה יְיָ אֱלֹהֵינוּ מֶלֶךְ הָעוֹלָם, אֲשֶׁר **בָּחַר בָּנוּ** מִכָּל הָעַמִּים וְנָתַן לָנוּ **אֶת תּוֹרָתוֹ.** בָּרוּךְ אַתָּה יְיָ, נוֹתֵן הַתּוֹרָה.

Bless **the Eternal One***, the blessed One.*
Blessed is the Eternal One, the blessed One, forever and ever.
Blessed are You, Eternal our God, Sovereign of the universe, who **chose us** *from all the peoples and gave to us* **God's {His} Torah.** *Blessed are You, Eternal One, Giver of the Torah.*

Genesis 1:1

בְּרֵאשִׁית בָּרָא אֱלֹהִים **אֵת הַשָּׁמַיִם וְאֵת הָאָרֶץ:**

In [the] beginning, God created **the heavens** *and* **the earth***.*

Blessing before the Haftarah Reading

בָּרוּךְ אַתָּה יְיָ אֱלֹהֵינוּ מֶלֶךְ הָעוֹלָם, אֲשֶׁר **בָּחַר בִּנְבִיאִים** טוֹבִים, וְרָצָה בְדִבְרֵיהֶם הַנֶּאֱמָרִים בֶּאֱמֶת, בָּרוּךְ אַתָּה יְיָ, **הַבּוֹחֵר בַּתּוֹרָה** וּבְמֹשֶׁה עַבְדּוֹ, **וּבְיִשְׂרָאֵל** עַמּוֹ, **וּבִנְבִיאֵי הָאֱמֶת** וָצֶדֶק.

Blessed are You, Eternal our God, Sovereign of the universe, who **chose** *good* **prophets** *and found favor in their words spoken in truth. Blessed are You, Eternal One,* **the [One who] chooses the Torah** *and* **Moses***, God's {His} servant, and* **Israel***, God's {His} people, and* **prophets of the truth** *and righteousness.*

From Our Texts

Secrets of Creation

Genesis 1:1

בְּרֵאשִׁית בָּרָא אֱלֹהִים אֵת הַשָּׁמַיִם וְאֵת הָאָרֶץ:

The first verse of the Torah, hinting at the mysteries of Creation, has given rise to perhaps more commentary than any other single verse. Here are two samplings:

Rabbi Dov Ber, the Maggid of Mezritch, writes: It is known in kabbalistic literature that the letters of the Aleph-Beis were created first of all. Thereafter, by use of the letters, the Holy One, Blessed is He, created all the worlds. This is the hidden meaning of the first phrase in the Torah, "In the beginning God created אֵת"—that is, God's first act was to create the letters from ת *to* א, *[the first and last letters of the Hebrew alphabet].*

"OR TORAH," QUOTED IN *THE WISDOM IN THE HEBREW ALPHABET: THE SACRED LETTERS AS A GUIDE TO JEWISH DEED AND THOUGHT*, RABBI MICHAEL MUNK. BROOKLYN: MESORAH PUBLICATIONS, 1983, PAGE 19.

The world was created on a foundation of אֱמֶת, *truth. This can be seen from the first three words of the Torah:* בְּרֵאשִׁית בָּרָא אֱלֹהִים *...If we take the final letter of each word, we have the letters of* אֱמֶת.

LETTERS OF FIRE: MYSTICAL INSIGHTS INTO THE HEBREW LANGUAGE, MATITYAHU GLAZERSON. JERUSALEM: FELDHEIM PUBLISHERS, 1991, PAGE 170.

Exercises

1. Draw a line connecting each Hebrew word to its English translation. For some words, there can be more than one correct translation.

English	Hebrew	
teaching	חַיִּים	
righteousness	צֶדֶק	
truth	עַם	
God	אֱלֹהִים	*God*
nation	מֹשֶׁה	*Moses*
justice	נָבִיא	*prophet*
Torah	עַמִּים	
prophet	תּוֹרָה	*teaching*
life	אֱמֶת	
Moses		
peoples		

2. The vocabulary words introduced in this chapter do not all have singular and plural forms. The following are those nouns that do have both singular and plural forms. Draw a line connecting each plural noun to its singular form. Translate both into English.

	Singular	Plural	
_____	נָבִיא	תּוֹרוֹת	_____
_____	עַם	אֱמִתּוֹת	_____
_____	תּוֹרָה	נְבִיאִים	_____
_____	אֱמֶת	עַמִּים	_____

3. Draw a line connecting the following singular participle forms to their plural counterparts. This list contains both masculine and feminine participles. Translate both into English.

	נוֹתֵן	בּוֹחֲרִים	
_____	שׁוֹמֶרֶת	אוֹכֶלֶת	_____
_____	בּוֹחֵר	שׁוֹמְעִים	_____
_____	מוֹלְכִים	שׁוֹמְרוֹת	_____
_____	אוֹכְלוֹת	נוֹתְנִים	_____
_____	שׁוֹמֵעַ	מוֹלֵךְ	_____

4. Read and translate the following sentences.

a. הַמֶּלֶךְ מוֹלֵךְ. _____

b. אֲנַחְנוּ מוֹלְכִים. _____

c. בְּנֵי הַמְּלָכִים מוֹלְכִים. _____

d. אֱלֹהִים בּוֹרֵא אֱמֶת וָצֶדֶק. _____

e. אֱלֹהֵי יִשְׂרָאֵל בּוֹרֵא יוֹם וָלַיְלָה. _____

f. אֱלֹהֵי יִשְׂרָאֵל בּוֹרֵא אֶת הָעוֹלָם. _____

g. אֱלֹהֵי יִשְׂרָאֵל בּוֹרֵא אֶת הַשָּׁמַיִם וְאֶת הָאָרֶץ. _____

_____

h. מֹשֶׁה בּוֹחֵר בְּנָבִיא. _____

i. אַתָּה בּוֹחֵר בִּנְבִיאִים. _____

j. מֹשֶׁה בּוֹחֵר בִּנְבִיאֵי הָאֱמֶת וָצֶדֶק. _____

k. שֵׁם הַנָּבִיא מֹשֶׁה. _____

l. שֵׁם הָעָם יִשְׂרָאֵל. _____

m. אֱלֹהִים נוֹתֵן אֶת הַתּוֹרָה וְאֶת הַמִּצְוֹת. _____

n. בָּרוּךְ נוֹתֵן הַתּוֹרָה. _____

o. הוּא נוֹתֵן הַחַיִּים. _____

אַתָּה שׁוֹמֵר אֶת הַשַּׁבָּת. .p _____

עַם יִשְׂרָאֵל שׁוֹמֵר מִצְוֹת. .q _____

עַם יִשְׂרָאֵל שׁוֹמֵר אֶת הַבְּרִית. .r _____

אָנוּ שׁוֹמְרֵי הַבְּרִית לְעוֹלָם וָעֶד. .s _____

אֲנַחְנוּ אוֹכְלִים אֶת הַמָּרוֹר וְאֶת הַמַּצָּה. .t _____

אָנוּ אוֹכְלֵי פְּרִי וְלֶחֶם. .u _____

5. Circle all the words in the following prayer book excerpt that have been introduced as vocabulary in this book. Some may have prefixes or suffixes attached. Underline the words that are derived from the roots שׁ־מ־ר‎, מ־ל־ך‎, ב־ר־ך, and שׁ־מ־ר.

From *Hashkiveinu*

כִּי אֵל שׁוֹמְרֵנוּ וּמַצִּילֵנוּ אָתָּה, כִּי אֵל מֶלֶךְ חַנּוּן וְרַחוּם אָתָּה. וּשְׁמוֹר צֵאתֵנוּ וּבוֹאֵנוּ לְחַיִּים וּלְשָׁלוֹם מֵעַתָּה וְעַד עוֹלָם. בָּרוּךְ אַתָּה יְיָ, הַפּוֹרֵשׂ סֻכַּת שָׁלוֹם עָלֵינוּ וְעַל כָּל עַמּוֹ יִשְׂרָאֵל וְעַל יְרוּשָׁלָיִם.

For God our Guardian and our Savior are You, for God a gracious and compassionate Sovereign are You. And guard our departing and our coming to life and to peace from now and unto eternity. Blessed are You, Eternal, the One who spreads a sukkah of peace over us and over all God's {His} people Israel and over Jerusalem.

6. The following prayer book excerpt contains two participles from the root ב־ר־א and two participles from roots you have not yet learned. Circle the four participle forms. Notice that these participles can be translated as either verbs or as nouns (except the last one, which must be a verb because it is followed by the direct object marker אֶת).

From *Yotzer*

בָּרוּךְ אַתָּה יְיָ, אֱלֹהֵינוּ מֶלֶךְ הָעוֹלָם, יוֹצֵר אוֹר, וּבוֹרֵא חֹשֶׁךְ, עֹשֶׂה שָׁלוֹם וּבוֹרֵא אֶת הַכֹּל.

Blessed are You, Eternal, our God, Sovereign of the universe,

translated as verbs: *[who] forms light and creates darkness, makes peace and creates the all {everything}.*

translated as nouns: *Former of light and Creator of darkness, Maker of peace and creating the all {everything}.*

7. Translate the following excerpts from the prayer book and the Bible. Check your translations against the English translations that follow.

   a. From *Ahavah Rabbah*

   | His {God's} *(attached suffix)* | — | וֹ־ |
   | with love | — | בְּאַהֲבָה |

   בָּרוּךְ אַתָּה יְיָ, הַבּוֹחֵר בְּעַמּוֹ יִשְׂרָאֵל בְּאַהֲבָה.

   _____

   b. From Ezekiel 33:4

will hear *(from the root* שׁ־מ־ע)	—	וְשָׁמַע
sound	—	קוֹל
shofar, horn	—	שׁוֹפָר

   וְשָׁמַע הַשֹּׁמֵעַ אֶת־קוֹל הַשּׁוֹפָר...

   _____

   c. From Exodus 16:29

gave *(from the root* נ־ת־ן)	—	נָתַן
to you	—	לָכֶם
therefore	—	עַל־כֵּן
on the sixth day	—	בַּיּוֹם הַשִּׁשִּׁי
two days	—	יוֹמָיִם

   ...יְהֹוָה נָתַן לָכֶם הַשַּׁבָּת עַל־כֵּן הוּא נֹתֵן לָכֶם בַּיּוֹם הַשִּׁשִּׁי לֶחֶם יוֹמָיִם...

   _____

d. From Deuteronomy 30:19

I call to witness against you today	—	הַעִדֹתִי בָכֶם הַיּוֹם
death	—	מָוֶת
I have given {placed} (from the root נ־ת־ן)	—	נָתַתִּי
before you	—	לְפָנֶיךָ
blessing (from the root ב־ר־ך)	—	בְּרָכָה
curse	—	קְלָלָה
choose (from the root ב־ח־ר)	—	וּבָחַרְתָּ

הַעִדֹתִי בָכֶם הַיּוֹם אֶת־הַשָּׁמַיִם וְאֶת־הָאָרֶץ הַחַיִּים וְהַמָּוֶת
נָתַתִּי לְפָנֶיךָ הַבְּרָכָה וְהַקְּלָלָה וּבָחַרְתָּ בַּחַיִּים...

_____

_____

Translations:

a. From *Ahavah Rabbah*—Blessed are You, Eternal, the One who chooses God's {His} people Israel with love.

b. From Ezekiel 33:4—The hearer will hear the sound of the shofar...

c. From Exodus 16:29—...the Eternal One gave to you the Sabbath; therefore God {He} is giving to you on the sixth day bread of two days {a two-day supply of bread}...

d. From Deuteronomy 30:19—I call to witness against you today the heavens and the earth; the life and the death I have placed before you, the blessing and the curse. Choose life...

EXTRA CREDIT

The Bible, the Torah, and the Honor of an Aliyah

The English word "Bible" is used by both Jews and Christians to refer to their sacred scriptures, but the word has a different meaning for each group. What Jews call the Bible is a body of Hebrew literature (with a bit of Aramaic included) spanning an almost thousand-year period from the eleventh or twelveth century B.C.E. to the second century B.C.E. The books that comprise the Jewish Bible (or Hebrew Scriptures, as it is often called) are divided into three sections. The Hebrew name for the Bible, the *Tanach*, תַּנַ״ךְ, is actually an acronym, a word formed from the first letters of the names of these three sections:

Writings — כְּתוּבִים   Prophets — נְבִיאִים   Torah — תּוֹרָה

The Christian Bible includes both the תַּנַ״ךְ, which Christians call the Old Testament, and the New Testament, a collection of Christian literature originally written in Greek, from the first two centuries of the common era. Roman Catholic and Greek Orthodox Bibles include the תַּנַ״ךְ and the New Testament as well as a third collection of books known as the Apocrypha. These are Jewish writings dating from the period immediately before the common era that were not accepted as part of the Bible by the Jewish community. While the Christian Old Testament contains the same books as the תַּנַ״ךְ, they are not divided into the three sections of the תַּנַ״ךְ, but are arranged in a somewhat different order.

The first section of the תַּנַ״ךְ, which is the Torah, consists of five books: Genesis, Exodus, Leviticus, Numbers, and Deuteronomy. These are sometimes called the Five Books of Moses, for Jewish tradition holds that the contents of these books were dictated by God to Moses at Mount Sinai. For this reason, the Torah is regarded as having the highest level of קְדוּשָׁה, "holiness." The Torah scrolls, which are housed in the אֲרוֹן הַקֹּדֶשׁ, "the holy ark," in the synagogue sanctuary, contain only these five books, not the entire תַּנַ״ךְ.

Every week, a section from the Torah is assigned to be read as the פָּרָשַׁת הַשָׁבוּעַ, "the weekly portion." A selection from נְבִיאִים (the Prophets, the second section of the תַּנַ״ךְ) is also assigned for each week. This prophetic selection is known as the Haftarah, הַפְטָרָה, which means "end" or "conclusion," as it is read at the conclusion of the Torah reading.

It is considered a great honor to say the blessings before and after a section is read from the Torah scroll. This honor is known as "having an *aliyah*." The word עֲלִיָה means "ascent," for one is seen as spiritually ascending when one comes forward to the Torah. There is a mystical notion that every reading of the Torah is a dramatic reenactment of the revelation at Mount Sinai. The individual called forward for an *aliyah* thus is seen as figuratively ascending Mount Sinai as a representative of the community, there assembled to receive God's Torah.

The word עֲלִיָה, "ascent," is also used in the phrase "making *aliyah*," which refers to one who is immigrating to Israel. Moving from any other land to אֶרֶץ הַקֹּדֶשׁ, "the Holy Land," is traditionally seen as a similar kind of spiritual ascent.

Review

In Chapter 4, eight vocabulary words and two Hebrew roots were introduced:

עַם תּוֹרָה אֱמֶת חַיִּים אֱלֹהִים נָבִיא צֶדֶק מֹשֶׁה

נ־ת־ן ב־ח־ר

The following Building Blocks were presented:

1. Hebrew participles can act as nouns or verbs.
2. A common participle pattern is: ⬛ ⬛ וֹ ⬛.
3. Hebrew participles have four forms: masculine singular, feminine singular, masculine plural, and feminine plural. The latter three forms are created through vowel changes and endings added to the basic, masculine singular form.
4. The word אֶת appears before the direct object of a verb when the direct object is a definite noun. The word אֶת does not translate into English.
5. Verbs from the root ב־ח־ר are never followed by the direct object marker אֶת. Instead, the prefix ב is attached to the word or words that in English would be considered the direct object.

Reading Practice

Avot

בָּרוּךְ אַתָּה יְיָ אֱלֹהֵינוּ וֵאלֹהֵי אֲבוֹתֵינוּ וְאִמּוֹתֵינוּ. אֱלֹהֵי

אַבְרָהָם, אֱלֹהֵי יִצְחָק, וֵאלֹהֵי יַעֲקֹב, אֱלֹהֵי שָׂרָה, אֱלֹהֵי

רִבְקָה, אֱלֹהֵי לֵאָה, וֵאלֹהֵי רָחֵל, הָאֵל הַגָּדוֹל הַגִּבּוֹר וְהַנּוֹרָא,

אֵל עֶלְיוֹן, גּוֹמֵל חֲסָדִים טוֹבִים וְקוֹנֵה הַכֹּל, וְזוֹכֵר חַסְדֵי

אָבוֹת וְאִמָּהוֹת, וּמֵבִיא גְאֻלָּה לִבְנֵי בְנֵיהֶם, לְמַעַן שְׁמוֹ

בְּאַהֲבָה. מֶלֶךְ עוֹזֵר וּמוֹשִׁיעַ וּמָגֵן. בָּרוּךְ אַתָּה יְיָ, מָגֵן

אַבְרָהָם וְעֶזְרַת שָׂרָה.

Blessed are You, Eternal One, our God and God of our fathers and our mothers, God of Abraham, God of Isaac, and God of Jacob, God of Sarah, God of Rebekah, God of Leah, and God of Rachel, the great, mighty, and awesome God, supreme God, doing good kindnesses and the Possesser of all, and remembering [the] kindnesses of [our] fathers and mothers, and bringing redemption to the children of their children, for the sake of God's {His} name in love. Sovereign, Helper and Savior and Shield. Blessed are You, Eternal One, Shield of Abraham and Help of Sarah.

Expressions and Greetings

Good morning!	בֹּקֶר טוֹב
Good night!	לַיְלָה טוֹב
[Have] a good week!	שָׁבוּעַ טוֹב
Good luck! {Congratulations!}	מַזָּל טוֹב
A good year! {Happy New Year!}	שָׁנָה טוֹבָה
Happy holiday!	חַג שָׂמֵחַ
A complete healing! {Get well soon!}	רְפוּאָה שְׁלֵמָה

The Fourth and Fifth Commandments (Exodus 20:8 and 20:12)

זָכוֹר אֶת־יוֹם הַשַּׁבָּת לְקַדְּשׁוֹ:

כַּבֵּד אֶת־אָבִיךָ וְאֶת־אִמֶּךָ...

Remember the day of the Sabbath to make it holy.
Honor your father and your mother...

Prayer Book Translations

Avot

Praised be our God, the God of our fathers and our mothers: God of Abraham, God of Isaac, and God of Jacob; God of Sarah, God of Rebekah, God of Leah, and God of Rachel; great, mighty, and awesome, God supreme.

Ruler of all the living, Your ways are ways of love. You remember the faithfulness of our ancestors, and in love bring redemption to their children's children for the sake of Your name.

You are our Sovereign and our Help, our Redeemer and our Shield. We praise You, Eternal One, Shield of Abraham, Protector of Sarah.

GATES OF PRAYER FOR SHABBAT AND WEEKDAYS: A GENDER SENSITIVE PRAYERBOOK, ED. CHAIM STERN. NEW YORK: CCAR PRESS, 1994.

Blessed are you, The Ancient One, our God, God of our ancestors,

God of Abraham	*God of Sarah*
God of Isaac	*God of Rebekah*
God of Jacob	*God of Rachel*
	and God of Leah;

Great, heroic, awesome God, supreme divinity, imparting deeds of kindness, begetter of all; mindful of the loyalty of Israel's ancestors, bringing, with love, redemption to their children's children for the sake of the divine name. REGAL ONE, our help, salvation and protector: Blessed are you, KIND ONE, the shield of Abraham and help of Sarah.

KOL HANESHAMAH: SHABBAT VEHAGIM. WYNCOTE, PA.: THE RECONSTRUCTIONIST PRESS, 1994

Praised are You Adonai, our God and God of our ancestors, God of Abraham, Isaac, and Jacob, Sarah, Rebecca, Rachel, and Leah, great, mighty, awesome, exalted God who bestows lovingkindness, Creator of all. You remember the pious deeds of our ancestors and will send a redeemer to their children's children because of Your loving nature.

You are the Sovereign who helps and guards, saves and shields. Praised are You Adonai, Shield of Abraham and Guardian of Sarah.

SIDDUR SIM SHALOM FOR SHABBAT AND FESTIVALS. NEW YORK: THE RABBINICAL ASSEMBLY, 1998.

Blessed art thou, Lord our God and God of our fathers, God of Abraham, God of Isaac and God of Jacob; great, mighty and revered God, sublime God, who bestowest lovingkindness, and art Master of all things; who rememberest the good deeds of our fathers, and who wilt graciously bring a redeemer to their children's children for the sake of thy name.

O King, Supporter, Savior and Shield. Blessed art thou, O Lord, Shield of Abraham.

DAILY PRAYER BOOK, TRANS. PHILLIP BIRNBAUM. NEW YORK: HEBREW PUBLISHING CO., 1949.

As mentioned previously in the Extra Credit section of Chapter 2, gender-sensitive versions of the *Avot* prayer, which include the names of our matriarchs as well as our patriarchs, were composed within the last quarter of the twentieth century. There is not a single fixed wording for these new gender-sensitive versions.

The Hebrew version included in this chapter is from the Reform Movement's prayer book *Gates of Prayer for Shabbat and Weekdays: A Gender Sensitive Prayerbook*. An identical version appears in the Reconstructionist prayer book *Kol Haneshamah*, except that the name Rachel is mentioned in the Hebrew before Leah and the plural form used for אֵם, "mother," is אִמּוֹת instead of אִמָּהוֹת.

The Conservative prayer book *Sim Shalom* offers two versions of the *Avot*, one with the traditional wording preserved and a gender-sensitive version that includes the matriarchs. The gender-sensitive version in *Sim Shalom* differs from the Hebrew version of this chapter in several small ways: the name Rachel is mentioned before Leah; the word וְאִמּוֹתֵינוּ, "and our mothers," is not added in the first line nor later in the prayer; the word גּוֹאֵל, "redeemer," appears in place of גְּאֻלָּה, "redemption"; the word פּוֹקֵד, "guards," is added in the second to last line; and God is described in the last line, not as עֶזְרַת שָׂרָה, "help of Sarah," but as פֹּקֵד שָׂרָה, "guardian of Sarah."

All of the other variations in the first three translations above are the result of differing interpretations by the translator, and not due to different Hebrew texts. The fourth and last translation above, from the *Daily Prayer Book*, is the traditional *Avot* text, without any of the gender-sensitive alterations made in recent years.

Vocabulary

Try to locate each of these words in the Reading Practice selections (*Avot*, expressions and greetings, the Fourth and Fifth Commandments). Some of these words appear with prefixes and/or suffixes attached. Some appear in word pairs.

father *m* (*plural:* fathers, ancestors)	—	אַב (אָבוֹת)
mother *f* (*plural:* mothers)	—	אֵם (אִמּוֹת, אִמָּהוֹת)
kindness *m* (*plural:* kindnesses)	—	חֶסֶד (חֲסָדִים)
God *m*	—	אֵל
big, great *adj*	—	גָּדוֹל
good *adj*	—	טוֹב

Note:

1. Both אִמּוֹת and אִמָּהוֹת are used as plural forms of אֵם, "mother."
2. The word חֶסֶד has a range of meanings: favor, goodness, love, loving-kindness, mercy, benevolence. You may see it translated in any of these ways.
3. The word אֵל is a form of the word אֱלֹהִים, "God," introduced in the last chapter.

The Hebrew names of our matriarchs and patriarchs appear in the *Avot* prayer. Now you can recognize them when you encounter them.

Abraham	—	אַבְרָהָם
Sarah	—	שָׂרָה
Isaac	—	יִצְחָק
Rebekah	—	רִבְקָה
Jacob	—	יַעֲקֹב
Leah	—	לֵאָה
Rachel	—	רָחֵל

Hebrew Roots

ע־ז־ר

The basic meaning of the root ע־ז־ר is "help." In Genesis 2:18, God decides to create an עֵזֶר, "helper" or "helpmate," for the first man. In Isaiah 50:9, the prophet states that the Eternal God יַעֲזָר־לִי, "will help me." In Psalm 118:7, the Psalmist finds reassurance in the Eternal One as עֹזְרִי, "my helper." There are many biblical names that are derived from this root:

Ezra {helper}	—	עֶזְרָא
Azriel {my help is God}	—	עַזְרִיאֵל
Azariah {Yah helped}	—	עֲזַרְיָה
Eliezer {my God is help}	—	אֱלִיעֶזֶר
Elazar {God helped}	—	אֶלְעָזָר

In the Reading Practice at the beginning of this chapter, the root ע־ז־ר appears twice, both times in the *Avot* prayer:

helper (*a participle, could also be translated as helping, helps, one who helps*)	—	עוֹזֵר
help (*noun*)	—	עֶזְרָה
help of Sarah	—	עֶזְרַת שָׂרָה

ז־כ־ר

The root ז־כ־ר has the basic meaning of "remember." In Genesis 9:16, God makes a covenant with Noah and his descendants never again to bring a flood to destroy the earth, and the rainbow is placed in the sky as a sign לִזְכֹּר, "to remember," this everlasting covenant. In Proverbs 10:7, we are taught זֵכֶר צַדִּיק לִבְרָכָה, "remembrance of a righteous one is a blessing." These words are often quoted at the conclusion of a eulogy or written in condolence cards and rendered in translation as "May the memory of the righteous be a blessing." On Yom Kippur, יִזְכֹּר, a "memorial" prayer, is said on behalf of our departed loved ones. (The name יִזְכֹּר comes from the first word of this memorial prayer: ...יִזְכֹּר אֱלֹהִים נִשְׁמַת, "May God remember the soul of....")

The following are words, both ancient and modern, derived from the root ז־כ־ר:

memorable	—	זָכִיר
remembrance	—	זְכִירָה
mentioning, reminding, recalling to memory	—	הַזְכָּרָה
secretary	—	מַזְכִּיר
souvenir, reminder	—	מַזְכֶּרֶת
memory, remembrance; trace, hint	—	זֵכֶר
in memory of	—	לְזֵכֶר
memory, remembrance, commemoration	—	זִכָּרוֹן
mnemonics	—	זִכְרוֹנִיּוּת
forget-me-not (plant)	—	זִכְרִינִי
Zechariah {*Yah* remembered}	—	זְכַרְיָה

In the Reading Practice at the beginning of this chapter, the root ז־כ־ר appears twice, once as a participle in the *Avot* prayer and once in the Fourth Commandment:

remembering, remembers, rememberer of	—	זוֹכֵר
and remembering [the] kindnesses of [our] fathers and mothers	—	וְזוֹכֵר חַסְדֵי אָבוֹת וְאִמָּהוֹת

CHAPTER 5

remember	—	זָכוֹר
Remember the day of the Sabbath to make it holy	—	זָכוֹר אֶת־יוֹם הַשַּׁבָּת לְקַדְּשׁוֹ

Building Blocks

Adjectives

Adjectives are words that describe nouns, such as "big" or "old" or "good." In English, the adjective is placed immediately before the noun it describes:

a great prophet or *a good name*

In Hebrew, the adjective is placed immediately after the noun it describes:

a great prophet	—	נָבִיא גָּדוֹל
a good name	—	שֵׁם טוֹב

In English there is only one form of each adjective. In Hebrew, each adjective has four forms: masculine singular, feminine singular, masculine plural, and feminine plural. The form of the adjective must match the noun it describes. Examples:

a good king *(masculine singular)*	—	מֶלֶךְ טוֹב
a good land *(feminine singular)*	—	אֶרֶץ טוֹבָה
good kings *(masculine plural)*	—	מְלָכִים טוֹבִים
good lands *(feminine plural)*	—	אֲרָצוֹת טוֹבוֹת

All of the Hebrew expressions and greetings introduced at the beginning of this chapter are adjective and noun combinations. The following are masculine singular combinations:

good morning	—	בֹּקֶר טוֹב
good night	—	לַיְלָה טוֹב
a good week	—	שָׁבוּעַ טוֹב
good luck {i.e., congratulations}	—	מַזָּל טוֹב
happy holiday	—	חַג שָׂמֵחַ

The following are feminine singular combinations:

| a good year | — | שָׁנָה טוֹבָה |
| a complete healing | — | רְפוּאָה שְׁלֵמָה |

The following masculine plural combinations appeared in the Reading Practice selections of this chapter and in Chapter 4:

| good kindnesses {good acts of kindness} | — | חֲסָדִים טוֹבִים |
| good prophets | — | נְבִיאִים טוֹבִים |

More on Plurals

As mentioned in Chapter 4, some words, such as the word חַיִּים, have the plural ending ים and follow rules for plural nouns even though they translate into English as singular nouns. Such nouns are described in Hebrew using plural adjectives. Examples:

| a good life | — | חַיִּים טוֹבִים |
| much compassion | — | רַחֲמִים רַבִּים |

Definite Nouns and Adjectives

We have already introduced the concept of definite nouns. Nouns that are preceded by the definite article הַ, meaning "the," are definite nouns. Possessive words like בֵּיתְךָ, "your house," and names of people and places are also definite nouns.

In Hebrew, adjectives that describe definite nouns are also definite, that is, they are preceded by the definite article הַ. The הַ attached to the adjective is not translated. Examples:

| the good mother | — | הָאֵם הַטּוֹבָה |
| the awesome days {the Days of Awe, the High Holy Days} | — | הַיָּמִים הַנּוֹרָאִים |

Adjectives as Nouns

In Hebrew, an adjective is sometimes used as a noun. When this occurs, the adjective is translated as "*adjective* one." Example:

holy	—	קָדוֹשׁ
the holy one	—	הַקָּדוֹשׁ
the Holy One, blessed is God {He}	—	הַקָּדוֹשׁ בָּרוּךְ הוּא

Reading Practice with Building Blocks

Following are some of the Reading Practice selections from this and previous chapters that contain adjectives. Reread these selections, noting the form of each adjective.

Avot

בָּרוּךְ אַתָּה יְיָ אֱלֹהֵינוּ וֵאלֹהֵי אֲבוֹתֵינוּ וְאִמּוֹתֵינוּ. אֱלֹהֵי אַבְרָהָם,
אֱלֹהֵי יִצְחָק, וֵאלֹהֵי יַעֲקֹב, אֱלֹהֵי שָׂרָה, אֱלֹהֵי רִבְקָה, אֱלֹהֵי לֵאָה,
וֵאלֹהֵי רָחֵל, **הָאֵל הַגָּדוֹל הַגִּבּוֹר וְהַנּוֹרָא, אֵל עֶלְיוֹן,**
גּוֹמֵל **חֲסָדִים טוֹבִים** וְקוֹנֵה הַכֹּל, וְזוֹכֵר חַסְדֵי אָבוֹת וְאִמָּהוֹת,
וּמֵבִיא גְאֻלָּה לִבְנֵי בְנֵיהֶם, לְמַעַן שְׁמוֹ בְּאַהֲבָה. מֶלֶךְ עוֹזֵר
וּמוֹשִׁיעַ וּמָגֵן. בָּרוּךְ אַתָּה יְיָ, מָגֵן אַבְרָהָם וְעֶזְרַת שָׂרָה.

*Blessed are You, Eternal One, our God and God of our fathers and our mothers, God of Abraham, God of Isaac, and God of Jacob, God of Sarah, God of Rebekah, God of Leah, and God of Rachel, **the great**, **mighty**, **and awesome God**, **supreme God**, doing **good kindnesses** and the Possesser of all, and remembering [the] kindnesses of [our] fathers and mothers, and bringing redemption to the children of their children, for the sake of God's {His} name in love. Sovereign, Helper and Savior and Shield. Blessed are You, Eternal One, Shield of Abraham and Help of Sarah.*

Va-anachnu

וַאֲנַחְנוּ כּוֹרְעִים וּמִשְׁתַּחֲוִים וּמוֹדִים, לִפְנֵי מֶלֶךְ מַלְכֵי הַמְּלָכִים,
הַקָּדוֹשׁ בָּרוּךְ הוּא.

*And we bend the knee and bow and give thanks before the Sovereign of sovereigns of sovereigns, **the Holy One**, blessed is God {He}.*

בָּרוּךְ אַתָּה יְיָ אֱלֹהֵינוּ מֶלֶךְ הָעוֹלָם, אֲשֶׁר בָּחַר בִּ**נְבִיאִים
טוֹבִים**, וְרָצָה בְדִבְרֵיהֶם הַנֶּאֱמָרִים בֶּאֱמֶת, בָּרוּךְ אַתָּה יְיָ,
הַבּוֹחֵר בַּתּוֹרָה וּבְמֹשֶׁה עַבְדּוֹ, וּבְיִשְׂרָאֵל עַמּוֹ, וּבִנְבִיאֵי הָאֱמֶת
וָצֶדֶק.

*Blessed are You, Eternal our God, Sovereign of the universe, who chose **good prophets**
and found favor in their words spoken in truth. Blessed are You, Eternal One, the [One
who] chooses the Torah and Moses, God's {His} servant, and Israel, God's {His} people,
and prophets of the truth and righteousness.*

GRAMMAR Enrichment

Adjective Chart

The following is a chart using the adjectives טוֹב and גָּדוֹל to illustrate the four forms of Hebrew adjectives: masculine singular, feminine
singular, masculine plural, and feminine plural. As you can see from the adjective גָּדוֹל, sometimes vowel changes occur when endings are attached. It is not
necessary to memorize these vowel changes, but it is important to be able to recognize adjectives
with endings.

big, great	good	
גָּדוֹל	טוֹב	*masculine singular*
גְּדוֹלָה	טוֹבָה	*feminine singular*
גְּדוֹלִים	טוֹבִים	*masculine plural*
גְּדוֹלוֹת	טוֹבוֹת	*feminine plural*

FROM OUR TEXTS

Honoring Father and Mother

In the following midrash, honoring one's father and mother is described as even more important than honoring God. For while the ways in which one shows honor to God may be limited by one's financial means, there is no such limitation placed on the ways in which one honors one's parents.

ר׳ שִׁמְעוֹן בֶּן יוֹחַאי אוֹמֵר: גָּדוֹל הוּא כִּבּוּד אָב וָאֵם, שֶׁהֶעֱדִיפוֹ הַקָּדוֹשׁ־בָּרוּךְ־הוּא יוֹתֵר מִכְּבוֹדוֹ, שֶׁבִּכְבוֹדוֹ שֶׁל הַקָּדוֹשׁ־בָּרוּךְ־הוּא כָּתוּב: "כַּבֵּד אֶת יְיָ מֵהוֹנֶךָ." כֵּיצַד מְכַבְּדוֹ מֵהוֹנוֹ? מַפְרִישׁ לֶקֶט שִׁכְחָה וּפֵאָה, תְּרוּמָה, מַעֲשֵׂר רִאשׁוֹן וּמַעֲשֵׂר שֵׁנִי וּמַעֲשַׂר עָנִי, וְחַלָּה, עוֹשֶׂה סֻכָּה וְלוּלָב וְשׁוֹפָר, וּתְפִלִּין וְצִיצִית, מַאֲכִיל רְעֵבִים, מַשְׁקֶה צְמֵאִים וּמַלְבִּישׁ עֲרֻמִּים. אִם יֵשׁ לְךָ אַתָּה חַיָּב בְּכָל אֵלוּ, וְאִם אֵין לְךָ אֵין אַתָּה חַיָּב בְּאַחַת מֵהֶן אֲבָל כְּשֶׁאַתָּה בָא אֵצֶל כִּבּוּד אָב וָאֵם, בֵּין שֶׁיֵּשׁ לְךָ הוֹן, בֵּין שֶׁאֵין לְךָ הוֹן "כַּבֵּד אֶת־אָבִיךָ וְאֶת־אִמֶּךָ."

R. Shimon ben Yochai says: Honoring one's father and mother is so important that the Holy One places it above giving honor to God. For, regarding giving honor to God, it is written: "Honor the Eternal One מֵהוֹנֶךָ *with your wealth" (Proverbs 3:9). How does one honor God with one's wealth?*

[A list of mitzvot follows, including offerings and tithes, religious practices such as building a sukkah, and ethical obligations such as feeding the hungry and clothing the naked.] *If you have the means, you are obligated to do all these things, but if you don't have the means, you are not obliged to do even one of them. However, when it comes to honoring one's father and mother, whether you have the means or not, you are commanded "Honor your father and mother" (Exodus 20:12).*

FROM PESIKTA RABBATI 23/24:2; MECHILTA, YITRO, BA-CHODESH, 8; PALESTINIAN TALMUD, PE-AH 1:1, 15D, AS QUOTED IN SEFER HA-AGGADAH, EDS. CHAYIM NACHMAN BIALIK AND YEHOSHUA HANA RAVNITZKY. TEL AVIV: DVIR PUBLISHING, 1952.

Exercises

1. Draw a line connecting each Hebrew word to its English translation. For some words, there can be more than one correct translation.

God	גָּדוֹל
great	אֵל
kindness	אַב
father	אִמָּהוֹת
big	חֶסֶד
good	אָבוֹת
mother	טוֹב
kindnesses	חֲסָדִים
ancestors	אֵם
mothers	
fathers	

2. Draw a line connecting each Hebrew name to its English equivalent.

Isaac	רָחֵל
Jacob	יִצְחָק
Rebekah	מֹשֶׁה
Rachel	אַבְרָהָם
Moses	רִבְקָה
Leah	שָׂרָה
Sarah	יַעֲקֹב
Abraham	לֵאָה

3. Following each noun below are three adjective forms. Circle the adjective that correctly matches the noun. Translate each phrase into English.

a. מֶלֶךְ (טוֹבִים, גְּדוֹלָה, טוֹב) _____

b. אִמּוֹת (טוֹבָה, גָּדוֹל, טוֹבוֹת) _____

c. אָבוֹת (טוֹבוֹת, גְּדוֹלִים, גָּדוֹל) _____

d. הַבָּנִים (טוֹבִים, הַטוֹבִים, גְּדוֹלוֹת) _____

e. רָחֵל (טוֹב, הַגְּדוֹלָה, גְּדוֹלוֹת) _____

f. הַחַיִּים (טוֹבִים, הַטוֹב, הַטוֹבִים) _____

4. Read and translate the following sentences.

a. הוּא זוֹכֵר אֶת הַבְּרִית. _____

b. אֲנַחְנוּ זוֹכְרִים אֶת הַיָּמִים הַטוֹבִים. _____
_____

c. יִצְחָק וְרִבְקָה זוֹכְרִים אֶת שָׂרָה וְאֶת אַבְרָהָם. _____
_____

d. הַנָּבִיא הַגָּדוֹל זוֹכֵר אֶת מִצְוֹת הַתּוֹרָה. _____
_____

e. עַם יִשְׂרָאֵל בּוֹחֵר בְּמֶלֶךְ טוֹב. _____
_____

f. בָּרוּךְ עוֹזֵר הָעָם. _____

g. יַעֲקֹב בּוֹחֵר בְּעוֹזְרֵי הָעָם. _____
_____

h. לֵאָה וּמֹשֶׁה אוֹכְלִים לֶחֶם טוֹב וּפְרִי טוֹב. _____
_____

i. הָאִמָּהוֹת הַטוֹבוֹת וְהָאָבוֹת הַטוֹבִים אוֹכְלִים מַצָּה, וְהַבָּנִים אוֹכְלִים חָמֵץ. _____

.j אָנוּ שׁוֹמְרֵי שַׁבָּת טוֹבִים.

.k הָאֵל הַגָּדוֹל בּוֹרֵא אֶת הָעוֹלָם יוֹם וָלַיְלָה.

.l אֱלֹהִים בּוֹרֵא חֶסֶד וֶאֱמֶת וָצֶדֶק.

5. Circle all the words that you know in the following prayer book excerpt. Some may have prefixes or suffixes attached. Underline the word that is derived from the root בּ־ר־ךּ. Underline twice the adjective and noun combination.

Insert to *Birkat Shalom* (in the *Amidah*) between Rosh HaShanah and Yom Kippur

בְּסֵפֶר חַיִּים וּבְרָכָה נִכָּתֵב לְחַיִּים טוֹבִים וּלְשָׁלוֹם.

In [the] Book of Life and Blessing may we be inscribed for a good life and for peace.

6. Circle the words in the following prayer book excerpt that have been introduced as vocabulary in this book. Some may have prefixes or suffixes attached. Underline the words that are derived from the roots שׁ־מ־ר, ז־כ־ר, שׁ־מ־ע, and .

First Verse of *L'chah Dodi*

שָׁמוֹר וְזָכוֹר בְּדִבּוּר אֶחָד, הִשְׁמִיעָנוּ אֵל הַמְּיֻחָד. יְיָ אֶחָד
וּשְׁמוֹ אֶחָד לְשֵׁם וּלְתִפְאֶרֶת וְלִתְהִלָּה.

Keep and remember, in one word, the unique God caused us to hear. The Eternal is One and God's {His} name is One, for a name [renown] and for glory and for praise.

7. Psalm 121 is included in certain liturgical settings, such as the Memorial Service in *Gates of Prayer* and *Gates of Repentance*. The first two verses have been set to music. Circle the words that have been introduced in this book. Underline the words that are derived from the root עָזַר.

Psalm 121:1–2

אֶשָּׂא עֵינַי אֶל־הֶהָרִים מֵאַיִן יָבֹא עֶזְרִי: עֶזְרִי מֵעִם יְהֹוָה עֹשֵׂה שָׁמַיִם וָאָרֶץ:

I lift my eyes to the mountains, from where will come my help. My help is from the Eternal One, Maker of heaven and earth.

8. Translate the following excerpts from the prayer book and the Bible. Check your translations against the English translations that follow.

a. High Holy Day Insert to *Hodaah* (in the *Amidah*)

inscribe	—	וּכְתוֹב
for *(attached prefix)*	—	לְ־
all	—	כָּל
your *(attached suffix)*	—	־ךָ

וּכְתוֹב לְחַיִּים טוֹבִים כָּל בְּנֵי בְרִיתֶךָ.

b. Psalm 109:26

help me *(from the root* עָזַר*)*	—	עָזְרֵנִי
my God *(from the word* אֱלֹהִים*)*	—	אֱלֹהָי
save me	—	הוֹשִׁיעֵנִי
as *(attached prefix)*	—	כְּ־
your *(attached suffix)*	—	־ךָ

עָזְרֵנִי יְהֹוָה אֱלֹהָי הוֹשִׁיעֵנִי כְחַסְדֶּךָ:

c. Deuteronomy 8:10

you shall eat *(from the root* א־כ־ל*)*	—	וְאָכַלְתָּ
and you shall be satisfied	—	וְשָׂבָעְתָּ
and you shall bless *(from the root* ב־ר־ך*)*	—	וּבֵרַכְתָּ
your God *(from the word* אֱלֹהִים*)*	—	אֱלֹהֶיךָ
on account of	—	עַל
that	—	אֲשֶׁר
he, it has given *(from the root* נ־ת־ן*)*	—	נָתַן
to you	—	לָךְ

וְאָכַלְתָּ וְשָׂבָעְתָּ וּבֵרַכְתָּ אֶת־יְהֹוָה אֱלֹהֶיךָ עַל־הָאָרֶץ הַטֹּבָה אֲשֶׁר נָתַן־לָךְ׃

---

d. From Deuteronomy 10:17

your God *(from the word* אֱלֹהִים*)*	—	אֱלֹהֵיכֶם
ruler of	—	אֲדֹנֵי
rulers	—	אֲדֹנִים
mighty	—	גִּבֹּר
awesome	—	נוֹרָא

יְהֹוָה אֱלֹהֵיכֶם הוּא אֱלֹהֵי הָאֱלֹהִים וַאֲדֹנֵי הָאֲדֹנִים הָאֵל הַגָּדֹל הַגִּבֹּר וְהַנּוֹרָא...

Translations:

a. High Holy Day insert to *Hodaah* (in the *Amidah*)—Inscribe for a good life all the children of Your covenant.

b. Psalm 109:26—Help me, Eternal One, my God, save me as Your kindness.

c. Deuteronomy 8:10—You shall eat and you shall be satisfied and you shall bless the Eternal One your God on account of the good land that God {He} has given to you.

d. From Deuteronomy 10:17—The Eternal One, your God, God {He} is God of the gods, and Ruler of the rulers, the great, mighty, and awesome God...

EXTRA CREDIT

Greetings and Expressions

Many of the greetings and expressions used in contemporary Jewish life are adjective and noun combinations. Those listed at the beginning of this chapter are fairly easy to understand; others, however, require a bit more explanation.

The standard Hebrew greeting for most Jewish festivals is חַג שָׂמֵחַ, "happy holiday." Yet one also often hears the greeting *gut yontiv*. *Gut yontiv* is a linguistic phrase that illustrates the evolution of Jewish language. *Yontiv* is a Yiddish pronunciation of the Hebrew adjective-noun combination יוֹם טוֹב, "a good day." As far back as the Bible, the phrase יוֹם טוֹב is used to refer to a holiday. When coupled with the Yiddish adjective גוּט, *gut*, meaning "good," גוּט יוֹם טוֹב became the Yiddish greeting meaning "a good holiday." Many who say the greeting are unaware that they are literally saying "a good good day."

On הַיָּמִים הַנּוֹרָאִים, "the awesome days" (the High Holy Days), we hear the greeting שָׁנָה טוֹבָה, "a good year." Sometimes people say לְשָׁנָה טוֹבָה, which literally means "for a good year." לְשָׁנָה טוֹבָה is actually the first two words of a three-word greeting: לְשָׁנָה טוֹבָה תִּכָּתֵבוּ, "For a good year may you be inscribed." This three-word greeting often appears on High Holy Day cards, along with variations such as:

| For a good and sweet year may you be inscribed | — | לְשָׁנָה טוֹבָה וּמְתוּקָה תִּכָּתֵבוּ |
| For a good year may you be inscribed and sealed | — | לְשָׁנָה טוֹבָה תִּכָּתֵבוּ וְתֵחָתֵמוּ |

This inscribing and sealing refers to the Book of Life, which tradition says is opened on Rosh HaShanah, with the fate of all the completely righteous and the completely wicked inscribed therein for the coming year. The fate of all others hangs in the balance until Yom Kippur and is affected by the depth and sincerity of our תְּשׁוּבָה, "repentance" or "turning back," during the ten-day period that spans Rosh HaShanah and Yom Kippur.

On Yom Kippur, the traditional greeting is גְּמַר חֲתִימָה טוֹבָה, which includes both a word pair, גְּמַר חֲתִימָה ("completion of sealing"), and a noun, טוֹבָה ("goodness" or "good things"), which is derived from the same root, ט־ו־ב, as the adjective טוֹב. The greeting means "[May the] completion of sealing be good things," reflecting the notion that one's fate for the coming year is sealed at the conclusion of the holy days.

On Chanukah, it is customary to play with a dreidel, a spinning top that has one of these Hebrew letters written on each of its four sides: שׁ, ה, ג, נ. These four letters stand for a four-word sentence, which includes an adjective-noun combination: נֵס גָּדוֹל, "a great miracle." The entire sentence is נֵס גָּדוֹל הָיָה שָׁם, "A great miracle happened there." The reference is to the Chanukah miracle of the oil, which happened in the Temple in Jerusalem. Dreidels made in Israel substitute the letter פ for the letter שׁ, to indicate that the miracle happened not שָׁם, "there," but פֹּה, "here."

And a last greeting worth mentioning is Happy Birthday, which in Hebrew consists of a word pair יוֹם הוֹלֶדֶת, "day of birth," coupled with the adjective שָׂמֵחַ, "happy." יוֹם הוֹלֶדֶת שָׂמֵחַ can be sung to the same tune as "Happy Birthday to You."

Review

In Chapter 5, six vocabulary words and two Hebrew roots were introduced:

אָב   אֵם   חֶסֶד   אֵל   גָּדוֹל   טוֹב

עֵזֵ־ר   ז־כ־ר

Seven Hebrew names were introduced:

אַבְרָהָם   שָׂרָה   יִצְחָק   רִבְקָה   יַעֲקֹב   לֵאָה   רָחֵל

The following Building Blocks were presented:

1. Adjectives come after the nouns they describe.
2. There are four forms of every adjective: masculine singular, feminine singular, masculine plural, and feminine plural.
3. The form of the adjective must match the type of noun it describes: masculine or feminine, singular or plural, definite or indefinite.

Reading Practice

V'ahavta (Deuteronomy 6:5–9)

וְאָהַבְתָּ אֵת יְיָ אֱלֹהֶיךָ בְּכָל־לְבָבְךָ וּבְכָל־נַפְשְׁךָ וּבְכָל־
מְאֹדֶךָ: וְהָיוּ הַדְּבָרִים הָאֵלֶּה אֲשֶׁר אָנֹכִי מְצַוְּךָ הַיּוֹם עַל־לְבָבֶךָ:
וְשִׁנַּנְתָּם לְבָנֶיךָ וְדִבַּרְתָּ בָּם בְּשִׁבְתְּךָ בְּבֵיתֶךָ וּבְלֶכְתְּךָ בַדֶּרֶךְ
וּבְשָׁכְבְּךָ וּבְקוּמֶךָ: וּקְשַׁרְתָּם לְאוֹת עַל־יָדֶךָ וְהָיוּ לְטֹטָפֹת בֵּין
עֵינֶיךָ: וּכְתַבְתָּם עַל מְזוּזוֹת בֵּיתֶךָ וּבִשְׁעָרֶיךָ:

You shall love the Eternal your God with all your heart and with all your soul and with all your being. And they will be, these words that I command you today, upon your heart. You shall teach them to your children and speak about them in your sitting {when you sit} in your house and in your walking {when you walk} on the way and in your lying down {when you lie down} and in your arising {when you arise}. You shall

*bind them for a sign upon your hand and they will be symbols between your eyes. You
shall write them upon the doorposts of your house and on your gates.*

L'ma-an Tizk'ru (Numbers 15:40–41)

לְמַעַן תִּזְכְּרוּ וַעֲשִׂיתֶם אֶת־כָּל־מִצְוֹתָי וִהְיִיתֶם קְדֹשִׁים
לֵאלֹהֵיכֶם: אֲנִי יְיָ אֱלֹהֵיכֶם אֲשֶׁר הוֹצֵאתִי אֶתְכֶם מֵאֶרֶץ
מִצְרַיִם לִהְיוֹת לָכֶם לֵאלֹהִים, אֲנִי יְיָ אֱלֹהֵיכֶם:

*In order that you will remember and do all My commandments and be holy to your
God. I am the Eternal your God, that I brought you out from the land of Egypt to be to
your God. I am the Eternal your God.*

Shalom Aleichem

שָׁלוֹם עֲלֵיכֶם, מַלְאֲכֵי הַשָּׁרֵת, מַלְאֲכֵי עֶלְיוֹן, מִמֶּלֶךְ מַלְכֵי
הַמְּלָכִים, הַקָּדוֹשׁ בָּרוּךְ הוּא.
בּוֹאֲכֶם לְשָׁלוֹם, מַלְאֲכֵי הַשָּׁלוֹם, מַלְאֲכֵי עֶלְיוֹן, מִמֶּלֶךְ מַלְכֵי
הַמְּלָכִים, הַקָּדוֹשׁ בָּרוּךְ הוּא.
בָּרְכוּנִי לְשָׁלוֹם, מַלְאֲכֵי הַשָּׁלוֹם, מַלְאֲכֵי עֶלְיוֹן, מִמֶּלֶךְ
מַלְכֵי הַמְּלָכִים, הַקָּדוֹשׁ בָּרוּךְ הוּא.
צֵאתְכֶם לְשָׁלוֹם, מַלְאֲכֵי הַשָּׁלוֹם, מַלְאֲכֵי עֶלְיוֹן, מִמֶּלֶךְ
מַלְכֵי הַמְּלָכִים, הַקָּדוֹשׁ בָּרוּךְ הוּא.

*Peace be upon you, the angels of service, angels of the Supreme One, from the
Sovereign of the sovereigns of the sovereigns, the Holy One, blessed is God {He}.
[May] your coming be in {to} peace, the angels of peace, angels of the Supreme One,
from the Sovereign of the sovereigns of the sovereigns, the Holy One, blessed is God
{He}.
Bless me for peace, the angels of peace....
[May] your leaving be in {to} peace, the angels of peace....*

Translations

V'ahavta

You shall love your Eternal God with all your heart, with all your mind, with all your being. Set these words, which I command you this day, upon your heart. Teach them faithfully to your children; speak of them in your home and on your way, when you lie down and when you rise up. Bind them as a sign upon your hand; let them be symbols before your eyes; inscribe them on the doorposts of your house, and on your gates.

GATES OF PRAYER FOR SHABBAT AND WEEKDAYS: A GENDER SENSITIVE PRAYERBOOK, ED. CHAIM STERN. NEW YORK: CCAR PRESS, 1994.

And you must love THE ONE, your God, with your whole heart, with every breath, with all you have. Take these words that I command you now to heart. Teach them intently to your children. Speak them when you sit inside your house or walk upon the road, when you lie down and when you rise. And bind them as a sign upon your hand, and keep them visible before your eyes. Inscribe them on the doorposts of your house and on your gates.

KOL HANESHAMAH: SHABBAT VEHAGIM. WYNCOTE, PA.: THE RECONSTRUCTIONIST PRESS, 1994.

You shall love Adonai your God with all your heart, with all your soul, with all your might. And these words, which I command you this day, you shall take to heart. Teach them, diligently, to your children, and recite them at home and away, night and day. Bind them as a sign upon your hand, and as a reminder above your eyes. Inscribe them upon the doorposts of your homes and upon your gates.

SIDDUR SIM SHALOM FOR SHABBAT AND FESTIVALS. NEW YORK: THE RABBINICAL ASSEMBLY, 1998.

You shall love the Lord your God with all your heart, and with all your soul, and with all your might. And these words which I command you today shall be in your heart. You shall teach them diligently to your children, and you shall speak of them when you are sitting at home and when you go on a journey, when you lie down and when you rise up. You shall bind them for a sign on your hand, and they shall be for frontlets between your eyes. You shall inscribe them on the doorposts of your house and on your gates.

DAILY PRAYER BOOK, TRANS. PHILLIP BIRNBAUM. NEW YORK: HEBREW PUBLISHING CO., 1949.

Vocabulary

Try to locate each of these words in the Reading Practice selections (*V'ahavta, L'ma-an Tizk'ru,* and *Shalom Aleichem*). Some appear with prefixes and/or suffixes attached. Some appear in word pairs.

heart *m*	—	לֵב, לֵבָב
soul, mind, breath *f*	—	נֶפֶשׁ
house *m*	—	בַּיִת
hand *f*	—	יָד
doorpost, mezuzah *f*	—	מְזוּזָה
peace *m*	—	שָׁלוֹם
angel, messenger *m*	—	מַלְאָךְ
holy, sacred *adj*	—	קָדוֹשׁ

Note:
1. There are two forms of the word "heart" in Hebrew: לֵב and לֵבָב. They are used interchangeably.
2. The word נֶפֶשׁ has a range of meanings, all related to what constitutes the essence of a living being: soul, life, spirit, mind, breath, person, human being, living creature. You may see it translated in any of these ways (as in the various translations of *V'ahavta* above).
3. The word מְזוּזָה, which originally meant "doorpost," has come to be used as the name of the religious object affixed to the doorposts of Jewish homes.
4. As with other adjectives, the word קָדוֹשׁ has four forms. It is not necessary to memorize them, but it is helpful to be able to recognize them:

קְדוֹשׁוֹת *f pl*   קְדוֹשִׁים *m pl*   קְדוֹשָׁה *f sg*   קָדוֹשׁ *m sg*

Hebrew Roots

א־ה־ב

The basic meaning of the root א־ה־ב is "love." In Leviticus 19:18, we are told וְאָהַבְתָּ לְרֵעֲךָ כָּמוֹךָ, "you shall love your neighbor as yourself." In Isaiah 1:23, the prophet bemoans the corruption of his society, where everyone אֹהֵב, "loves," bribes. In Song of Songs 3:1–4, a young lover refers to her beloved as one שֶׁאָהֲבָה נַפְשִׁי, "whom my soul loves."

The following are words, both ancient and modern, derived from the root אָהַבׁ:

lover	—	אוֹהֵב
sweetheart, beloved	—	אָהוּב
suitor, lover	—	מְאַהֵב
flirtation	—	אֲהַבְהָבִים
philanderer	—	אַהֲבָן
enamored, lovesick	—	מְאֹהָב

The root אָהַבׁ appears only once in the Reading Practice at the beginning of this chapter:

you shall love	—	וְאָהַבְתָּ

דָּבַרׁ

The root דָּבַרׁ has the basic meaning of "speak" or "talk." The fifth book of the Torah, known in English as Deuteronomy, is דְּבָרִים, "words," derived from the opening words of the book: אֵלֶּה הַדְּבָרִים, "These are the words...." The last books of the Bible, Chronicles, are known in Hebrew as דִּבְרֵי הַיָּמִים, "the Words of the Days." The Hebrew term for the Ten Commandments is עֲשֶׂרֶת הַדִּבְּרוֹת, "the Ten Sayings." A sermon providing commentary on the Torah portion is called a דְּבַר תּוֹרָה, "word of Torah."

The following are words, both ancient and modern, derived from the root דָּבַרׁ:

word, thing	—	דָּבָר
speaker	—	דֹּבֵר
orator	—	דַּבְּרָן
speech	—	דִּבּוּר
colloquial, spoken	—	דִּבּוּרִי
uttered, said	—	דָּבוּר

In the Reading Practice at the beginning of this chapter, the root דָּבַרׁ appears twice in the *V'ahavta*:

these words	—	הַדְּבָרִים הָאֵלֶּה
and speak of them	—	וְדִבַּרְתָּ בָּם

Building Blocks

The Endings ךָ and כֶם

In English, possession is indicated by using separate words that come before a noun and indicate to whom that noun belongs:

my hand   *your* house   *our* father

In Hebrew, possession is indicated by endings that are attached directly to the noun. When endings are attached to a Hebrew word, the vowels of that word often change. The Hebrew ending ךָ means "your." Examples:

your heart	—	לְבָבְךָ	**heart**	—	לֵבָב
your soul	—	נַפְשְׁךָ	**soul**	—	נֶפֶשׁ
your house	—	בֵּיתְךָ	**house**	—	בַּיִת

The Hebrew ending כֶם also means "your," but it refers to a group of people, as opposed to a single individual. The Hebrew words לְבָבְךָ and לְבַבְכֶם both mean "your heart," but the Hebrew has an added nuance that is lost in the English translation:

your *(a single individual)* **heart**	—	לְבָבְךָ
your *(a group of people)* **heart**	—	לְבַבְכֶם

There is another nuance in the Hebrew that is lost in the English translation. There are actually four different endings in Hebrew that mean "your": masculine singular, feminine singular, masculine plural, and feminine plural. The ending ךָ is the masculine singular ending, and כֶם is the masculine plural ending. (The feminine singular and plural endings are included in the Grammar Enrichment section of Chapter 9.) Because there is no gender-neutral way to say "your" in Hebrew, the masculine plural ending כֶם is used for both all-male and mixed-gender groups. The masculine singular ending ךָ is used to refer to a single male but can also be interpreted as addressing a single individual of unspecified gender.

Adding ךְ and כֶם to Plural Nouns

When the ךְ or כֶם endings are added to nouns that already have the ִים plural ending attached, the final ם disappears but the י remains. There may be additional vowel changes.

children	—	בָּנִים
your *(a single individual)* children	—	בָּנֶיךָ
your *(a group of people)* children	—	בְּנֵיכֶם
God	—	אֱלֹהִים
your *(a single individual)* God	—	אֱלֹהֶיךָ
your *(a group of people)* God	—	אֱלֹהֵיכֶם

When the ךְ or כֶם endings are added to nouns that already have the וֹת plural ending attached, the וֹת ending remains with a י added after the וֹת ending. There may be additional vowel changes.

fathers, ancestors	—	אָבוֹת
your *(a single individual)* fathers your *(a single individual)* ancestors	—	אֲבוֹתֶיךָ
your *(a group of people)* fathers your *(a group of people)* ancestors	—	אֲבוֹתֵיכֶם

The Prefix בְּ

In English, prepositions are separate words that come before a noun or a pronoun or a noun phrase, such as the following:

under the bed   *by* my side   *to* the store   *for* me   *with* great appreciation

In Hebrew, some prepositions are separate words, and some are prefixes that are attached to words. The Hebrew letter בְּ is used as a prefix to indicate the preposition "in" or "with." Because prepositions do not translate exactly from one language to another, it is sometimes also translated as "at" or "on." It usually appears with the ִ vowel, though it can also appear with the ַ or ָ or ָ or ֶ vowels. Sometimes it appears without a dot in the middle as בְ.

Adding the Prefix בְּ to words with the Prefix הַ

When the prefix בְּ is added to a word that already has the prefix הַ, meaning "the," attached, the two prefixes combine. The prefix הַ disappears, but the vowel under the הַ (which is usually ◌ַ but occasionally ◌ָ or ◌ֶ) remains, written under the בְּ. Example:

the land	—	הָאָרֶץ
in the land	—	בְּ + הָאָרֶץ = בָּאָרֶץ

Pronoun Endings

GRAMMAR Enrichment

The ךָ and כֶם and other possessive endings are not only used with nouns in Hebrew. These same endings are also used as pronoun endings on Hebrew prepositions and verbs.

In Hebrew, subject pronouns such as אַתָּה, "you" (and all the other subject pronouns included in the Grammar Enrichment section of Chapter 1), are *never* used following a preposition. A word like בְּאַתָּה does not exist. Instead, the meaning "in you" or "with you" is expressed by attaching the pronoun ending ךָ, "you," to the preposition בְּ to form the word בְּךָ.

Similarly, subject pronouns such as אַתָּה, "you," are *never* used as the direct object following a verb. One cannot say "I command you" in Hebrew by using the word אַתָּה for "you." Instead, the pronoun ending ךָ is attached either directly to the verb or to the direct object marker אֶת.

The following examples come from the *V'ahavta* and *L'ma-an Tizk'ru*:

I *(subject pronoun)*	—	אָנֹכִי
command	—	מְצַוֶּה
I command you	—	אָנֹכִי מְצַוְּךָ

I brought out	—	הוֹצֵאתִי
direct object marker	—	אֶת
I brought out you from the land	—	הוֹצֵאתִי אֶתְכֶם מֵאֶרֶץ
of Egypt	—	מִצְרַיִם

Reading Practice with Building Blocks

Following are the Reading Practice selections for this chapter, as well as one from Chapter 5, reprinted with the new Building Blocks highlighted. Reread these selections, noting each appearance of the ךָ and כֶם endings and the prefix בָּ or בְּ.

The Fifth Commandment (Exodus 20:12)

כַּבֵּד אֶת־אָבִ֫יךָ וְאֶת־אִמֶּ֫ךָ...

*Honor **your** father and **your** mother…*

V'ahavta (Deuteronomy 6:5–9)

וְאָהַבְתָּ אֵת יְיָ אֱלֹהֶ֫יךָ בְּכָל־לְבָבְךָ וּבְכָל־נַפְשְׁךָ וּבְכָל־
מְאֹדֶ֫ךָ: וְהָיוּ הַדְּבָרִים הָאֵ֫לֶּה אֲשֶׁר אָנֹכִי מְצַוְּךָ הַיּוֹם עַל־לְבָבֶ֫ךָ:
וְשִׁנַּנְתָּם לְבָנֶ֫יךָ וְדִבַּרְתָּ בָּם בְּשִׁבְתְּךָ בְּבֵיתֶ֫ךָ וּבְלֶכְתְּךָ בַדֶּ֫רֶךְ
וּבְשָׁכְבְּךָ וּבְקוּמֶ֫ךָ: וּקְשַׁרְתָּם לְאוֹת עַל־יָדֶ֫ךָ וְהָיוּ לְטֹטָפֹת בֵּין
עֵינֶ֫יךָ: וּכְתַבְתָּם עַל מְזוּזֹת בֵּיתֶ֫ךָ וּבִשְׁעָרֶ֫יךָ:

*You shall love the Eternal **your** God **with** all **your** heart and **with** all **your** soul and **with** all **your** being. And they will be, these words that I command **you** today, upon **your** heart. You shall teach them to **your** children and speak **about** them **in your** sitting {when you sit} **in your** house and **in your** walking {when you walk} on the way and **in your** lying down {when you lie down} and **in your** arising {when you arise}. You shall bind them for a sign upon **your** hand and they will be symbols between **your** eyes. You shall write them upon the doorposts of **your** house and **on your** gates.*

L'ma-an Tizk'ru (Numbers 15:40–41)

לְמַ֫עַן תִּזְכְּרוּ וַעֲשִׂיתֶם אֶת־כָּל־מִצְוֹתָי וִהְיִיתֶם קְדֹשִׁים
לֵאלֹהֵיכֶם: אֲנִי יְיָ אֱלֹהֵיכֶם אֲשֶׁר הוֹצֵ֫אתִי אֶתְכֶם מֵאֶ֫רֶץ
מִצְרַ֫יִם לִהְיוֹת לָכֶם לֵאלֹהִים, אֲנִי יְיָ אֱלֹהֵיכֶם:

*In order that you will remember and do all My commandments and be holy to **your** God. I am the Eternal **your** God, that I brought **you** out from the land of Egypt to be to **your** God. I am the Eternal **your** God.*

שָׁלוֹם עֲלֵיכֶם, מַלְאֲכֵי הַשָּׁרֵת, מַלְאֲכֵי עֶלְיוֹן, מִמֶּלֶךְ מַלְכֵי הַמְּלָכִים, הַקָּדוֹשׁ בָּרוּךְ הוּא.

בּוֹאֲכֶם לְשָׁלוֹם, מַלְאֲכֵי הַשָּׁלוֹם, מַלְאֲכֵי עֶלְיוֹן, מִמֶּלֶךְ מַלְכֵי הַמְּלָכִים, הַקָּדוֹשׁ בָּרוּךְ הוּא.

בָּרְכוּנִי לְשָׁלוֹם, מַלְאֲכֵי הַשָּׁלוֹם, מַלְאֲכֵי עֶלְיוֹן, מִמֶּלֶךְ מַלְכֵי הַמְּלָכִים, הַקָּדוֹשׁ בָּרוּךְ הוּא.

צֵאתְכֶם לְשָׁלוֹם, מַלְאֲכֵי הַשָּׁלוֹם, מַלְאֲכֵי עֶלְיוֹן, מִמֶּלֶךְ מַלְכֵי הַמְּלָכִים, הַקָּדוֹשׁ בָּרוּךְ הוּא.

*Peace be upon **you**, the angels of service, angels of the Supreme One, from the Sovereign of the sovereigns of the sovereigns, the Holy One, blessed is God {He}.*
*[May] **your** coming be in {to} peace, the angels of peace, angels of the Supreme One, from the Sovereign of the sovereigns of the sovereigns, the Holy One, blessed is God {He}.*
Bless me for peace, the angels of peace....
*[May] **your** leaving be in {to} peace, the angels of peace....*

FROM OUR TEXTS

With Your Whole Heart: Good and Evil

Every human being has both a יֵצֶר טוֹב, "good inclination," inspiring us to perform noble and selfless acts, and a יֵצֶר רָע, "evil inclination," which fuels our baser lusts and cravings. The challenge that we face is not to eradicate our evil inclination, for it is regarded as a powerful motivating force, but rather to channel and direct it toward constructive purposes. This lesson is derived in the following passage by playing upon the use of the word לְבָב, "heart," which has a double ב, instead of the word לֵב, "heart."

חַיָּב אָדָם לְבָרֵךְ עַל הָרָעָה כְּשֵׁם שֶׁהוּא מְבָרֵךְ עַל הַטּוֹבָה, שֶׁנֶּאֱמַר (דברים ו) וְאָהַבְתָּ אֵת יְיָ אֱלֹהֶיךָ בְּכָל-לְבָבְךָ וּבְכָל-נַפְשְׁךָ וּבְכָל-מְאֹדֶךָ. בְּכָל לְבָבְךָ, בִּשְׁנֵי יְצָרֶיךָ, בְּיֵצֶר טוֹב וּבְיֵצֶר רָע.

One should bless the evil just as one blesses the good. For it is written, "You shall love the Eternal your God with all your heart and with all your soul and with all your being" (Deuteronomy 6:5). "With all לְבָבְךָ your heart" means "with your two inclinations": וּבְיֵצֶר רָע, *with the good inclination,* בְּיֵצֶר טוֹב, *and with the evil inclination.*

BERACHOT 9:5

Exercises

1. Draw a line connecting each Hebrew word to its English translation. For some words, there can be more than one correct translation.

soul	יָד
hand	לֵב
angel	מַלְאָךְ
sacred	מְזוּזָה
heart	נֶפֶשׁ
holy	קָדוֹשׁ
peace	שָׁלוֹם
breath	לֵבָב
messenger	בַּיִת
doorpost	
house	

2. The following are all the nouns introduced in this chapter. Draw a line connecting each singular noun to its plural form. Translate both into English.

_____	נְפָשׁוֹת	לֵב	_____
_____	לְבָבוֹת	בַּיִת	_____
_____	יָדַיִם	שָׁלוֹם	_____
_____	מְזוּזוֹת	לֵבָב	_____
_____	מַלְאָכִים	יָד	_____
_____	לִבּוֹת	נֶפֶשׁ	_____
_____	בָּתִּים	מַלְאָךְ	_____
_____	שְׁלוֹמִים	מְזוּזָה	_____

Following each noun below are three adjective forms. Circle the adjective that correctly matches the noun. Translate each phrase into English.

a. מַלְאָךְ (טוֹבִים, גְּדוֹלָה, קָדוֹשׁ) _____

b. נְפָשׁוֹת (קְדוֹשָׁה, גָּדוֹל, טוֹבוֹת) _____

c. לְבָבוֹת (טוֹבִים, הַגְּדוֹלָה, קְדוֹשָׁה) _____

d. הַיָּד (קְדוֹשׁוֹת, הַגְּדוֹלָה, טוֹבִים) _____

e. בֵּיתְךָ (הַקָּדוֹשׁ, גְּדוֹלִים, טוֹבָה) _____

f. הַשָּׁלוֹם (קְדוֹשָׁה, הַטּוֹבִים, הַגָּדוֹל) _____

4. Read and translate the following sentences. Masculine and feminine participle forms are used.

a. בִּנְךָ הַגָּדוֹל אוֹהֵב אֶת רִבְקָה. _____
your son

_____

b. רָחֵל אוֹהֶבֶת אֶת מֹשֶׁה. _____

c. לֵאָה וְשָׂרָה אוֹהֲבוֹת אֶת שׁוֹמְרֵי בֵּיתְךָ. _____

_____

d. הַמֶּלֶךְ אוֹהֵב אֶת שׁוֹמְעֵי הָאֱמֶת וְדֹבְרֵי צֶדֶק. _____

_____

e. אָנוּ אוֹכְלִים פֵּרוֹת וְלֶחֶם בַּשַּׁבָּת. _____

_____

f. אֲנַחְנוּ זוֹכְרִים אֶת אֲבוֹתֵיכֶם הַנְּבִיאִים. _____

_____

g. אַבְרָהָם וְיִצְחָק זוֹכְרִים אֶת בְּרִיתְךָ. _____

_____

h. אֱלֹהֵיכֶם זוֹכֵר אֶת חַסְדֵי אִמּוֹתֵיכֶם. _____

_____

i. ‏בָּרוּךְ הַלֵּב הַזּוֹכֵר אֶת הָאֱמֶת לְעוֹלָם וָעֶד.‏ _____

_____

j. ‏הוּא בּוֹחֵר בְּדוֹבְרֵי צֶדֶק.‏ _____

k. ‏מַלְאֲכֵי הַשָּׁלוֹם שׁוֹמְרִים אֶת בֵּיתְכֶם בַּשַּׁבָּת.‏ _____

_____

l. ‏הוּא שׁוֹמֵר אֶת מְזוּזוֹת הַבַּיִת בַּיּוֹם וּבַלַּיְלָה.‏ _____

_____

m. ‏אֱלֹהֶיךָ בּוֹרֵא אֶת הַתּוֹרָה בַּשָּׁמַיִם וּבָאָרֶץ.‏ _____

_____

n. ‏נַפְשְׁכֶם וְחַיֵּיכֶם בְּיַד הָאֵל.‏ _____

_____

o. ‏יַד אֱלֹהִים בָּעוֹלָם בַּשָּׁמַיִם וּבָאָרֶץ.‏ _____

_____

p. ‏אַתָּה עוֹזֵר עַמְּךָ וְנוֹתֵן בִּלְבָבְךָ וּבְנַפְשֶׁךָ.‏ _____

_____

5. Circle the words in the following prayer book excerpt that have possessive endings
attached. Underline the word that is derived from the same root as the adjective ‏טוֹב‏.
Underline twice the words that are names you have learned.

Mah Tovu **(Numbers 24:5)**

‏מַה טֹּבוּ אֹהָלֶיךָ יַעֲקֹב מִשְׁכְּנֹתֶיךָ יִשְׂרָאֵל:‏

How goodly are your tents, Jacob, your dwelling places, Israel.

6. Circle and translate the words in the following prayer book excerpt that have been introduced as vocabulary in this book. Underline the words that are derived from the roots
ד־ב־ר ,מ־ל־ך, and ב־ר־ך.

Blessing for Torah Study

בָּרוּךְ אַתָּה יְיָ אֱלֹהֵינוּ מֶלֶךְ הָעוֹלָם, אֲשֶׁר קִדְּשָׁנוּ בְּמִצְוֹתָיו,
וְצִוָּנוּ לַעֲסוֹק בְּדִבְרֵי תוֹרָה.

*Blessed are You, Eternal our God, Sovereign of the universe, who makes us holy with
God's {His} mitzvot and commands us to occupy ourselves with words of Torah.*

7. Circle and translate the words in the following prayer book excerpt that have been introduced as vocabulary in this book. Some have possessive endings attached. Underline the
word that is derived from the root א־ה־ב.

From *Ahavah Rabbah*

וְהָאֵר עֵינֵינוּ בְּתוֹרָתֶךָ, וְדַבֵּק לִבֵּנוּ בְּמִצְוֹתֶיךָ, וְיַחֵד לְבָבֵנוּ
לְאַהֲבָה וּלְיִרְאָה אֶת שְׁמֶךָ.

*Enlighten our eyes with your Torah, and make our hearts cling to your mitzvot, and
unite our hearts to love and to revere your name.*

8. Translate the following excerpts from the prayer book and the Bible. Check your translations against the English translations that follow.

   a. **From *Ahavat Olam***

   love *(noun from the root* א־ה־ב*)* — אַהֲבָה

   you have loved *(verb from the
   root* א־ה־ב*)* — אָהַבְתָּ

   אַהֲבַת עוֹלָם בֵּית יִשְׂרָאֵל עַמְּךָ אָהָבְתָּ...

   b. *K'dushat Hashem*—from the *Amidah*

   holy ones *(adjective used as a
   plural noun)* — קְדוֹשִׁים

every	—	כָּל
[they] praise	—	יְהַלְלוּ
selah (concluding word in certain Psalms, liturgy)	—	סֶלָה

אַתָּה קָדוֹשׁ וְשִׁמְךָ קָדוֹשׁ וּקְדוֹשִׁים בְּכָל יוֹם יְהַלְלוּךָ, סֶלָה. בָּרוּךְ אַתָּה יְיָ, הָאֵל הַקָּדוֹשׁ.

---

c. **Deuteronomy 10:19**

you *(plural)* shall love (from the root אֿהֿב)	—	וַאֲהַבְתֶּם
stranger	—	גֵּר
because	—	כִּי
you *(plural)* were	—	הֱיִיתֶם
Egypt	—	מִצְרָיִם

וַאֲהַבְתֶּם אֶת־הַגֵּר כִּי־גֵרִים הֱיִיתֶם בְּאֶרֶץ מִצְרָיִם:

---

d. **From Ecclesiastes 3:7–8**

time	—	עֵת
to be silent	—	לַחֲשׁוֹת
to speak *(from the root* דֿבֿר)	—	לְדַבֵּר
to love *(from the root* אֿהֿב)	—	לֶאֱהֹב
to hate	—	לִשְׂנֹא
war	—	מִלְחָמָה

...עֵת לַחֲשׁוֹת וְעֵת לְדַבֵּר: עֵת לֶאֱהֹב וְעֵת לִשְׂנֹא עֵת מִלְחָמָה וְעֵת שָׁלוֹם:

---

e. Psalm 128:5–6

English		Hebrew
may *(he, it)* bless *(from the root* ב־ר־ך *)*	—	יְבָרֶךְ
may *(he, it)* bless you *(with possessive ending attached)*	—	יְבָרֶכְךָ
from Zion	—	מִצִּיּוֹן
may you see	—	רְאֵה
goodness *(noun from the same root as the adjective* טוֹב *)*	—	טוּב
Jerusalem	—	יְרוּשָׁלָם
all	—	כֹּל
for *(attached preposition)*	—	לְ
upon	—	עַל

יְבָרֶכְךָ יְהֹוָה מִצִּיּוֹן וּרְאֵה בְּטוּב יְרוּשָׁלָם כֹּל יְמֵי חַיֶּיךָ:
וּרְאֵה־בָנִים לְבָנֶיךָ שָׁלוֹם עַל־יִשְׂרָאֵל:

_____

_____

Translations:

a. From *Ahavat Olam*—[With] a love of eternity {eternal love}, You have loved the house of Israel, Your people...

b. *K'dushat Hashem*—from the *Amidah*—You are holy and Your name is holy and holy ones every day praise You, selah. Blessed are You, Eternal One, the holy God.

c. Deuteronomy 10:19—You shall love the stranger because you were strangers in the land of Egypt.

d. From Ecclesiastes 3:7–8—...a time to be silent and a time to speak, a time to love and a time to hate, a time of war and a time of peace.

e. Psalm 128:5–6—May the Eternal One bless you from Zion and may you see the goodness of Jerusalem all the days of your life. And may you see children for your children {i.e., your grandchildren}, peace upon Israel.

You may have noticed that the singular pronoun ending ךָ appears throughout the *V'ahavta*, while the plural pronoun ending כֶם appears in *L'ma-an Tizk'ru*. The *V'ahavta* and *L'ma-an Tizk'ru* paragraphs are presented in sequence in the Reform liturgy, but they are actually two separate biblical excerpts.

The *V'ahavta* comes from the fifth book of the Torah, Deuteronony 6:5–9, immediately after the following line:

שְׁמַע יִשְׂרָאֵל יְהֹוָה אֱלֹהֵינוּ יְהֹוָה אֶחָד:

Hear, Israel: the Eternal is our God, the Eternal is One. (Deuteronomy 6:4)

This passage is addressed to יִשְׂרָאֵל, "Israel," a grammatically masculine singular noun. For this reason, the entire *V'ahavta* passage is worded using the masculine singular pronoun ending ךָ. The "you" or "your" signified by the singular pronoun ךָ is the entire community of Israel, addressed as a single entity.

Because the *V'ahavta* is worded in this way, it sounds as if a single person is being addressed or as if an entire community is being addressed not as a group, but as individuals (somewhat analogous to saying in English "each of you" as opposed to "all of you"). This language imparts a subtle nuance: each of you, as an individual and as part of the community of Israel, faces the individual imperative to love the Eternal One and to reflect that love in the actions enumerated in the *V'ahavta* passage.

The *L'ma-an Tizk'ru* paragraph comes from the fourth book of the Torah, Numbers 15:40–41. In this context, Moses is directed to דַּבֵּר אֶל־בְּנֵי יִשְׂרָאֵל, "speak to the Children of Israel" (Numbers 15:38). Because *L'ma-an Tizk'ru* is addressed to בְּנֵי יִשְׂרָאֵל, "the Children of Israel," a grammatically masculine plural group, the entire passage is worded using the masculine plural pronoun ending כֶם. (Males and females are included within masculine plural forms in Hebrew, as mentioned earlier in this chapter.)

When the two passages are placed together in the Reform liturgy, the switch in language from the singular forms of the *V'ahavta* to the plural forms of *L'ma-an Tizk'ru* imparts a lesson that is not apparent in a separate reading of each passage: we demonstrate our love for God through our individual performance of the actions described in the *V'ahavta*, but it is through our participation in the group, the community of faith joined in the remembrance and performance of mitzvot, that we become a holy people.

Review

In Chapter 6, nine vocabulary words and two Hebrew roots were introduced:

לֵב לֵבָב נֶפֶשׁ בַּיִת יָד מְזוּזָה שָׁלוֹם מַלְאָךְ קָדוֹשׁ

א־ה־ב ד־ב־ר

The following Building Blocks were presented:
1. The endings ךָ (singular) and כֶם (plural) both mean "your" when attached to a noun.
2. The prefix בְּ generally indicates the English preposition "in" or "with."
3. The endings ךָ and כֶם mean "you" when attached to a preposition or verb.

Reading Practice

Avinu Malkeinu

אָבִינוּ מַלְכֵּנוּ, שְׁמַע קוֹלֵנוּ...
אָבִינוּ מַלְכֵּנוּ, חָנֵּנוּ וַעֲנֵנוּ, כִּי אֵין בָּנוּ מַעֲשִׂים, עֲשֵׂה עִמָּנוּ
צְדָקָה וָחֶסֶד וְהוֹשִׁיעֵנוּ.

Our God {our Father}, our Sovereign, hear our voice…
Our God {our Father}, our Sovereign, favor us and answer us, for there are not in us
[good] deeds. Act with us [with] righteousness and kindness and save us.

Ein Keloheinu

אֵין כֵּאלֹהֵינוּ, אֵין כַּאדוֹנֵינוּ, אֵין כְּמַלְכֵּנוּ, אֵין כְּמוֹשִׁיעֵנוּ.

מִי כֵאלֹהֵינוּ, מִי כַאדוֹנֵינוּ, מִי כְמַלְכֵּנוּ, מִי כְמוֹשִׁיעֵנוּ.

נוֹדֶה לֵאלֹהֵינוּ, נוֹדֶה לַאדוֹנֵינוּ, נוֹדֶה לְמַלְכֵּנוּ, נוֹדֶה לְמוֹשִׁיעֵנוּ.

בָּרוּךְ אֱלֹהֵינוּ, בָּרוּךְ אֲדוֹנֵינוּ, בָּרוּךְ מַלְכֵּנוּ, בָּרוּךְ מוֹשִׁיעֵנוּ. אַתָּה הוּא אֱלֹהֵינוּ, אַתָּה הוּא אֲדוֹנֵינוּ, אַתָּה הוּא מַלְכֵּנוּ, אַתָּה הוּא מוֹשִׁיעֵנוּ.

There is none like our God, there is none like our Ruler, there is none like our Sovereign, there is none like our Savior.
Who is like our God, who is like our Ruler, who is like our Sovereign, who is like our Savior?
We give thanks to our God, we give thanks to our Ruler, we give thanks to our Sovereign, we give thanks to our Savior.
Blessed is our God, blessed is our Ruler, blessed is our Sovereign, blessed is our Savior.
You are our God, You are our Ruler, You are our Sovereign, You are our Savior.

Ein Kamocha (Psalm 86:8)

אֵין כָּמוֹךָ בָאֱלֹהִים אֲדֹנָי וְאֵין כְּמַעֲשֶׂיךָ:

There is none like You among the gods, Eternal One, and there are none like Your deeds.

Mi Chamochah (Exodus 15:11)

מִי כָמֹכָה בָּאֵלִים יְיָ, מִי כָּמֹכָה נֶאְדָּר בַּקֹּדֶשׁ, נוֹרָא תְהִלֹּת, עֹשֵׂה פֶלֶא:

Who is like You among the gods, Eternal One, who is like You, majestic in holiness, awesome One of praises, doing wonders?

Mi Chamochah

PRAYER BOOK Translations

Who is like You, Eternal One, among the gods that are wor-shipped? Who is like You, majestic in holiness, awesome in splen-dor, doing wonders?

GATES OF PRAYER FOR SHABBAT AND WEEKDAYS: A GENDER SENSITIVE PRAYERBOOK, ED. CHAIM STERN. NEW YORK: CCAR PRESS, 1994.

Who among the mighty can compare to you, WISE ONE? Who can compare to you, adorned in holiness, awesome in praises, acting wondrously?

KOL HANESHAMAH: SHABBAT VEHAGIM. WYNCOTE, PA.: THE RECONSTRUCTIONIST PRESS, 1994.

Who is like You, Adonai, among all that is worshipped? Who is, like You, majestic in holi-ness, awesome in splendor, working wonders?

SIDDUR SIM SHALOM FOR SHABBAT AND FESTIVALS. NEW YORK: THE RABBINICAL ASSEMBLY, 1998.

Who is like thee, O Lord, among the mighty? Who is like thee, glorious in holiness, awe-inspiring in renown, doing wonders?

DAILY PRAYER BOOK, TRANS. PHILLIP BIRNBAUM. NEW YORK: HEBREW PUBLISHING CO., 1949.

Vocabulary

Try to locate each of these words in the Reading Practice selections (*Avinu Malkeinu, Ein Keloheinu, Ein Kamocha,* and *Mi Chamochah*). Some appear with prefixes and/or suffixes attached.

there is/are not, there is/are none	—	אֵין
deed, act *m*	—	מַעֲשֶׂה
righteousness, justice, *tzedakah f*	—	צְדָקָה
lord, ruler *m*	—	אָדוֹן
savior, deliverer *m*	—	מוֹשִׁיעַ
who	—	מִי
holiness, sanctity *m*	—	קֹדֶשׁ

Note: The word צְדָקָה is sometimes translated as "charity," for it is used to refer to monetary assistance to the poor. The act of giving *tzedakah* is viewed in the Jewish tradition as an act of righteousness and economic justice. It is not merely something we might choose to do, but is a "mitzvah," a commandment, which we are obligated to do.

Hebrew Roots

ק־ד־שׁ

The noun קֹדֶשׁ, "holiness, sanctity," and the adjective קָדוֹשׁ, "holy, sacred," both come from the root ק־ד־שׁ. The basic meaning of this root is "holy," "sacred," or "set apart" from the ordinary. There are many terms in Jewish life that are derived from this root. The blessing said over a cup of wine or grape juice to sanctify Shabbat or a holiday is called קִדּוּשׁ, "sanctifica-tion." The prayer recited by mourners (and included at other times in Jewish liturgy) is called the קַדִּישׁ, the Aramaic word for "holy." The Jewish communal organization that is responsible for washing and preparing bodies for burial is known as the חֶבְרָא קַדִּישָׁא, "holy society." The following are several other terms derived from the root ק־ד־שׁ.

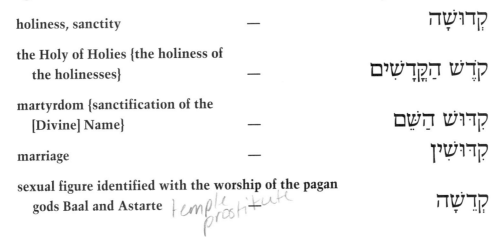

holiness, sanctity	—	קְדוּשָׁה
the Holy of Holies {the holiness of the holinesses}	—	קֹדֶשׁ הַקֳּדָשִׁים
martyrdom {sanctification of the [Divine] Name}	—	קִדּוּשׁ הַשֵּׁם
marriage	—	קִדּוּשִׁין
sexual figure identified with the worship of the pagan gods Baal and Astarte *[handwritten: temple prostitute]*	—	קְדֵשָׁה

The root ק־ד־שׁ appears only once in the Reading Practice at the beginning of this chapter, in *Mi Chamochah*:

majestic in holiness	—	נֶאְדָּר בַּקֹּדֶשׁ

ע־שׂ־ה

The root ע־שׂ־ה has the basic meaning of "make" or "do" or "act." In Genesis 2:2, God rests on the seventh day from all the creative work that God עָשָׂה, "had done." In Ezekiel 18:31, God urges the people of Israel to cast away transgressions and וַעֲשׂוּ לָכֶם ,לֵב חָדָשׁ "make yourselves a new heart." In Joshua 2:12, Rahab reminds the Israelite spies whom she has saved עָשִׂיתִי עִמָּכֶם חָסֶד, "I have done with you kindness

[I have acted kindly toward you]." In the last two examples, the final root letter הָ does not appear. When the letter הָ is the last letter of a root, it is omitted in some words formed from that root.

The following are words, both ancient and modern, derived from the root עָ־שָׂ־הָ. In some of the examples below, the last root letter הָ is omitted, and only the root letters עָ and שָׂ remain.

activator / *doer*	—	מַעֲשֶׂה
practical, feasible, workable	—	מַעֲשִׂי *often an "i" ending*
tale, legend, fairy-tale	—	מַעֲשִׂיָּה
practicability, feasibility	—	מַעֲשִׂיּוּת
industry, manufacture, production	—	תַּעֲשִׂיָּה
Creation {the act of Creation}	—	מַעֲשֵׂה בְרֵאשִׁית
actually, in fact	—	לְמַעֲשֶׂה
there's nothing to be done; it can't be helped	—	אֵין מַה לַעֲשׂוֹת

In the Reading Practice at the beginning of this chapter, the root עָ־שָׂ־הָ appears four times:

there are not in us [good] deeds	—	אֵין בָּנוּ מַעֲשִׂים
act with us [with] righteousness and kindness	—	עֲשֵׂה עִמָּנוּ צְדָקָה וָחֶסֶד
and there are none like your deeds	—	וְאֵין כְּמַעֲשֶׂיךָ
doing wonders	—	עֹשֵׂה פֶלֶא

Building Blocks

The Pronoun Ending נוּ

In the last chapter, we introduced the pronoun endings ךָ and כֶם. In this chapter, we introduce the pronoun ending נוּ. When it is attached to a noun, the ending נוּ means "our." There are often vowel changes in Hebrew words when endings are attached.

sovereign, king	—	מֶלֶךְ
our sovereign, our king	—	מַלְכֵּנוּ

When the ending נוּ is added to a plural noun that already has the יִם plural ending attached, the final ם disappears, but the י remains. When the ending נוּ is added to a plural noun that already has the וֹת plural ending attached, the וֹת ending remains, with a י added after the וֹת ending. There may be additional vowel changes.

God	—	אֱלֹהִים
our God	—	אֱלֹהֵינוּ
fathers, ancestors	—	אָבוֹת
our fathers, our ancestors	—	אֲבוֹתֵינוּ

The Ending נוּ on Prepositions

Some Hebrew prepositions are separate words and some are prefixes, such as the בְּ prefix introduced in the last chapter. Both types of Hebrew prepositions can have pronoun endings attached. When the pronoun ending נוּ is attached to a preposition, it means "us." The following examples come from *Avinu Malkeinu*:

in	—	בְּ
in us	—	בָּנוּ
with	—	עִם
with us	—	עִמָּנוּ

Two Irregular Forms

Two irregular forms appear in the Reading Practice selections at the beginning of this chapter. One is the term meaning "our father":

father	—	אָב
our father	—	אָבִינוּ

The word אָבִינוּ contains a י before the נוּ ending even though the ending is not attached to a plural noun. This is an exception to the usual rule stated above. Despite the presence of the י, the word אָבִינוּ is singular: "our father." The plural form "our fathers" is אֲבוֹתֵינוּ.

The word אָדוֹן, "lord" or "ruler," introduced in this chapter's vocabulary, is used as a human title; it is also used to refer to God, as in the phrase אֲדוֹן עוֹלָם, "Ruler of eternity." Often, however, when the word refers to God, it appears in the plural though it is translated as a singular term (similar to the use of the plural word אֱלֹהִים to refer to God). Such usage appears in *Ein Keloheinu*:

ruler	—	אָדוֹן
rulers	—	אֲדוֹנִים
our rulers [our Ruler]	—	אֲדוֹנֵינוּ

Another example of such usage is the word אֲדֹנָי, "Adonai," used as a substitute for the unpronounceable four-letter name of God. This is actually a plural form of the word אָדוֹן with the ending meaning "my" attached. אֲדֹנָי literally means "my lords" or "my rulers," and in the past it was almost always translated as "Lord." Since, however, "Lord" is a masculine term, contemporary gender-sensitive prayer books have sought other ways to render אֲדֹנָי in English, such as "God" or "Eternal One."

The Ending נוּ on Verbs

When the ending נוּ is attached to a verb, there are two possible meanings. In prayer book Hebrew, the ending נוּ most often means "us" and indicates the direct object of the verb. There are often vowel changes when this ending is attached. The following examples appear in the blessing for performing a mitzvah:

has made holy, has sanctified	—	קִדֵּשׁ
has made us holy, has sanctified us	—	קִדְּשָׁנוּ

has commanded	—	צִוָּה
has commanded us	—	צִוָּנוּ

אֲשֶׁר קִדְּשָׁנוּ בְּמִצְוֹתָיו וְצִוָּנוּ

who has made us holy with his commandments and has commanded us

The ending נוּ, when attached to a verb, can also mean "we." This only occurs with verbs in the perfect tense, a tense that generally, but not always, corresponds to our past tense. One of the best examples appears in *Ashamnu*, the alphabetical confession of sins recited on Yom Kippur:

we have transgressed	—	אָשַׁמְנוּ
we have betrayed	—	בָּגַדְנוּ
we have robbed	—	גָּזַלְנוּ
we have defamed {we have spoken scorn}	—	דִּבַּרְנוּ דֹפִי

אָשַׁמְנוּ, בָּגַדְנוּ, גָּזַלְנוּ, דִּבַּרְנוּ דֹפִי...

Another example is provided in the introduction to *Birkat HaMazon*, the Blessing after Meals:

we have eaten	—	אָכַלְנוּ
we have lived	—	חָיִינוּ

בָּרוּךְ אֱלֹהֵינוּ שֶׁאָכַלְנוּ מִשֶּׁלּוֹ וּבְטוּבוֹ חָיִינוּ.

Blessed is our God that we have eaten from that which is God's {His} and with God's {His} goodness we live.

The Prepositions כְּמוֹ and כ

As stated in Chapter 6, some Hebrew prepositions are separate words, and some are prefixes. The prepositions "like" or "as" can be expressed in Hebrew both ways: by the Hebrew letter כ used as a prefix, or by the word כְּמוֹ. These can appear without the dot in the letter כ, as in the prefix כ or as in כְּמוֹ.

Reading Practice with Building Blocks

Following are the Reading Practice selections for this chapter, reprinted with the new Building Blocks highlighted. Reread these selections, noting each appearance of the נוּ ending and the prepositions כְּ and כְּמוֹ.

Avinu Malkeinu

אָבִינוּ מַלְכֵּנוּ, שְׁמַע קוֹלֵנוּ...
אָבִינוּ מַלְכֵּנוּ, חָנֵּנוּ וַעֲנֵנוּ, כִּי אֵין בָּנוּ מַעֲשִׂים, עֲשֵׂה עִמָּנוּ צְדָקָה וָחֶסֶד וְהוֹשִׁיעֵנוּ.

Our God {*our Father*}, *our* Sovereign, hear *our* voice...
Our God {*our Father*}, *our* Sovereign, favor *us* and answer *us*, for there are not in *us* [good] deeds. Act with *us* [with] righteousness and kindness and save *us*.

Ein Keloheinu

אֵין כֵּאלֹהֵינוּ, אֵין כַּאדוֹנֵינוּ, אֵין כְּמַלְכֵּנוּ, אֵין כְּמוֹשִׁיעֵנוּ.
מִי כֵאלֹהֵינוּ, מִי כַאדוֹנֵינוּ, מִי כְמַלְכֵּנוּ, מִי כְמוֹשִׁיעֵנוּ.
נוֹדֶה לֵאלֹהֵינוּ, נוֹדֶה לַאדוֹנֵינוּ, נוֹדֶה לְמַלְכֵּנוּ, נוֹדֶה לְמוֹשִׁיעֵנוּ.
בָּרוּךְ אֱלֹהֵינוּ, בָּרוּךְ אֲדוֹנֵינוּ, בָּרוּךְ מַלְכֵּנוּ, בָּרוּךְ מוֹשִׁיעֵנוּ.
אַתָּה הוּא אֱלֹהֵינוּ, אַתָּה הוּא אֲדוֹנֵינוּ, אַתָּה הוּא מַלְכֵּנוּ, אַתָּה הוּא מוֹשִׁיעֵנוּ.

There is none **like our** *God, there is none* **like our** *Ruler, there is none* **like our** *Sovereign, there is none* **like our** *Savior.*
Who is **like our** *God, who is* **like our** *Ruler, who is* **like our** *Sovereign, who is* **like our** *Savior?*
We give thanks to **our** *God, we give thanks to* **our** *Ruler, we give thanks to* **our** *Sovereign, we give thanks to* **our** *Savior.*
Blessed is **our** *God, blessed is* **our** *Ruler, blessed is* **our** *Sovereign, blessed is* **our** *Savior.*
You are **our** *God, You are* **our** *Ruler, You are* **our** *Sovereign, You are* **our** *Savior.*

Ein Kamocha (Psalm 86:8)

אֵין כָּמֽוֹךָ בָאֱלֹהִים אֲדֹנָי וְאֵין כְּמַעֲשֶׂיךָ:

*There is none **like** You among the gods, Eternal One, and there are none **like** Your deeds.*

Mi Chamochah (Exodus 15:11)

מִי כָמֹֽכָה בָּאֵלִם יְיָ, מִי כָּמֹֽכָה נֶאְדָּר בַּקֹּֽדֶשׁ, נוֹרָא תְהִלֹּת, עֹֽשֵׂה פֶֽלֶא:

*Who is **like** You among the gods, Eternal One, who is **like** You, majestic in holiness, awesome One of praises, doing wonders!*

The Extra Pronoun

The last verse of the song *Ein Keloheinu*, included as one of this chapter's Reading Practice selections, reads as follows:

אַתָּה הוּא אֱלֹהֵינוּ, אַתָּה הוּא אֲדוֹנֵינוּ,
אַתָּה הוּא מַלְכֵּנוּ, אַתָּה הוּא מוֹשִׁיעֵנוּ.

Each phrase in this verse contains two pronouns, אַתָּה, "you," and הוּא, "he," although only the pronoun אַתָּה is reflected in the translation: "You are our God, you are our Ruler...."

The extra pronoun הוּא is not necessary, but it is sometimes included in Hebrew sentences or phrases that have no verb. In such cases, the extra pronoun appears where the words "is," "am," or "are," which do not exist in Hebrew, would appear in the English translation.

When an extra pronoun is used, it must match the subject of the sentence. The pronouns הוּא ("he"—masculine singular), הִיא ("she"—feminine singular), הֵם or הֵמָּה ("they"—masculine plural), and הֵן or הֵנָּה ("they"—feminine plural) can all be used as the extra pronoun depending upon the subject of the sentence.

The following examples come from the Bible. The passage from Deuteronomy appears in the High Holy Day prayer book at the end of *N'ilah*, the concluding service on Yom Kippur. This phrase is repeated seven times before the final blast of the shofar that brings the fast day to an end.

From Deuteronomy 4:39 (included at the end of *N'ilah*)

Eternal One *(the unpronounceable four-letter name of God)*	—	יְהֹוָה
The Eternal One is the God.		יְהֹוָה הוּא הָאֱלֹהִים.

Genesis 25:16

these	—	אֵלֶּה
Ishmael	—	יִשְׁמָעֵאל
These are the children of Ishmael.		אֵלֶּה הֵם בְּנֵי יִשְׁמָעֵאל:

Job 28:28

reverence, awe	—	יִרְאָה
wisdom	—	חָכְמָה
Reverence of the Eternal One is wisdom.		יִרְאַת אֲדֹנָי הִיא חָכְמָה:

FROM OUR TEXTS

ק-ד-ש Holiness as Union

The performance of a mitzvah provides an avenue through which we draw closer to God. The blessing said before performing a mitzvah includes the root ק-ד-ש in the phrase אֲשֶׁר קִדְּשָׁנוּ בְּמִצְוֹתָיו, "who has made us holy with mitzvot." This root is generally understood to mean "holy," "sacred," or "set apart from the ordinary." It is also the root of the noun קִדּוּשִׁין, "marriage," and the verb מְקַדֵּשׁ, which can mean "betroth" (as well as "sanctify" or "make holy"). The following Chasidic teaching plays with these meanings of the root ק-ד-ש to suggest that the performance of mitzvot does not merely make us holy but actually provides an avenue for our souls to become one with God, to merge in perfect union with the Infinite One.

וְזֶה שֶׁאָמַר: "אֲשֶׁר קִדְּשָׁנוּ בְּמִצְוֹתָיו", כְּאָדָם הַמְקַדֵּשׁ אִשָּׁה לִהְיוֹת מְיוּחֶדֶת עִמּוֹ בְּיִחוּד גָּמוּר כְּמוֹ שֶׁכָּתוּב: "וְדָבַק בְּאִשְׁתּוֹ וְהָיוּ לְבָשָׂר אֶחָד" ...כִּי עַל יַד יִחוּד הַנֶּפֶשׁ וְהִתְכַּלְלוּתָהּ בְּאוֹר אֵין סוֹף בָּרוּךְ הוּא הֲרֵי הִיא בְּמַעֲלַת וּמַדְרֵגַת קְדוּשַׁת אֵין סוֹף בָּרוּךְ הוּא מַמָּשׁ מֵאַחַר שֶׁמִּתְיַחֶדֶת וּמִתְכַּלֶּלֶת בּוֹ יִתְבָּרַךְ וְהָיוּ לַאֲחָדִים מַמָּשׁ. וְזֶה שֶׁאוֹמֵר: "וַעֲשִׂיתֶם אֶת-כָּל-מִצְוֹתָי וִהְיִיתֶם קְדֹשִׁים לֵאלֹהֵיכֶם: אֲנִי יְהוָה אֱלֹהֵיכֶם..."

And this is the meaning of the blessing phrase: אֲשֶׁר **קִדְּשָׁנוּ** בְּמִצְוֹתָיו, *"who has made us holy (who has betrothed us) with mitzvot." It is like a man* הַמְ**קַדֵּשׁ**, *"who betroths," a woman to be joined with him in a perfect union, as it is written: "...he shall cling to his wife and they shall become one flesh" (Genesis 2:24)... For through the union of the soul with and its absorption into the light of the blessed Infinite One, it attains the height and degree of* **קְדוּשַׁת**, *"holiness of (betrothal with/joining with)" the blessed Infinite One, since it unites with and is absorbed into the One Who is Blessed and they become one in reality. And this is the meaning of the verse...*
"You shall do all my mitzvot and be **קְדֹשִׁים** *[holy (betrothed/joined into one with)] to your God: I am Adonai your God..." (Exodus 15:40–41).*

LIKUTEI AMARIM TANYA, RABBI SCHNEUR ZALMAN OF LIADI, REVISED EDITION. BROOKLYN: KEHOT PUBLICATION SOCIETY, 1984, CHAPTER 46, PAGES 243–245.

Exercises

1. Draw a line connecting each Hebrew word to its English translation. For some words, there can be more than one correct translation.

deed	אָדוֹן
lord	מִי
savior	מַעֲשֶׂה
righteousness	מוֹשִׁיעַ
who	אֵין
holiness	קֹדֶשׁ
ruler	צְדָקָה
there is not	
act	
justice	

2. The following are all the nouns introduced in this chapter. Draw a line connecting each singular noun to its plural form. Translate both into English.

_____	אֲדוֹנִים	מַעֲשֶׂה	_____
_____	צְדָקוֹת	מוֹשִׁיעַ	_____
_____	קֳדָשִׁים	אָדוֹן	_____
_____	מוֹשִׁיעִים	צְדָקָה	_____
_____	מַעֲשִׂים	קֹדֶשׁ	_____

3. Read and translate the following sentences. Masculine and feminine participle forms are used.

a. אֵין נָבִיא כְּמשֶׁה. _____

b. אֵין חָמֵץ בְּבֵיתֵנוּ. _____

c. מִי הָאָדוֹן בְּאַרְצֵנוּ? _____

d. מִי זוֹכֵר אֶת בֵּית קָדְשֶׁךָ? _____

.e מִי עוֹשֶׂה חֶסֶד וּצְדָקָה וּמַעֲשִׂים טוֹבִים? _____

_____

.f אֲנַחְנוּ בּוֹחֲרִים בְּךָ כְּמוֹשִׁיעֵנוּ. _____

_____

.g לְבָבֵנוּ וְנַפְשֵׁנוּ בְּיָדְךָ. _____

_____

.h אַתָּה אוֹהֵב אֶת רִבְקָה כְּמוֹ אִמְּךָ. _____

_____

.i אָנוּ אוֹהֲבוֹת אֶת מֹשֶׁה כְּאָבִינוּ. _____

_____

.j אָנוּ אוֹכְלִים אֶת לַחְמְךָ וְאַתָּה אוֹכֵל אֶת מִצְוֹתֵינוּ. _____

_____

.k אֱלֹהֵינוּ שׁוֹמֵר אֶת חַיֵּיכֶם. _____

.l אִמֵּנוּ שׁוֹמֶרֶת אֶת חַיֵּינוּ. _____

.m שֵׁם אָבִינוּ יִצְחָק וְהוּא זוֹכֵר אֶת שְׁמוֹת בְּנֵיכֶם. _____

_____

.n אֵין שׁוֹמְרֵי מִצְוֹתֶיךָ וְאֵין אֱמֶת וָצֶדֶק. _____

_____

.o בָּרוּךְ הָעוֹשֶׂה מַעֲשֶׂה קָדוֹשׁ. _____

_____

.p בָּרוּךְ בּוֹרֵא עוֹלָמֵנוּ לְעוֹלָם וָעֶד. _____

_____

4. Underline and translate the words in the following prayer book excerpt that have been introduced as vocabulary in this book. Circle the words that are derived from the root ע־ש־ה.

Oseh Shalom

עֹשֶׂה שָׁלוֹם בִּמְרוֹמָיו הוּא יַעֲשֶׂה שָׁלוֹם עָלֵינוּ וְעַל כָּל יִשְׂרָאֵל, וְאִמְרוּ אָמֵן.

Maker of peace in God's {His} heights, may God {He} make peace upon us and upon all Israel, and say: Amen.

5. Underline and translate the words in the following prayer book excerpt that have been introduced as vocabulary in this book. Circle the words that have pronoun endings attached. Note the use of the extra pronoun in the phrase אַתָּה הוּא מֶלֶךְ.

Shalom Rav

שָׁלוֹם רָב עַל יִשְׂרָאֵל עַמְּךָ תָּשִׂים לְעוֹלָם, כִּי אַתָּה הוּא מֶלֶךְ אָדוֹן לְכָל הַשָּׁלוֹם. וְטוֹב בְּעֵינֶיךָ לְבָרֵךְ אֶת עַמְּךָ יִשְׂרָאֵל וְאֶת כָּל הָעַמִּים בְּכָל עֵת וּבְכָל שָׁעָה בִּשְׁלוֹמֶךָ.

Abundant peace upon Israel Your people may You place forever, for You are Sovereign Ruler of all the peace. And [it is] good in Your eyes to bless Your people Israel and all the peoples at every time and in every hour with Your peace.

6. Underline and translate the words in the following prayer book excerpt that have been introduced as vocabulary in this book. Circle the words that are derived from the root ק־ד־ש. Underline twice the words that have pronoun endings attached.

R'tzei Vim'nuchateinu

אֱלֹהֵינוּ וֵאלֹהֵי אֲבוֹתֵינוּ וְאִמּוֹתֵינוּ, רְצֵה בִמְנוּחָתֵנוּ. קַדְּשֵׁנוּ בְּמִצְוֹתֶיךָ וְתֵן חֶלְקֵנוּ בְּתוֹרָתֶךָ. שַׂבְּעֵנוּ מִטּוּבֶךָ וְשַׂמְּחֵנוּ בִּישׁוּעָתֶךָ, וְטַהֵר לִבֵּנוּ לְעָבְדְּךָ בֶּאֱמֶת. וְהַנְחִילֵנוּ, יְיָ אֱלֹהֵינוּ, בְּאַהֲבָה וּבְרָצוֹן שַׁבַּת קָדְשֶׁךָ, וְיָנוּחוּ בָהּ יִשְׂרָאֵל מְקַדְּשֵׁי שְׁמֶךָ. בָּרוּךְ אַתָּה יְיָ, מְקַדֵּשׁ הַשַּׁבָּת.

Our God and God of our fathers and our mothers, be pleased with our rest. Sanctify us with Your mitzvot and grant our portion in Your Torah. Satisfy us with Your goodness and gladden us with Your salvation, and purify our hearts to serve You in truth. And bequeath us {let be our heritage}, Eternal our God, with love and with favor, Your holy Sabbath {the Shabbat of Your holiness}, that Israel, those who sanctify Your name, may rest on it. Blessed are You, Eternal One, who sanctifies the Sabbath {Sanctifier of the Sabbath}.

7. The following two songs are part of the *Havdalah* ritual. Many also sing *Eliyahu HaNavi* at the Passover seder. Underline and translate the words in these songs that have been introduced as vocabulary. Circle the words that have pronoun endings or the preposition כְּ attached.

Eliyahu HaNavi

אֵלִיָּֽהוּ הַנָּבִיא, אֵלִיָּֽהוּ הַתִּשְׁבִּי,

אֵלִיָּֽהוּ, אֵלִיָּֽהוּ, אֵלִיָּֽהוּ הַגִּלְעָדִי.

בִּמְהֵרָה בְיָמֵֽינוּ, יָבֹא אֵלֵֽינוּ,

עִם מָשִֽׁיחַ בֶּן דָּוִד, עִם מָשִֽׁיחַ בֶּן דָּוִד.

Elijah the prophet, Elijah the Tishbite, Elijah, Elijah, Elijah the Gileadite, soon in our days may he come to us with the Messiah son of David, with the Messiah son of David.

Hamavdil

הַמַּבְדִּיל בֵּין קֹֽדֶשׁ לְחוֹל חַטֹּאתֵֽינוּ הוּא יִמְחַל

זַרְעֵֽנוּ וְכַסְפֵּֽנוּ יַרְבֶּה כַחוֹל וְכַכּוֹכָבִים בַּלָּֽיְלָה. שָׁבֽוּעַ טוֹב.

The One who distinguishes between holy and ordinary, our sins may God {He} pardon. Our offspring and our wealth may God {He} increase like the sand and like the stars at night. A good week!

8. Translate the following excerpts from the prayer book and the Bible. Check your translations against the English translations that follow.

   a. **From *Ein Adir***

mighty	—	אַדִּיר
Amram (the father of Moses)	—	עַמְרָם

its interpreters {interpreters of it}	—	דַּרְשָׁנֶיהָ
from the mouth of	—	מִפִּי
may [he, it] be blessed *(verb from the root* בּ־ר־ך*)*	—	יְבָרֵךְ
all	—	כָּל

אֵין אַדִּיר כַּיְיָ וְאֵין בָּרוּךְ כְּבֶן עַמְרָם.
אֵין גְדוֹלָה כַּתּוֹרָה וְאֵין דַּרְשָׁנֶיהָ כְּיִשְׂרָאֵל.
מִפִּי אֵל וּמִפִּי אֵל יְבָרֵךְ כָּל יִשְׂרָאֵל.

_____

_____

_____

b. From *Ki Anu Amecha* (in the Yom Kippur Liturgy)

for	—	כִּי
flock	—	צֹאן
shepherd	—	רוֹעֶה
beloved, friend	—	רַעְיָה
beloved, loved one	—	דּוֹד

כִּי אָנוּ עַמֶּךָ, וְאַתָּה מַלְכֵּנוּ _____

אָנוּ בָנֶיךָ, וְאַתָּה אָבִינוּ... _____

אָנוּ צֹאנֶךָ, וְאַתָּה רוֹעֵנוּ... _____

אָנוּ רַעְיָתֶךָ, וְאַתָּה דוֹדֵנוּ. _____

c. Genesis 2:4

these	—	אֵלֶּה
chronicles	—	תוֹלְדוֹת
their being created *(from the root* בּ־ר־א*)*	—	הִבָּרְאָם
the making of *(from the root* עֲ־שׂ־ה*)*	—	עֲשׂוֹת

אֵלֶּה תוֹלְדוֹת הַשָּׁמַיִם וְהָאָרֶץ בְּהִבָּרְאָם בְּיוֹם עֲשׂוֹת יְהוָֹה אֱלֹהִים אֶרֶץ וְשָׁמָיִם:

---

d. **Leviticus 19:18**

no, not	—	לֹא
you shall take vengeance	—	תִקֹּם
you shall bear a grudge against	—	תִטֹּר
you shall love (from the root א־ה־ב)	—	וְאָהַבְתָּ לְ-
neighbor, fellow human being	—	רֵעַ
I	—	אֲנִי

לֹא־תִקֹּם וְלֹא־תִטֹּר אֶת־בְּנֵי עַמֶּךָ וְאָהַבְתָּ לְרֵעֲךָ כָּמוֹךָ אֲנִי יְהוָֹה:

---

e. **From II Samuel 7:22–23**

besides, except for	—	זוּלָת
all	—	כֹּל
that	—	אֲשֶׁר
we have heard (from the root ש־מ־ע)	—	שָׁמַעְנוּ
ear	—	אֹזֶן
nation, people	—	גּוֹי
one	—	אֶחָד

...אֵין כָּמוֹךָ וְאֵין אֱלֹהִים זוּלָתֶךָ בְּכֹל אֲשֶׁר־שָׁמַעְנוּ בְּאָזְנֵינוּ: וּמִי כְעַמְּךָ כְּיִשְׂרָאֵל גּוֹי אֶחָד בָּאָרֶץ...

---

f.   From I Kings 8:23

above	—	מִמַּעַל
upon	—	עַל
below	—	מִתַּחַת
servant	—	עֶבֶד
who walk	—	הַהֹלְכִים
before	—	לִפְנֵי
all	—	כָּל
לֵב *with pronoun ending meaning* their	—	לִבָּם

...יְהוָֹה אֱלֹהֵי יִשְׂרָאֵל אֵין־כָּמוֹךָ אֱלֹהִים בַּשָּׁמַיִם מִמַּעַל
וְעַל־הָאָרֶץ מִתַּחַת שֹׁמֵר הַבְּרִית וְהַחֶסֶד לַעֲבָדֶיךָ הַהֹלְכִים
לְפָנֶיךָ בְּכָל־לִבָּם:

_____

_____

_____

Translations:

a. From *Ein Adir*—There is none mighty as the Eternal One and there is none blessed as the son of Amram {Moses}. There is none great as the Torah and there are no interpreters of it like Israel. From the mouth of God and from the mouth of God, may all Israel be blessed.

b. From *Ki Anu Amecha*—For we are Your people and You are our Sovereign, we are Your children and You are our Father,... we are Your flock and You are our Shepherd,... we are Your beloved and You are our Loved One.

c. Genesis 2:4—These are the chronicles of the heavens and the earth in their being created {when they were created}, in the day of the Eternal God's making of earth and heavens {when the Eternal God made earth and heavens}.

d. Leviticus 19:18—You shall not take vengeance and you shall not bear a grudge against the children of your people; you shall love your neighbor as you {yourself}; I am the Eternal One.

e. From II Samuel 7:22–23—There is none like You and there is no God besides You in all that we have heard with our ears. And who is like Your people, like Israel, one nation on earth...

f. From I Kings 8:23—...Eternal One, God of Israel, there is none like You God in the heavens above and upon the earth below, Keeper of the covenant and the kindness to Your servants who walk before You with all their heart.

EXTRA CREDIT

Avinu Malkeinu

Avinu Malkeinu is one of the most well-known High Holiday prayers. It consists of a series of statements, each beginning with the words אָבִינוּ מַלְכֵּנוּ. Sung to an evocative melody, it expresses our yearning for forgiveness and reconciliation, for blessing and goodness despite our shortcomings and failures.

The prayer is based upon a supplication of Rabbi Akiva's recorded in the Talmud (*Taanit* 25b). It is said that during a severe drought, Rabbi Akiva prayed the following prayer, and rain fell:

אָבִינוּ מַלְכֵּנוּ, אֵין לָנוּ מֶלֶךְ אֶלָּא אַתָּה.

אָבִינוּ מַלְכֵּנוּ, לְמַעַנְךָ רַחֵם עָלֵינוּ.

Our Father, our King, we have no king but You.
Our Father, our King, for Your sake have mercy upon us.

The linking of the words אָבִינוּ and מַלְכֵּנוּ conveys both the closeness and intimacy that we experience with the Eternal One, as well as distance and awe. The term אָבִינוּ, "our father," evokes a father's love and concern; the term מַלְכֵּנוּ, "our king," evokes a ruler's power and authority.

For some, these are powerful metaphors that speak to the heart of their experience of God. For others, these metaphors are problematic, couched in masculine language that interferes with their connection with the Divine. And so, there are several different ways of approaching this prayer.

In some communities, the Hebrew phrase אָבִינוּ מַלְכֵּנוּ has been left unchanged, but the English translation of the phrase avoids using exclusively masculine language, utilizing instead gender-neutral language such as "our God, our Beloved," or alternating masculine with feminine language, such as "our God, our Father...our God, our Mother." Some prayer books, such as the gender-sensitive *Gates of Repentance*, leave the words אָבִינוּ מַלְכֵּנוּ untranslated in the English, as *Avinu Malkeinu*. This approach avoids altogether the literal meaning of the words, treating them instead as a title or opening phrase.

Other communities have addressed the Hebrew itself, attempting to create new metaphors to express our varied relationship with the Eternal. A liberal congregation in Israel created a version of this prayer that uses the phrase שְׁכִינָה מְקוֹר חַיֵּינוּ in place of אָבִינוּ מַלְכֵּנוּ. (This version is included in the back of the gender-sensitive Reform *Gates of Repentance* as an alternative option.) The word שְׁכִינָה is a grammatically feminine term that refers to the indwelling presence of the Divine. The phrase מְקוֹר חַיֵּינוּ means "Source of our lives." The linking of the terms שְׁכִינָה and מְקוֹר חַיֵּינוּ expresses the concepts of intimacy with and awe of the Eternal One differently than do the words אָבִינוּ מַלְכֵּנוּ. God is both an intimate presence dwelling within each of us, as near to us as the next breath we take, and beyond each of us, the Source of all our lives.

Review

In Chapter 7, seven vocabulary words and two Hebrew roots were introduced:

אֵין מַעֲשֶׂה צְדָקָה אָדוֹן מוֹשִׁיעַ מִי קֹדֶשׁ

ק־ד־שׁ ע־שׂ־ה

The following Building Blocks were presented:

1. The ending נוּ means "our" when it is attached to a noun.
2. The ending נוּ means "us" when it is attached to a preposition.
3. When it is attached to a verb, the ending נוּ generally means "us" in prayer book Hebrew and indicates the direct object of the verb. On certain verb forms, the ending נוּ means "we."
4. The prefix כְּ and the word כְּמוֹ indicate the English prepositions "like" or "as."

Reading Practice

Chanukah Candle Lighting Blessings

בָּרוּךְ אַתָּה יְיָ אֱלֹהֵינוּ מֶלֶךְ הָעוֹלָם, אֲשֶׁר קִדְּשָׁנוּ
בְּמִצְוֹתָיו וְצִוָּנוּ לְהַדְלִיק נֵר שֶׁל חֲנֻכָּה.
בָּרוּךְ אַתָּה יְיָ אֱלֹהֵינוּ מֶלֶךְ הָעוֹלָם, שֶׁעָשָׂה נִסִּים לַאֲבוֹתֵינוּ
בַּיָּמִים הָהֵם בַּזְּמַן הַזֶּה.
בָּרוּךְ אַתָּה יְיָ אֱלֹהֵינוּ מֶלֶךְ הָעוֹלָם, שֶׁהֶחֱיָנוּ וְקִיְּמָנוּ וְהִגִּיעָנוּ
לַזְּמַן הַזֶּה.

Blessed are You, Eternal our God, Sovereign of the universe, who makes us holy with God's {His} mitzvot and commands us to kindle the light of Chanukah.
Blessed are You, Eternal our God, Sovereign of the universe, who did miracles for our ancestors in those days at this time.
Blessed are You, Eternal our God, Sovereign of the universe, who has given us life and sustained us and brought us to this time.

Al Hanisim

הַנֵּרוֹת הַלָּלוּ אֲנַחְנוּ מַדְלִיקִים עַל הַנִּסִּים וְעַל הַפֻּרְקָן וְעַל הַגְּבוּרוֹת וְעַל הַתְּשׁוּעוֹת וְעַל הַמִּלְחָמוֹת, שֶׁעָשִׂיתָ לַאֲבוֹתֵינוּ וְשֶׁעָשִׂיתָ לְאִמּוֹתֵינוּ בַּיָּמִים הָהֵם בַּזְּמַן הַזֶּה.

These lights we kindle on [account of] the miracles and on [account of] the deliverance and on [account of] the heroism and on [account of] the salvation and on [account of] the battles that You did for our fathers and that You did for our mothers in those days at this season.

Aleinu

עָלֵינוּ לְשַׁבֵּחַ לַאֲדוֹן הַכֹּל, לָתֵת גְּדֻלָּה לְיוֹצֵר בְּרֵאשִׁית, שֶׁלֹּא עָשָׂנוּ כְּגוֹיֵי הָאֲרָצוֹת, וְלֹא שָׂמָנוּ כְּמִשְׁפְּחוֹת הָאֲדָמָה, שֶׁלֹּא שָׂם חֶלְקֵנוּ כָּהֶם, וְגֹרָלֵנוּ כְּכָל הֲמוֹנָם.

It is [incumbent] upon us to praise the Ruler of all, to give greatness to the Fashioner of Creation, who did not make us as the nations of the lands, and did not place us as the families of the earth, who did not place our portion as theirs nor our destiny as all their multitude.

PRAYER BOOK

Translations

Aleinu

We must praise the God of all, the Maker of heaven and earth, who has set us apart from the other families of earth, giving us a destiny unique among the nations.

GATES OF PRAYER FOR SHABBAT AND WEEKDAYS: A GENDER SENSITIVE PRAYERBOOK, ED. CHAIM STERN. NEW YORK: CCAR PRESS, 1994.

It is up to us to offer praises to the Source of all, to declare the greatness of the author of Creation, who has made us different from the other nations of the earth, and situated us in quite a different spot, and made our daily lot another kind from theirs, and given us a destiny uncommon in this world.

KOL HANESHAMAH: SHABBAT VEHAGIM. WYNCOTE, PA.: THE RECONSTRUCTIONIST PRESS, 1994.

We rise to our duty to praise the Master of all, to acclaim the Creator. God made our lot unlike that of other people, assigning to us a unique destiny.

SIDDUR SIM SHALOM FOR SHABBAT AND FESTIVALS. NEW YORK: THE RABBINICAL ASSEMBLY, 1998.

It is our duty to praise the Master of all, to exalt the Creator of the universe, who has not made us like the nations of the world and has not placed us like the families of the earth; who has not designed our destiny to be like theirs, nor our lot like that of all their multitude.

DAILY PRAYER BOOK, TRANS. PHILLIP BIRNBAUM. NEW YORK: HEBREW PUBLISHING CO., 1949.

Vocabulary

Try to locate each of these words in the Reading Practice selections (Chanukah candle lighting blessings, *Al Hanisim*, and *Aleinu*). Some of these words appear with prefixes and/or suffixes attached. Some appear in word pairs.

who, that, which	—	אֲשֶׁר
light, candle, lamp *m*	—	נֵר
on, about	—	עַל
all, every	—	כֹּל, כָּל
Creation, in the beginning	—	בְּרֵאשִׁית
nation, people *m*	—	גּוֹי
family *f*	—	מִשְׁפָּחָה
earth, ground *f*	—	אֲדָמָה
Chanukah, dedication *f*	—	חֲנֻכָּה

Note:

1. The preposition עַל has a wide range of meanings. It can indicate physical relationship: "above," "on," "upon," "over." It can mean "about," "regarding," "concerning." In some contexts it can mean "because of" or "on account of" (as in *Al Hanisim* on page 128). This preposition appears with the כֶם ending in the greeting שָׁלוֹם עֲלֵיכֶם, "peace [be] upon you."

2. Both כֹּל and כָּל are pronounced *kol*. The dot in the letter כ sometimes disappears when prefixes are attached (such as כְּכָל in *Aleinu* above).

3. The word רֵאשִׁית means "beginning." The first word in the Torah is בְּרֵאשִׁית, "in [the] beginning." The word בְּרֵאשִׁית is used as the Hebrew name for the first book of the Bible (Genesis). It has also come to be used as a noun meaning Creation as a whole (i.e., everything created by God), in word pairs such as מַעֲשֵׂה בְרֵאשִׁית, "the act of Creation" or שֵׁשֶׁת יְמֵי בְרֵאשִׁית, "the six days of Creation."

4. The Hebrew word גּוֹי means "nation" or "people." In the Bible, this word is applied to the people of Israel as well as other peoples. Its plural גּוֹיִים, "nations" or "peoples," entered the Yiddish language and was used to refer to non-Jewish peoples. The singular form גּוֹי thus came to mean, in Yiddish, an individual non-Jew.

Hebrew Roots

חָ־יָ־ה

The root חָ־יָ־ה has the basic meaning of "live" or "be alive." When the letter ה is the last letter of a root, it is omitted in some words formed from that root. From the root חָ־יָ־ה comes the word חַי meaning "live" or "living"; necklaces featuring this word as an affirmation of life are a popular type of ethnic Jewish jewelry. The Jewish drinking toast לְחַיִּים, "to life," is also derived from this root. In Genesis 3:20, Adam names his wife חַוָּה, "Chava" (Eve), a variant of the root חָ־יָ־ה, because she was the אֵם כָּל חָי, "mother of all living." In Genesis 3:22, God worries that Adam and Eve, after eating from the forbidden tree of knowledge, may also eat from עֵץ הַחַיִּים, "the tree of life," וְחַי לְעֹלָם, "and live forever." In Esther 4:11, only those to whom the king extends his golden sceptre וְחָיָה, "may live." In Ezekiel 37:6, the Eternal prophesies to the dry bones: I will put breath into you וִחְיִיתֶם, "and you shall live."

The following are words, both ancient and modern, derived from the root חָ־יָ־ה:

animal, beast	—	חַיָּה
zoo, zoological garden {garden of animals}	—	גַּן חַיּוֹת
lively, vivacious	—	חַיָּה
vital, indispensable	—	חִיּוּנִי
vitality	—	חִיּוּת
life	—	חַיִּים
eternal life {life of eternity}	—	חַיֵּי עוֹלָם
means of livelihood, subsistence	—	מִחְיָה

The root חָ־יָ־ה appears only once in the Reading Practice at the beginning of this chapter, in the *Shehecheyanu* blessing (third Chanukah candle lighting blessing):

who	—	שֶׁ־
has given life	—	הֶחֱיָה
has given us life	—	הֶחֱיָנוּ

שֶׁהֶחֱיָנוּ וְקִיְּמָנוּ וְהִגִּיעָנוּ לַזְּמַן הַזֶּה...

...who has given us life and sustained us and brought us to this time.

צ־ו־ה

The root צ־ו־ה has the basic meaning of "command" or "order." The word מִצְוָה, "commandment," comes from this root. In Genesis 7:9, Noah brings the animals into the ark as God צִוָּה, "commanded," him. In Leviticus 14:4, the priest וְצִוָּה, "shall order," the birds used in the ritual of purification for a person who has been healed from the affliction of *tzaraat*. (The meaning of this Hebrew term is uncertain, though it is often translated as "leprosy.") In Genesis 18:19, God says that Abraham יְצַוֶּה, "will command," his children and his household to keep the way of the Eternal and do what is right and just.

The following are examples of Hebrew words formed from the root צ־ו־ה. When the letter ה is the last letter of a root, it is omitted in some words formed from that root. In one of the examples below, the letter ה has dropped out, and only the root letters ו and צ remain.

Bar Mitzvah {a young man who has reached the age of responsibility for the observance of mitzvot}	—	בַּר מִצְוָה
Bat Mitzvah {a young woman who has reached the age of responsibility for the observance of mitzvot}	—	בַּת מִצְוָה
commander, governor	—	מְצַוֶּה
bound to, obliged to, ordered	—	מְצֻוֶּה
he commanded	—	צִוָּה
command, order, imperative	—	צִוּוּי

The root צ־ו־ה appears twice in the blessing for the performance of a mitzvah such as lighting Shabbat or Chanukah candles:

mitzvot	—	מִצְוֹת
his mitzvot	—	מִצְוֹתָיו
with his mitzvot	—	בְּמִצְוֹתָיו
has commanded	—	צִוָּה
has commanded us	—	צִוָּנוּ
and has commanded us	—	וְצִוָּנוּ

...אֲשֶׁר קִדְּשָׁנוּ בְּמִצְוֹתָיו וְצִוָּנוּ...

...who has made us holy with God's {His} commandments and has commanded us...

Building Blocks

The Word אֲשֶׁר and the Prefix שֶׁ

The word מִי introduced in the last chapter means "who" when asking a question:

Who is like you? — מִי כָמוֹךָ?

The word אֲשֶׁר introduced in this chapter means "who" (or "that" or "which") when introducing a clause within a sentence. The following example appeared in a Reading Practice selection in Chapter 6:

From *V'ahavta* (Deuteronomy 6:6)

וְהָיוּ הַדְּבָרִים הָאֵלֶּה **אֲשֶׁר** אָנֹכִי מְצַוְּךָ הַיּוֹם עַל־לְבָבֶךָ:

*And they will be, these words **which** I command you today, upon your heart.*

The word אֲשֶׁר often appears in blessings, as the following prayer book selection illustrates. This passage appeared in a Reading Practice selection in Chapter 4.

From the Blessing after the Reading of the Torah

בָּרוּךְ אַתָּה יְיָ אֱלֹהֵינוּ מֶלֶךְ הָעוֹלָם, **אֲשֶׁר** נָתַן לָנוּ תּוֹרַת אֱמֶת...

*Blessed are You, Eternal our God, Sovereign of the universe, **who** gave to us a Torah of truth...*

A short form of the word אֲשֶׁר is the prefix שֶׁ. There are several examples of the use of the prefix שֶׁ in the Reading Practice selections for this chapter.

The Preposition לְ

The Hebrew letter לְ is used as a prefix to indicate the preposition "to" or "for." Like the preposition בְּ, it combines with the prefix הַ when attached to a word that already has that prefix:

the land	—	הָאָרֶץ
to the land *or* **for the land**	—	לְ + הָאָרֶץ = לָאָרֶץ

Like other Hebrew prepositions, the preposition ל can have pronoun endings attached. When such endings are attached, the prefix ל and the pronoun ending form a full word:

to, for	—	־לְ
to us, for us	—	לָנוּ
to you, for you *(singular)*	—	לְךָ
to you, for you *(plural)*	—	לָכֶם

Translating Prepositions

Prepositions do not always translate smoothly from one language to another. Sometimes a different preposition must be used in the translation. Sometimes a preposition is best left untranslated. We have already seen an example of this with the root ב־ח־ר; verbs formed from this root are followed by the preposition בְּ, which is not translated into English:

He chooses good prophets.	הוּא בּוֹחֵר בִּנְבִיאִים טוֹבִים.—

Similarly, verbs formed from the root ע־ז־ר, "help," which was introduced in Chapter 5, are often followed by a preposition ל, which is best left untranslated:

He is helping Sarah.	—	הוּא עוֹזֵר לְשָׂרָה.
He is helping us.	—	הוּא עוֹזֵר לָנוּ.

Of course, if the participles in the above sentences were translated as the noun "helper," then it would not sound awkward to translate the preposition ל into English:

He is a helper for Sarah.	—	הוּא עוֹזֵר לְשָׂרָה.
He is a helper for us.	—	הוּא עוֹזֵר לָנוּ.

Reading Practice with Building Blocks

Following are the Reading Practice selections for this chapter, reprinted with the new Building Blocks highlighted. Reread these selections, noting each appearance of the preposition לְ, the word אֲשֶׁר, and its short form as the prefix שֶׁ.

Chanukah Candle Lighting Blessings

בָּרוּךְ אַתָּה יְיָ אֱלֹהֵינוּ מֶלֶךְ הָעוֹלָם, **אֲשֶׁר** קִדְּשָׁנוּ
בְּמִצְוֹתָיו וְצִוָּנוּ **לְהַדְלִיק** נֵר שֶׁל חֲנֻכָּה.
בָּרוּךְ אַתָּה יְיָ אֱלֹהֵינוּ מֶלֶךְ הָעוֹלָם, **שֶׁ**עָשָׂה נִסִּים **לַ**אֲבוֹתֵינוּ
בַּיָּמִים הָהֵם בַּזְּמַן הַזֶּה.
בָּרוּךְ אַתָּה יְיָ אֱלֹהֵינוּ מֶלֶךְ הָעוֹלָם, **שֶׁ**הֶחֱיָנוּ וְקִיְּמָנוּ וְהִגִּיעָנוּ
לַזְּמַן הַזֶּה.

*Blessed are You, Eternal our God, Sovereign of the universe, **who** makes us holy with God's {His} mitzvot and commands us **to** kindle the light of Chanukah.*
*Blessed are You, Eternal our God, Sovereign of the universe, **who** did miracles **for** our ancestors in those days at this time.*
*Blessed are You, Eternal our God, Sovereign of the universe, **who** has given us life and sustained us and brought us **to** this time.*

Al Hanisim

הַנֵּרוֹת הַלָּלוּ אֲנַחְנוּ מַדְלִיקִים עַל הַנִּסִּים וְעַל הַפֻּרְקָן וְעַל
הַגְּבוּרוֹת וְעַל הַתְּשׁוּעוֹת וְעַל הַמִּלְחָמוֹת, **שֶׁ**עָשִׂיתָ
לַאֲבוֹתֵינוּ וְ**שֶׁ**עָשִׂיתָ **לְ**אִמּוֹתֵינוּ בַּיָּמִים הָהֵם בַּזְּמַן הַזֶּה.

*These lights we kindle on [account of] the miracles and on [account of] the deliverance and on [account of] the heroism and on [account of] the salvation and on [account of] the battles **that** You did **for** our fathers and **that** You did **for** our mothers in those days at this season.*

עָלֵינוּ לְשַׁבֵּחַ לַאֲדוֹן הַכֹּל, לָתֵת גְּדֻלָּה לְיוֹצֵר בְּרֵאשִׁית,
שֶׁלֹּא עָשָׂנוּ כְּגוֹיֵי הָאֲרָצוֹת, וְלֹא שָׂמָנוּ כְּמִשְׁפְּחוֹת הָאֲדָמָה,
שֶׁלֹּא שָׂם חֶלְקֵנוּ כָּהֶם, וְגוֹרָלֵנוּ כְּכָל הֲמוֹנָם.

*It is [incumbent] upon us **to** praise the Ruler of all, **to** give greatness **to** the Fashioner of
Creation, **who** did not make us as the nations of the lands, and did not place us as the
families of the earth, **who** did not place our portion as theirs nor our destiny as all their
multitude.*

GRAMMAR Enrichment

The Word כֹּל or כָּל with Endings

The word כֹּל or כָּל, meaning "all" or "every," is included among
the vocabulary words for this chapter. Although this word is not a noun,
verb, or preposition, it sometimes appears with pronoun endings attached.
When this occurs, the vowel changes to ▓. The following examples appear in the
Passover Four Questions, included as a Reading Practice selection in Chapter 2:

all of us	—	כֻּלָּנוּ	
all of it	—	כֻּלּוֹ	

Passover Four Questions (First and Fourth)

מַה נִּשְׁתַּנָּה הַלַּיְלָה הַזֶּה מִכָּל הַלֵּילוֹת?
שֶׁבְּכָל הַלֵּילוֹת אָנוּ אוֹכְלִין חָמֵץ וּמַצָּה. הַלַּיְלָה הַזֶּה **כֻּלּוֹ** מַצָּה....
שֶׁבְּכָל הַלֵּילוֹת אָנוּ אוֹכְלִין בֵּין יוֹשְׁבִין וּבֵין מְסֻבִּין. הַלַּיְלָה
הַזֶּה **כֻּלָּנוּ** מְסֻבִּין.

What differentiates this night from all the [other] nights?
*that on all the [other] nights we eat leavened foods and matzah; this night—**all of it** is*
matzah....
*that on all the [other] nights we eat either sitting or reclining; this night—**all of us** are*
reclining.

FROM OUR TEXTS

The Dreidel

In Chapter 5, under Extra Credit, we explained that the letters on the four sides of the Chanukah dreidel stand for the Hebrew sentence: נֵס גָּדוֹל הָיָה שָׁם, "A great miracle happened there." In the following passage, the Chasidic Rabbi Nachman of Bratzlav provides a different interpretation:

All creation is like a rotating wheel, revolving and oscillating.

At one time something can be on top like a head with another on bottom like a foot.

Then the situation is reversed. Head becomes foot, and foot becomes head. Man becomes angel, and angel becomes man…

For the world is like a rotating wheel. It spins like a Dreidel, with all things emanating from one root…

The letters on the Dreidel are Heh, Nun, Gimel, Shin.

*Heh is Hiyuli (*הִיּוּלִי *primordial), the Hyle* (the first matter of the universe).

*Nun is Nivdal (*נִבְדָּל *separate), the transcendental.*

*Gimel is Galgal (*גַּלְגַּל *the heavenly sphere), the celestial.*

*Shin is Shafal (*שָׁפָל *base, lowly), the physical.*

The Dreidel thus includes all creation. It goes in cycles, alternating and revolving, one thing becoming another.

SICHOS HARAN 40, INCLUDED IN RABBI NACHMAN'S WISDOM, TRANSLATED AND ANNOTATED BY RABBI ARYEH KAPLAN. JERUSALEM: THE BRESLOV RESEARCH INSTITUTE, 1973, PAGES 143–145.

Exercises

1. Draw a line connecting each Hebrew word to its English translation. For some words, there can be more than one correct translation.

Creation	אֲדָמָה
every	נֵר
nation	גּוֹי
light	
who	מִשְׁפָּחָה
family	כֹּל
on	
earth	אֲשֶׁר
all	
about	בְּרֵאשִׁית
candle	עַל
that	
Chanukah	חֲנֻכָּה

CHAPTER 8

2. The following are all the nouns introduced in this chapter. Draw a line connecting each singular noun to its plural form. Translate both into English.

_____	גּוֹיִים	נֵר	_____
_____	מִשְׁפָּחוֹת	גּוֹי	_____
_____	נֵרוֹת	אֲדָמָה	_____
_____	אֲדָמוֹת	מִשְׁפָּחָה	_____

3. Read and translate the following sentences. Masculine and feminine participle forms are used.

a. יִצְחָק שׁוֹמֵעַ לְמַלְאֲכֵי הַמֶּלֶךְ.

_____

b. הוּא שׁוֹמֵעַ לְדִבְרֵי הָאֱמֶת.

_____

c. אַבְרָהָם וְלֵאָה שׁוֹמְעִים לָנוּ וַאֲנַחְנוּ שׁוֹמְעוֹת לָכֶם.

_____

_____

d. מִי מוֹשִׁיעֵנוּ? אֵין עֹזֵר לְיִשְׂרָאֵל.

_____

_____

e. הַנֵּרוֹת וְהַלֶּחֶם עוֹזְרִים לְשׁוֹמְרֵי הַשַּׁבָּת.

_____

_____

f. בָּרוּךְ הָאֵל הַשּׁוֹמֵר עַל חַיֵּינוּ וְעַל נַפְשׁוֹתֵינוּ.

_____

_____

g. בָּרוּךְ עוֹשֶׂה מַעֲשֵׂה בְרֵאשִׁית.

_____

h. אָנוּ אוֹהֲבִים אֶת כָּל בְּנֵי מִשְׁפַּחְתֵּנוּ.

_____

i. אַתָּה וְרָחֵל זוֹכְרִים אֶת נֵרוֹת הַחֲנֻכָּה אֲשֶׁר בְּבֵיתְכֶם.

_____

_____

j. רִבְקָה זוֹכֶרֶת אֶת הָאֲדָמָה הַטּוֹבָה שֶׁאַתָּה אוֹהֵב.

_____

_____

k. אָנוּ זוֹכְרִים אֶת בְּרִיתְךָ הַקְּדוֹשָׁה בְּלִבֵּנוּ. _____

_____

l. שָׁלוֹם עָלֶיךָ וְעַל בֵּיתֶךָ. _____

m. אֲבוֹתֵינוּ שׁוֹמְרִים עָלֵינוּ לְעוֹלָם וָעֶד. _____

_____

n. אֵין מְזוּזָה בְּבֵית הַקֹּדֶשׁ. _____

o. יַד אֱלֹהִים בָּעוֹלָם כְּיַד הָאֵם עַל הַבָּנִים. _____

_____

p. מִי הַגּוֹי הָעוֹשֶׂה חֶסֶד וְצֶדֶק וּמַעֲשִׂים טוֹבִים? _____

_____

q. בְּכָל יוֹם וּבְכָל לַיְלָה בּוֹרֵא הָאֵל אֶת הַשָּׁמַיִם וְאֶת הָאָרֶץ. _____

_____

r. אֲדוֹן הָאָרֶץ נוֹתֵן לָנוּ פֵּרוֹת וּמְרוֹרִים. _____

_____

s. מֹשֶׁה הַנָּבִיא נוֹתֵן לָנוּ אֶת הַתּוֹרָה וְאֶת מִצְוֹת הָאֵל. _____

_____

4. Underline and translate the words in the following prayer book excerpt that have been introduced as vocabulary. Circle the words from the roots ע־שׂ־ה and מ־ל־ך and ב־ר־א.

Adon Olam

אֲדוֹן עוֹלָם אֲשֶׁר מָלַךְ, בְּטֶרֶם כָּל יְצִיר נִבְרָא,
לְעֵת נַעֲשָׂה בְחֶפְצוֹ כֹּל, אֲזַי מֶלֶךְ שְׁמוֹ נִקְרָא.

Eternal Ruler [Ruler of eternity] who reigned before every being was created,
At the time was made by God's {His} will all {at the time all was made by God's will},
then Sovereign was God's {His} name called.

5. Underline and translate the words in the following prayer book excerpt that have been introduced as vocabulary in this book. Circle the words that have attached prefixes.

V'zot HaTorah

וְזֹאת הַתּוֹרָה אֲשֶׁר שָׂם מֹשֶׁה לִפְנֵי בְּנֵי יִשְׂרָאֵל עַל פִּי יְיָ בְּיַד מֹשֶׁה.

And this is the Torah that Moses placed before the Children of Israel by the mouth of the Eternal with the hand of Moses.

6. Underline and translate the words in the following prayer book excerpt that have been introduced as vocabulary in this book. Circle the words that have attached prepositions or pronoun endings. (Notice that the word כָּל appears with the נוּ ending as כֻּלָּנוּ, meaning "all of us.") Underline twice all the words that come from the roots ב־ר־ך and נ־ת־ן and א־ה־ב and ח־י־ה.

Sim Shalom

שִׂים שָׁלוֹם, טוֹבָה וּבְרָכָה, חֵן וָחֶסֶד וְרַחֲמִים, עָלֵינוּ וְעַל כָּל יִשְׂרָאֵל עַמֶּךָ. בָּרְכֵנוּ, אָבִינוּ, כֻּלָּנוּ כְּאֶחָד בְּאוֹר פָּנֶיךָ, כִּי בְאוֹר פָּנֶיךָ נָתַתָּ לָּנוּ, יְיָ אֱלֹהֵינוּ, תּוֹרַת חַיִּים, וְאַהֲבַת חֶסֶד, וּצְדָקָה וּבְרָכָה וְרַחֲמִים וְחַיִּים וְשָׁלוֹם. וְטוֹב בְּעֵינֶיךָ לְבָרֵךְ אֶת עַמְּךָ יִשְׂרָאֵל וְאֶת כָּל הָעַמִּים בְּכָל עֵת וּבְכָל שָׁעָה בִּשְׁלוֹמֶךָ.

Place peace, goodness and blessing, grace and kindness and compassion, upon us and upon all Israel Your people. Bless us, our God {our Father}, all of us as one with the light of Your face, for with the light of Your face You have given us, Eternal our God, a Torah of life, and a love of kindness, and righteousness and blessing and compassion and life and peace. And [it is] good in Your eyes to bless Your people Israel and all the peoples at every time and in every hour with Your peace.

7. Underline and translate the words in the following prayer book excerpt that have been introduced as vocabulary. Circle the words that have attached prepositions or pronoun endings. Underline twice all the words from the roots ד־ב־ר and צ־ו־ה and א־ה־ב.

From V'ahavta (Deuteronomy 6:5–6)

וְאָהַבְתָּ אֵת יְיָ אֱלֹהֶיךָ בְּכָל־לְבָבְךָ וּבְכָל־נַפְשְׁךָ וּבְכָל־מְאֹדֶךָ:
וְהָיוּ הַדְּבָרִים הָאֵלֶּה אֲשֶׁר אָנֹכִי מְצַוְּךָ הַיּוֹם עַל־לְבָבֶךָ:

You shall love the Eternal your God with all your heart and with all your soul and with all your being. And they will be, these words that I command you today, upon your heart.

8. Translate the following excerpts from the Bible. Check your translations against the English translations that follow.

   a. **From Genesis 21:22**

with	—	עִם
do, are doing *(participle from the root ע־שׂ־ה)*	—	עֹשֶׂה

   ...אֱלֹהִים עִמְּךָ בְּכֹל אֲשֶׁר־אַתָּה עֹשֶׂה:

   ---

   b. **Genesis 6:22**

[he, it] did *(verbs from the root ע־שׂ־ה)*	—	וַיַּעַשׂ, עָשָׂה
Noah	—	נֹחַ
[he, it] commanded *(from the root צ־ו־ה)*	—	צִוָּה
him *(direct object marker אֵת with pronoun ending)*	—	אֹתוֹ
so, thus	—	כֵּן

   וַיַּעַשׂ נֹחַ כְּכֹל אֲשֶׁר צִוָּה אֹתוֹ אֱלֹהִים כֵּן עָשָׂה:

   ---

c. Genesis 18:18

[he, it] will surely become	—	הָיוֹ יִהְיֶה לְ-
numerous	—	עָצוּם
[they] will be blessed (from the root ‏בָּ-ר-ךְ‏)	—	נִבְרְכוּ
in him, through him (attached preposition ‏בְּ‏ with pronoun ending)	—	בוֹ

וְאַבְרָהָם הָיוֹ יִהְיֶה לְגוֹי גָּדוֹל וְעָצוּם, וְנִבְרְכוּ-בוֹ כֹּל גּוֹיֵי הָאָרֶץ:

---

d. From Genesis 22:2

take	—	קַח-נָא
your only one	—	יְחִידְךָ
you love (from the root ‏אָ-ה-ב‏)	—	אָהַבְתָּ

...קַח-נָא אֶת-בִּנְךָ אֶת-יְחִידְךָ אֲשֶׁר-אָהַבְתָּ אֶת-יִצְחָק...

---

e. From Genesis 1:29–30

I have given (from the root ‏נָ-ת-ן‏)	—	נָתַתִּי
seed-bearing plant	—	עֵשֶׂב זֹרֵעַ זֶרַע
face	—	פְּנִים
it will be	—	יִהְיֶה
food (from the root ‏אָ-כָ-ל‏)	—	אָכְלָה
animal of (from the root ‏חָ-י-ה‏)	—	חַיַּת
bird	—	עוֹף
creeper, thing that creeps	—	רוֹמֵשׂ
in it (attached preposition ‏בְּ‏ with pronoun ending)	—	בוֹ
living (adjective from the root ‏חָ-י-ה‏)	—	חַיָּה

vegetation, green plants	—	יֶרֶק עֵשֶׂב
and it was so	—	וַיְהִי־כֵן

...נָתַתִּי לָכֶם אֶת־כָּל־עֵשֶׂב זֹרֵעַ זֶרַע אֲשֶׁר עַל־פְּנֵי כָל־הָאָרֶץ...

לָכֶם יִהְיֶה לְאָכְלָה: וּלְכָל־חַיַּת הָאָרֶץ וּלְכָל־עוֹף הַשָּׁמַיִם וּלְכֹל

רוֹמֵשׂ עַל־הָאָרֶץ אֲשֶׁר־בּוֹ נֶפֶשׁ חַיָּה אֶת־כָּל־יֶרֶק עֵשֶׂב לְאָכְלָה

וַיְהִי־כֵן:

_____

_____

_____

f. Psalm 146:5–6

happy, fortunate	—	אַשְׁרֵי
who {*best translated here as the one who*}	—	שֶׁ־
his help (*from the root* עֶ־ז־ר)	—	בְּעֶזְרוֹ
his hope	—	שִׂבְרוֹ
the Eternal One (*the unpronounceable four-letter name of God*)	—	יְהֹוָה
his God	—	אֱלֹהָיו
sea	—	יָם
in them (*attached preposition* בְּ *with pronoun ending*)	—	בָּם

אַשְׁרֵי שֶׁאֵל יַעֲקֹב בְּעֶזְרוֹ, שִׂבְרוֹ עַל־יְהֹוָה אֱלֹהָיו: עֹשֶׂה שָׁמַיִם

וָאָרֶץ, אֶת הַיָּם וְאֶת כָּל אֲשֶׁר בָּם, הַשֹּׁמֵר אֱמֶת לְעוֹלָם:

_____

_____

Translations:

a. From Genesis 21:22—…God is with you in all that you do.

b. Genesis 6:22—Noah did as {according to} all that God commanded him, so he did.

c. Genesis 18:18—And Abraham will surely become a great and numerous nation, and they will be blessed through him all the nations of the earth {all the nations of the earth will be blessed through him}.

d. From Genesis 22:2—…Take your son, your only one, whom you love, Isaac…

e. From Genesis 1:29–30—…I have given to you every seed-bearing plant that is on the face of all the earth…for you it will be for food. And to every animal of the land and to every bird of the sky and to every thing that creeps on the earth that in it is living breath {in which there is living breath}, all green plants for food. And it was so.

f. Psalm 146:5–6—Happy is the one who the God of Jacob is his help, his hope is upon the Eternal One his God, Maker of heaven and earth, the sea and all that is in them, the One who keeps truth forever.

EXTRA CREDIT

Aleinu

The *Aleinu* was originally included within the Rosh HaShanah liturgy, as part of the מַלְכֻוִיּוֹת, "sovereignty," section of praise of God in the *Amidah*. It was first placed in the daily service in the twelfth century in the *Machzor Vitry*; this inclusion was said to honor the memory of a group of martyrs in Blois, France, falsely accused of ritual murder, who went to their deaths chanting the words of this prayer. The *Aleinu* eventually came to be said at the conclusion of almost every prayer service.

The contents of the *Aleinu* reflect both universal and particular elements of Jewish religious belief. Underlying the text of the *Aleinu* is the Jewish concept of chosenness, the idea that the Jewish people were chosen by God for a special and unique role in God's plan for all humanity. The Jewish people were given the gift of the Torah and the corresponding obligation to communicate its teachings to the rest of the world by example. This notion has evoked varying responses from both Jews and non-Jews, some of whom enthusiastically embrace it, while others regard it as chauvinistic or elitist.

The first section of the *Aleinu* speaks of our duty to praise the Creator of the universe, "who has not made us as the nations of the lands… has not placed us as the families of the earth… has not placed our portion as theirs nor our destiny as all their multitude." Some have found this negative language problematic, implying that others are inferior. This section has been abridged or reworded in several liberal prayer books, including the Reform *Gates of Prayer* and the Reconstructionist *Kol Haneshamah*, both of which offer various alternatives. *Gates of Prayer* presents the original Hebrew as an option, but alters the translation to eliminate the negative formulation of the Hebrew, providing instead a positively worded statement of Jewish uniqueness: "who has set us apart from the other families of earth, giving us a destiny unique among the nations."

The second section of the *Aleinu* (which was not included in this chapter) articulates a universal vision encompassing all humankind. It envisions a time of wholeness, of repair of the world, when all will be united in reverence of the Divine. The culminating line of the prayer is a quote from the prophet Zechariah 14:9:

וְנֶאֱמַר, וְהָיָה יְיָ לְמֶלֶךְ עַל כָּל הָאָרֶץ, בַּיּוֹם הַהוּא יִהְיֶה יְיָ אֶחָד, וּשְׁמוֹ אֶחָד:

And it has been said: "The Eternal One will be Sovereign over all the earth. On that day, the Eternal One will be One and God's {His} name One."

Though the *Shema* asserts that the Eternal is One, now and not at some future time, the last line of the *Aleinu* reminds us that the oneness of God is related to the oneness of the world. As long as our world is broken and fragmented, God is, in a sense, not yet One. The opening words of the *Aleinu* state that it is our task לָתֵת גְּדֻלָּה, "to give greatness," to God. The actions we take to improve our world, to repair its brokenness and bring healing and wholeness to all its inhabitants, also affect the realm of the Divine. The recitation of the *Aleinu* at the conclusion of our prayer service reminds us of this task as we rise from our prayers and go out into the world.

Review

In Chapter 8, nine vocabulary words and two Hebrew roots were introduced:

אֲשֶׁר נֵר עַל כָּל בְּרֵאשִׁית גּוֹי מִשְׁפָּחָה אֲדָמָה חֲנֻכָּה

ח־י־ה צ־ו־ה

The following Building Blocks were presented:

1. The word אֲשֶׁר means "who" or "that" or "which" and introduces a clause within a sentence. The prefix שֶׁ is a short from of אֲשֶׁר.

2. The prefix לְ generally indicates the prepositions "to" or "for." As with other Hebrew prepositions, pronoun endings can be attached to indicate the object of the preposition.

3. Prepositions do not always translate smoothly from one language to another. Sometimes it is best to leave a Hebrew preposition untranslated.

Reading Practice

Psalm 150

הַלְלוּיָהּ הַלְלוּ־אֵל בְּקָדְשׁוֹ, הַלְלוּהוּ בִּרְקִיעַ עֻזּוֹ:

הַלְלוּהוּ בִגְבוּרֹתָיו, הַלְלוּהוּ כְּרֹב גֻּדְלוֹ:

הַלְלוּהוּ בְּתֵקַע שׁוֹפָר, הַלְלוּהוּ בְּנֵבֶל וְכִנּוֹר:

הַלְלוּהוּ בְּתֹף וּמָחוֹל, הַלְלוּהוּ בְּמִנִּים וְעוּגָב:

הַלְלוּהוּ בְּצִלְצְלֵי־שָׁמַע, הַלְלוּהוּ בְּצִלְצְלֵי תְרוּעָה:

כֹּל הַנְּשָׁמָה תְּהַלֵּל יָהּ הַלְלוּיָהּ:

Praise Yah, praise God in God's {His} holiness, praise God {Him} in the expanse of
God's {His} strength.
Praise God {Him} in God's {His} might, praise God {Him} as {in accordance with} the
abundance of God's {His} greatness.
Praise God {Him} with a blast of [the] shofar, praise God {Him} with harp and lyre.

Praise God {Him} with drum and dance, praise God {Him} with strings and pipe.
Praise God {Him} with cymbals sounding, praise God {Him} with cymbals blasting.
Every living being {all the breath} let it praise Yah. Praise Yah!

Mi Shebeirach for Healing
(For a Male)

מִי שֶׁבֵּרַךְ אֲבוֹתֵינוּ, אַבְרָהָם, יִצְחָק וְיַעֲקֹב, וְאִמּוֹתֵינוּ, שָׂרָה,
רִבְקָה, רָחֵל וְלֵאָה, הוּא יְבָרֵךְ וִירַפֵּא אֶת הַחוֹלֶה: _____
בֶּן _____ . הַקָּדוֹשׁ בָּרוּךְ הוּא יְמָלֵא רַחֲמִים עָלָיו, לְהַחֲלִימוֹ
וּלְרַפְּאתוֹ וּלְהַחֲזִיקוֹ וּלְהַחֲיוֹתוֹ, וְיִשְׁלַח לוֹ בִּמְהֵרָה רְפוּאָה
שְׁלֵמָה, רְפוּאַת הַנֶּפֶשׁ, וּרְפוּאַת הַגּוּף, בְּתוֹךְ שְׁאָר חוֹלֵי
יִשְׂרָאֵל, הַשְׁתָּא בַּעֲגָלָא וּבִזְמַן קָרִיב. וְנֹאמַר אָמֵן.

(For a Female)

מִי שֶׁבֵּרַךְ אֲבוֹתֵינוּ, אַבְרָהָם, יִצְחָק וְיַעֲקֹב, וְאִמּוֹתֵינוּ, שָׂרָה,
רִבְקָה, רָחֵל וְלֵאָה, הוּא יְבָרֵךְ וִירַפֵּא אֶת הַחוֹלָה: _____
בַּת _____ . הַקָּדוֹשׁ בָּרוּךְ הוּא יְמָלֵא רַחֲמִים עָלֶיהָ, לְהַחֲלִימָהּ
וּלְרַפְּאתָהּ, וּלְהַחֲזִיקָהּ וּלְהַחֲיוֹתָהּ, וְיִשְׁלַח לָהּ בִּמְהֵרָה רְפוּאָה
שְׁלֵמָה, רְפוּאַת הַנֶּפֶשׁ, וּרְפוּאַת הַגּוּף, בְּתוֹךְ שְׁאָר חוֹלֵי
יִשְׂרָאֵל, הַשְׁתָּא בַּעֲגָלָא וּבִזְמַן קָרִיב. וְנֹאמַר אָמֵן.

Who that {the One who} blessed our fathers Abraham, Isaac, and Jacob, and our moth-
ers Sarah, Rebekah, Rachel, and Leah, may God {He} bless and heal the sick one:
_____ son of/daughter of _____. The
Holy One, blessed is God {He}, may God {He} be filled [with] compassion upon
him/her, to restore him/her and to heal him/her and to strengthen him/her and to keep
alive him/her, and may God {He} send to him/her with haste complete healing, healing
of the soul and healing of the body, within {among} the rest of the sick of Israel, now,
speedily, and soon {in a near time}. And let us say: amen.

עֵץ חַיִּים הִיא לַמַּחֲזִיקִים בָּהּ, וְתֹמְכֶיהָ מְאֻשָּׁר: דְּרָכֶיהָ דַרְכֵי נֹעַם, וְכָל נְתִיבוֹתֶיהָ שָׁלוֹם:

A tree of life it is to those who grasp it, and its upholders are fortunate. Its ways are ways of pleasantness, and all its paths are peace.

PRAYER BOOK Translations

Eitz Chayyim Hi

It is a tree of life to those who hold it fast, and all who cling to it find happiness. Its ways are ways of pleasantness, and all its paths are peace.

GATES OF PRAYER FOR SHABBAT AND WEEKDAYS: A GENDER SENSITIVE PRAYERBOOK, ED. CHAIM STERN. NEW YORK: CCAR PRESS, 1994.

It is a Tree of Life to those that hold fast to it, all who uphold it may be counted fortunate. Its ways are ways of pleasantness, and all its paths are peace.

KOL HANESHAMAH: SHABBAT VEHAGIM. WYNCOTE, PA.: THE RECONSTRUCTIONIST PRESS, 1994.

It is a tree of life for those who grasp it, and all who uphold it are blessed. Its ways are pleasant, and all its paths are peace.

SIDDUR SIM SHALOM FOR SHABBAT AND FESTIVALS. NEW YORK: THE RABBINICAL ASSEMBLY, 1998.

It is a tree of life to those who take hold of it, and happy are those who support it. Its ways are pleasant ways, and all its paths are peace.

DAILY PRAYER BOOK, TRANS. PHILLIP BIRNBAUM. NEW YORK: HEBREW PUBLISHING CO., 1949.

Vocabulary

Try to locate each of these words in the Reading Practice selections (Psalm 150, *Mi Shebeirach*, or *Eitz Chayyim Hi*). Some of these words appear with prefixes and/or suffixes attached. Some appear in word pairs.

hallelujah, praise *Yah*!	—	הַלְלוּיָה
shofar, ram's horn, horn *m*	—	שׁוֹפָר
living being, soul, breath, breathing *f*	—	נְשָׁמָה
sick, ill *m*	—	חוֹלֶה
sick, ill *f*	—	חוֹלָה
compassion, mercy *m*	—	רַחֲמִים
healing *f*	—	רְפוּאָה
way, road, path *m* and *f*	—	דֶּרֶךְ

Note:

1. The word הַלְלוּיָה is often translated as "praise God!" or "praise the Eternal!" It is actually a combination of the command הַלְלוּ, "praise!" and יָהּ, *Yah* (the first two letters of the unpronounceable four-letter name of God). The phrase הַלְלוּ אֵל, which appears in the first verse of Psalm 150, means "praise God."

2. The word נְשָׁמָה is derived from the root נ־שׁ־ם, meaning to "breathe" or "inhale," and so means "breath" or "breathing." As it is used to refer to the breath of life, the life force that distinguishes a living, breathing being from one that is not, it is also translated as "living being" or "soul."

3. The words חוֹלֶה and חוֹלָה are masculine and feminine participles from the root ח־ל־ה. Hence they are used as both adjectives ("sick" or "ill") and nouns ("one who is sick" or "the sick one"). The Hebrew phrase for the mitzvah of "visiting the sick," בִּקּוּר חוֹלִים, uses חוֹלִים, the plural of חוֹלָה, as a noun.

4. The word רַחֲמִים, like the words שָׁמַיִם and חַיִּים and אֱלֹהִים, is grammatically plural, even though it translates into English as a singular noun.

Hebrew Roots

ה-ל-ל

The root ה-ל-ל has the basic meaning of "praise." The new vocabulary word הַלְלוּיָה, "hallelujah," which has entered English and other languages, is derived from this Hebrew root. The group of psalms in praise of the Eternal that are recited on festivals, Psalms 113–118, is called הַלֵּל, *Hallel*. The name of a famous rabbi in the Mishnah is הִלֵּל, *Hillel*; the national campus organization for Jewish college students is named after this Sage.

The following words are derived from the root ה-ל-ל. Note that only one ל appears in some of these words.

praise	—	מַהֲלָל
praised, blessed, commended	—	מְהֻלָּל
praising	—	הִלּוּל
praise, song of praise	—	תְּהִלָּה
Book of Psalms, psalms	—	תְּהִלִּים

The root ה-ל-ל appears several times in Psalm 150, one of the Reading Practice selections at the beginning of this chapter:

praise *Yah*	—	הַלְלוּיָה
praise God	—	הַלְלוּ אֵל
praise him, it	—	הַלְלוּהוּ
let her praise, let it praise	—	תְּהַלֵּל

ר-פ-א

The root ר-פ-א has the basic meaning of "heal" or "cure." The word רְפוּאָה, "healing," is derived from this root. In Exodus 21:19, a man who strikes and injures his fellow is obligated to provide that וְרַפֹּא יְרַפֵּא, "he be completely healed." In Jeremiah 17:14, the prophet cries out: רְפָאֵנִי יהוה, "Heal me, Eternal One," וְאֵרָפֵא, "and I shall be healed." In Psalm 147:3, God is described as הָרֹפֵא לִשְׁבוּרֵי לֵב, "the Healer of the heartbroken."

The following are several words, both ancient and modern, derived from the root ר-פ-א:

physician, doctor *m*	—	רוֹפֵא
physician, doctor *f*	—	רוֹפְאָה
medicine, cure	—	רְפָאוּת

medicinal, therapeutic	—	רְפוּאִי
curable	—	רָפִיא
curability	—	רְפִיאוּת
Raphael (angel of healing)	—	רְפָאֵל

The root ר-פ-א appears several times in the *Mi Shebeirach* for healing:

and may he heal	—	וִירַפֵּא
and to heal him	—	וּלְרַפֹּאתוֹ
and to heal her	—	וּלְרַפֹּאתָה
complete healing	—	רְפוּאָה שְׁלֵמָה
healing of the soul	—	רְפוּאַת הַנֶּפֶשׁ
and healing of the body	—	וּרְפוּאַת הַגּוּף

Building Blocks

The Endings וֹ and הָ

We have already introduced the endings ךָ and כֶם and נוּ. In this chapter, we introduce the endings וֹ and הָ. When attached to a noun, the ending וֹ means "his" and the ending הָ means "her." Both endings can also mean "its." There are often vowel changes in a word when endings are attached. Examples:

house	—	בַּיִת
his house, its house	—	בֵּיתוֹ
her house, its house	—	בֵּיתָהּ
kindness	—	חֶסֶד
his kindness	—	חַסְדּוֹ
her kindness	—	חַסְדָּהּ

The ending הָ is used to mean "its" with reference to grammatically feminine words, such as אֲדָמָה, "earth"; the ending וֹ is used to mean "its" with reference to grammatically masculine words, such as עַם, "people":

the earth and its fruit	—	הָאֲדָמָה וּפְרִיָהּ
the nation and its covenant	—	הָעָם וּבְרִיתוֹ

When the וֹ or הָ or other pronoun endings are attached to a word that ends with the letter ה, such as the word תּוֹרָה, the final letter ה is replaced by a ת: תּוֹרַת־.

his Torah	—	תּוֹרָתוֹ
her Torah	—	תּוֹרָתָהּ
your Torah	—	תּוֹרָתְךָ

Endings on Plural Nouns

The וֹ and הָ endings take a slightly different form when attached to words that already have the יִם or וֹת plural ending. In such cases, they appear as יו, pronounced "av," and יהָ. These endings replace the יִם plural ending:

deeds	—	מַעֲשִׂים
his deeds	—	מַעֲשָׂיו
her deeds	—	מַעֲשֶׂיהָ

These endings do not replace the וֹת plural ending. Instead, they are attached to the וֹת plural ending:

commandments	—	מִצְוֹת
his commandments	—	מִצְוֹתָיו
her commandments	—	מִצְוֹתֶיהָ

Endings on Prepositions

When attached to a preposition, the endings יו and וֹ mean "him." The endings הָ and יהָ mean "her." These endings can also mean "it." A preposition uses either the וֹ and הָ endings, or it uses the יו and יהָ endings:

to, for	—	לְ-
to him, to it, for him, for it	—	לוֹ
to her, to it, for her, for it	—	לָהּ
on, about	—	עַל
on him, on it, about him, about it	—	עָלָיו
on her, on it, about her, about it	—	עָלֶיהָ

Endings on Verbs

When attached to a verb, the וֹ ending means "him" or "it." The הָ ending means "her" or "it." Sometimes the ending הוּ appears on a verb instead of וֹ, as in the word הַלְלוּהוּ, "praise him."

Reading Practice with Building Blocks

Following are Reading Practice selections from this and previous chapters that contain the new endings. Reread these selections, noting the form of each ending.

Passover Seder—Blessing over Matzah

בָּרוּךְ אַתָּה יְיָ אֱלֹהֵינוּ מֶלֶךְ הָעוֹלָם, אֲשֶׁר קִדְּשָׁנוּ בְּמִצְוֹתָיו וְצִוָּנוּ עַל אֲכִילַת מַצָּה.

Blessed are You, Eternal our God, Sovereign of the universe, who makes us holy with **God's {His}** *mitzvot and commands us regarding eating of matzah.*

בְּרוּכָה אַתְּ יָהּ אֱלֹהֵינוּ רוּחַ הָעוֹלָם, אֲשֶׁר קִדְּשַׁתְנוּ בְּמִצְוֹתֶיהָ וְצִוַּתְנוּ עַל אֲכִילַת מַצָּה.

Blessed are You, Yah *our God, Soul {Spirit} of the world, who makes us holy with* **God's {Her}** *mitzvot and commands us regarding eating of matzah.*

The Fourth Commandment (Exodus 20:8)

זָכוֹר אֶת־יוֹם הַשַּׁבָּת לְקַדְּשׁוֹ:

Remember the day of the Sabbath to make **it** *holy.*

Psalm 150

הַלְלוּיָהּ הַלְלוּ־אֵל בְּקָדְשׁוֹ, הַלְלוּ**הוּ** בִּרְקִיעַ עֻזּוֹ:
הַלְלוּ**הוּ** בִגְבוּרֹתָיו, הַלְלוּ**הוּ** כְּרֹב גֻּדְלוֹ:
הַלְלוּ**הוּ** בְּתֵקַע שׁוֹפָר, הַלְלוּ**הוּ** בְּנֵבֶל וְכִנּוֹר:
הַלְלוּ**הוּ** בְּתֹף וּמָחוֹל, הַלְלוּ**הוּ** בְּמִנִּים וְעוּגָב:
הַלְלוּ**הוּ** בְצִלְצְלֵי־שָׁמַע, הַלְלוּ**הוּ** בְּצִלְצְלֵי תְרוּעָה:
כֹּל הַנְּשָׁמָה תְּהַלֵּל יָהּ הַלְלוּיָהּ:

Praise Yah, *praise God in* **God's {His}** *holiness, praise* **God {Him}** *in the expanse of* **God's {His}** *strength.*
Praise **God {Him}** *in* **God's {His}** *might, praise* **God {Him}** *as {in accordance with} the abundance of* **God's {His}** *greatness.*
Praise **God {Him}** *with a blast of [the] shofar, praise* **God {Him}** *with harp and lyre.*
Praise **God {Him}** *with drum and dance, praise* **God {Him}** *with strings and pipe.*

*Praise **God** {Him} with cymbals sounding, praise **God** {Him} with cymbals blasting.*
Every living being {all the breath} let it praise Yah. Praise Yah!

Mi Shebeirach for Healing
(For a Male)

מִי שֶׁבֵּרַךְ אֲבוֹתֵינוּ, אַבְרָהָם, יִצְחָק וְיַעֲקֹב, וְאִמּוֹתֵינוּ, שָׂרָה,

רִבְקָה, רָחֵל וְלֵאָה, הוּא יְבָרֵךְ וִירַפֵּא אֶת הַחוֹלֶה: _____

בֶּן _____ . הַקָּדוֹשׁ בָּרוּךְ הוּא יְמַלֵּא רַחֲמִים עָלָיו, לְהַחֲלִימוֹ

וּלְרַפֹּאתוֹ וּלְהַחֲזִיקוֹ וּלְהַחֲיוֹתוֹ, וְיִשְׁלַח לוֹ בִּמְהֵרָה רְפוּאָה

שְׁלֵמָה, רְפוּאַת הַנֶּפֶשׁ, וּרְפוּאַת הַגּוּף, בְּתוֹךְ שְׁאָר חוֹלֵי

יִשְׂרָאֵל, הַשְׁתָּא בַּעֲגָלָא וּבִזְמַן קָרִיב. וְנֹאמַר אָמֵן.

(For a Female)

מִי שֶׁבֵּרַךְ אֲבוֹתֵינוּ, אַבְרָהָם, יִצְחָק וְיַעֲקֹב, וְאִמּוֹתֵינוּ, שָׂרָה,

רִבְקָה, רָחֵל וְלֵאָה, הוּא יְבָרֵךְ וִירַפֵּא אֶת הַחוֹלָה: _____

בַּת _____ . הַקָּדוֹשׁ בָּרוּךְ הוּא יְמַלֵּא רַחֲמִים עָלֶיהָ,

לְהַחֲלִימָה וּלְרַפֹּאתָה, וּלְהַחֲזִיקָה וּלְהַחֲיוֹתָהּ, וְיִשְׁלַח לָהּ

בִּמְהֵרָה רְפוּאָה שְׁלֵמָה, רְפוּאַת הַנֶּפֶשׁ, וּרְפוּאַת הַגּוּף, בְּתוֹךְ

שְׁאָר חוֹלֵי יִשְׂרָאֵל, הַשְׁתָּא בַּעֲגָלָא וּבִזְמַן קָרִיב. וְנֹאמַר אָמֵן.

Who that {the One who} blessed our fathers Abraham, Isaac, and Jacob, and our moth-
ers Sarah, Rebekah, Rachel, and Leah, may God {He} bless and heal the sick one:
_____ son of/daughter of _____. The
Holy One, blessed is God {He}, may God {He} be filled [with] compassion upon
***him/her**, to restore **him/her** and to heal **him/her** and to strengthen **him/her** and to keep*
*alive **him/her**, and may God {He} send to **him/her** with haste complete healing, healing*
of the soul and healing of the body, within {among} the rest of the sick of Israel, now,
speedily, and soon {in a near time}. And let us say: amen.

עֵץ חַיִּים הִיא לַמַּחֲזִיקִים **בָּהּ**, וְתֹמְכֶ**יהָ** מְאֻשָּׁר: דְּרָכֶ**יהָ** דַרְכֵי נֹעַם, וְכָל נְתִיבוֹתֶ**יהָ** שָׁלוֹם:

*A tree of life it is to those who grasp **it**, and **its** upholders are fortunate. **Its** ways are ways of pleasantness, and all **its** paths are peace.*

The Full Paradigm of Pronoun Endings

This book has now introduced several pronoun endings. The ones presented were chosen because they appear in key prayers or biblical passages. A chart of all the basic pronoun endings in Hebrew is included here for your general information. (This chart does not include any irregular forms or variations.) It is not necessary to memorize all these pronoun endings, but it is helpful to be able to recognize them.

Object Pronoun (attached to a verb or preposition)	Possessive Pronoun (attached to a noun)	Pronoun Endings	Corresponding Subject Pronoun
me	my	ִי or ַי or נִי ָ	I אֲנִי, אָנֹכִי
you *(m, sg)*	your *(m, sg)*	ְךָ or ֶיךָ	you *(m, sg)* אַתָּה
you *(f, sg)*	your *(f, sg)*	ֵךְ or ַיִךְ	you *(f, sg)* אַתְּ
him, it	his, its	וֹ or ָיו or הוּ	he, it הוּא
her, it	her, its	ָהּ or ֶיהָ or ָה	she, it הִיא
us	our	ֵנוּ or נוּ	we אֲנַחְנוּ, אָנוּ
you *(m, pl)*	your *(m, pl)*	כֶם or ֵיכֶם	you *(m, pl)* אַתֶּם
you *(f, pl)*	your *(f, pl)*	כֶן or ֵיכֶן	you *(f, pl)* אַתֶּן
them *(m)*	their *(m)*	ָם or ֵיהֶם	they *(m)* הֵם, הֵמָּה
them *(f)*	their *(f)*	ָן or ֵיהֶן	they *(f)* הֵן, הֵנָּה

The different endings listed above as alternatives are not used interchangeably. There are various grammatical reasons why one or another ending is used in a given instance.

FROM OUR TEXTS

Connections through ב and ל

Sefer Yetzirah, one of the oldest kabbalistic texts, begins with the assertion that Creation occurred through thirty-two mystical paths of wisdom. In his commentary on *Sefer Yetzirah*, Aryeh Kaplan explains that these thirty-two paths are manifest as the twenty-two letters and ten vowels of the Hebrew alphabet and explores various connections that can be discerned between numbers, letters, and the name of God.

In Hebrew, the number 32 is written Lamed Bet (לב). [The letter ל represents the number 30; the letter ב represents the number 2.] This spells Lev, *the Hebrew word for heart...*

The Torah is seen as the heart of creation. The first letter of the Torah is the Bet (ב) of Bereshit *(בראשית)—"In the beginning" (Genesis 1:1). The last letter of the Torah is the Lamed (ל) of* Yisrael *(ישראל)—"Israel" (Deuteronomy 34:12). Together, these two letters also spell out* Lev *(לב), meaning heart...*

The two letters Lamed (ל) and Bet (ב) also share another unique distinction. As a prefix, Lamed means "to" and Bet means "in." The three letters of the Tetragrammaton [the unpronounceable four-letter name of God], Yud (י), Heh (ה), and Vav (ו), can also serve as suffixes for personal pronouns. The suffix Yud means "me," Heh means "her," and Vav means "him."

In the entire alphabet, there are only two letters to which these suffixes can be joined [to form complete words], and these are Lamed and Bet. These then spell out the words:

Li	לִי	to me	Bi	בִּי	in me
Lah	לָהּ	to her	Bah	בָּהּ	in her
Lo	לוֹ	to him	Bo	בּוֹ	in him

The two letters, Lamed and Bet, are the only ones in the entire alphabet which combine with the letters of the divine name in this manner.

SEFER YETZIRAH: THE BOOK OF CREATION, TRANSLATED AND COMMENTARY BY ARYEH KAPLAN. YORK BEACH, MAINE: SAMUEL WEISER, 1990, PAGES 9–10.

Exercises

1. Draw a line connecting each Hebrew word to its English translation. For some words, there can be more than one correct translation.

<table>
<tr><td>ill</td><td>שׁוֹפָר</td></tr>
<tr><td>healing</td><td>חוֹלָה</td></tr>
<tr><td>breath</td><td>רְפוּאָה</td></tr>
<tr><td>horn</td><td>רַחֲמִים</td></tr>
<tr><td>way</td><td>דֶּרֶךְ</td></tr>
<tr><td>compassion</td><td>חוֹלֶה</td></tr>
<tr><td>sick</td><td>הַלְלוּיָהּ</td></tr>
<tr><td>path</td><td>נְשָׁמָה</td></tr>
<tr><td>soul</td><td></td></tr>
<tr><td>praise</td><td></td></tr>
<tr><td>Yah!</td><td></td></tr>
<tr><td>mercy</td><td></td></tr>
</table>

2. The following are all the nouns introduced in this chapter that have both singular and plural forms. Draw a line connecting each singular noun to its plural form. Translate both into English.

_____ רְפוּאוֹת	שׁוֹפָר _____
_____ חוֹלוֹת	חוֹלֶה _____
_____ שׁוֹפָרוֹת	נְשָׁמָה _____
_____ דְּרָכִים	רְפוּאָה _____
_____ נְשָׁמוֹת	חוֹלָה _____
_____ חוֹלִים	דֶּרֶךְ _____

3. Read and translate the following groups of words.

c. אָבוֹת _____	b. מֶלֶךְ _____	a. שֵׁם _____
אֲבוֹתֶיהָ _____	מַלְכָּה _____	שְׁמוֹ _____
אֲבוֹתָיו _____	מַלְכּוֹ _____	שְׁמָהּ _____
אֲבוֹתֵיכֶם _____	מַלְכֵּךְ _____	שִׁמְךָ _____
אֲבוֹתֵינוּ _____	מַלְכְּכֶם _____	שְׁמֵנוּ _____
אֲבוֹתֶיךָ _____	מַלְכֵּנוּ _____	שִׁמְכֶם _____

f. נֶפֶשׁ _____	e. רְפוּאָה _____	d. בָּנִים _____
נַפְשְׁךָ _____	רְפוּאָתֵךְ _____	בָּנָיו _____
נַפְשׁוֹ _____	רְפוּאָתוֹ _____	בָּנֶיךָ _____
נַפְשָׁהּ _____	רְפוּאָתָהּ _____	בָּנֶיהָ _____
נַפְשׁוֹתֵינוּ _____	רְפוּאָתֵנוּ _____	בְּנֵיכֶם _____
נַפְשׁוֹתֵיכֶם _____	רְפוּאַתְכֶם _____	בָּנֵינוּ _____

h. מִשְׁפָּחָה _____	g. דֶּרֶךְ _____
מִשְׁפַּחְתָּהּ _____	דַּרְכּוֹ _____
מִשְׁפַּחְתּוֹ _____	דַּרְכָּהּ _____
מִשְׁפַּחְתֵּנוּ _____	דְּרָכָיו _____
מִשְׁפְּחוֹתֵינוּ _____	דְּרָכֶיהָ _____
מִשְׁפְּחוֹתָיו _____	דַּרְכֵיכֶם _____

4. Read and translate the following groups of sentences. Masculine and feminine participle forms are used.

a. הוּא שׁוֹמֵעַ לְיַעֲקֹב. _____

הוּא שׁוֹמֵעַ לוֹ. _____

יִצְחָק שׁוֹמֵעַ לְאִמּוֹ. _____

הוּא שׁוֹמֵעַ לָהּ. _____

אֲנַחְנוּ שׁוֹמְעִים לְאִמּוֹתֵינוּ. _____

b. הַמֶּלֶךְ מוֹלֵךְ עַל עַמּוֹ. _____

הַמֶּלֶךְ מוֹלֵךְ עָלָיו. _____

הַמֶּלֶךְ מוֹלֵךְ עַל כָּל הָאָרֶץ. _____

הַמֶּלֶךְ מוֹלֵךְ עָלֶיהָ. _____

c. הוּא זוֹכֵר אֶת בְּרִית הַגּוֹיִים. _____

הוּא זוֹכֵר אֹתָהּ יוֹם וָלַיְלָה. _____

רָחֵל זוֹכֶרֶת אֹתוֹ כָּל יוֹם. _____

הָאָדוֹן זוֹכֵר אֶת יוֹם הַשַּׁבָּת. _____

הָאָדוֹן זוֹכֵר אֹתוֹ. _____

d. הַנָּבִיא אוֹכֵל בַּדֶּרֶךְ. _____

הוּא אוֹכֵל אֶת לַחְמוֹ וְאֶת פִּרְיוֹ. _____

כָּל הַנְּבִיאִים אוֹכְלִים בַּדֶּרֶךְ. _____

אַתָּה אוֹכֵל אֶת לַחְמְךָ בַּדֶּרֶךְ. _____

e. מִי הַמּוֹשִׁיעַ לַחוֹלִים? _____

מִי הַמּוֹשִׁיעַ לָכֶם וּלְמִשְׁפְּחוֹתֵיכֶם? _____

מִי נוֹתֵן רְפוּאָה לָאָרֶץ? _____

מִי נוֹתֶנֶת רְפוּאָה לְכָל מִשְׁפְּחוֹתֶיהָ? _____

אֵין רוֹפֵא וְאֵין רְפוּאָה בְּיָמֵינוּ. _____

f. הוּא עוֹשֶׂה שָׁלוֹם. _____

הוּא עוֹשֶׂה מַעֲשִׂים טוֹבִים. _____

שָׂרָה וְאַבְרָהָם עוֹשִׂים מַעֲשִׂים טוֹבִים. _____

שָׂרָה וְלֵאָה עוֹשׂוֹת לָכֶם מַעֲשִׂים טוֹבִים. _____

אַבְרָהָם עוֹשֶׂה לָהּ מַעֲשִׂים טוֹבִים. _____

g. הוּא רוֹפֵא אֶת הַחוֹלִים. _____

הוּא רוֹפֵא אֶת לִבְבוֹת כָּל הָאוֹהֲבִים. _____

הוּא רוֹפֵא אֶת לִבְבוֹתֵיכֶם. _____

הוּא רוֹפֵא אֶת לִבָּהּ וְאֶת נַפְשָׁהּ. _____

h. הַלְלוּיָהּ! בָּרוּךְ שֵׁם קָדְשׁוֹ לְעוֹלָם וָעֶד. _____

בָּרוּךְ הוּא וּבָרוּךְ שְׁמוֹ. _____

רַחֲמָיו עַל כָּל מַעֲשָׂיו וּלְעוֹלָם חַסְדּוֹ. _____

בָּרוּךְ הָעוֹלָם וְכָל אֲשֶׁר בּוֹ. _____

i. הָרַחֲמִים בְּלֵב הָאֵם עַל כָּל בָּנֶיהָ. _____

רַחֲמֶיהָ עַל בְּנָהּ הַחוֹלֶה. _____

הוּא עוֹזֵר לְאִמּוֹ הַחוֹלָה. _____

רִבְקָה עוֹזֶרֶת לְבָנֶיהָ הַחוֹלִים. _____

הוּא עוֹזֵר לִבְנוֹ הַגָּדוֹל שֶׁהוּא אוֹהֵב בְּכָל לִבּוֹ. _____

5. Underline and translate the words in the following prayer book excerpt that have been introduced as vocabulary. Circle all words that have the feminine pronoun ending הָ attached. Underline twice the words that are derived from the roots ב־ר־א and נ־ת־ן and ח־י־ה and ע־ש־ה and שׁ־מ־ר.

Elohai N'shamah

אֱלֹהַי, נְשָׁמָה שֶׁנָּתַתָּ בִּי טְהוֹרָה הִיא. אַתָּה בְרָאתָהּ, אַתָּה יְצַרְתָּהּ, אַתָּה נְפַחְתָּהּ בִּי, וְאַתָּה מְשַׁמְּרָהּ בְּקִרְבִּי. כָּל זְמַן שֶׁהַנְּשָׁמָה בְקִרְבִּי, מוֹדֶה אֲנִי לְפָנֶיךָ, יְיָ אֱלֹהַי וֵאלֹהֵי אֲבוֹתַי וְאִמּוֹתַי, רִבּוֹן כָּל הַמַּעֲשִׂים, אֲדוֹן כָּל הַנְּשָׁמוֹת. בָּרוּךְ אַתָּה יְיָ, אֲשֶׁר בְּיָדוֹ נֶפֶשׁ כָּל חַי וְרוּחַ כָּל בְּשַׂר אִישׁ.

My God, [the] soul that You placed in me, pure is it. You created it, You formed it, You breathed it in me, and You keep it within me. All [the] time that the soul is within me, I give thanks before You, Eternal my God and God of my fathers and my mothers, Master of all the deeds, Ruler of all the souls {living beings}. Blessed are You, Eternal One, that in God's {His} hand {in whose hand} is [the] soul of every life and [the] spirit of all flesh of man.

6. Underline and translate the words in the following prayer book excerpt that have been introduced as vocabulary in this book. Circle all words that have the וֹ or יו masculine pronoun endings attached. Underline twice the words that are derived from the roots ב־ר־ך and ה־ל־ל.

From *Ashrei* (Psalms 84:5; 144:15; 145:1–3)

אַשְׁרֵי יוֹשְׁבֵי בֵיתֶךָ, עוֹד יְהַלְלוּךָ סֶּלָה:
אַשְׁרֵי הָעָם שֶׁכָּכָה לּוֹ, אַשְׁרֵי הָעָם שֶׁיְיָ אֱלֹהָיו:
תְּהִלָּה לְדָוִד, אֲרוֹמִמְךָ אֱלוֹהַי הַמֶּלֶךְ, וַאֲבָרְכָה שִׁמְךָ לְעוֹלָם וָעֶד:
בְּכָל יוֹם אֲבָרְכֶךָ, וַאֲהַלְלָה שִׁמְךָ לְעוֹלָם וָעֶד:
גָּדוֹל יְיָ וּמְהֻלָּל מְאֹד, וְלִגְדֻלָּתוֹ אֵין חֵקֶר:

Fortunate are the dwellers of Your house, still they praise You selah.
Fortunate is the nation that [it is] like this for it, fortunate is the nation that the Eternal One is its God.

Praise of David {or a psalm of David} I will exalt You my God the sovereign, and I will bless Your name forever and ever.
In every day I will bless You, and I will praise Your name forever and ever.
Great is the Eternal One and praised much, and to God's {His} greatness there is no measure.

7. *Eishet Chayil* (Proverb 31:10–31) is recited in some Jewish homes on Shabbat evening. In the following excerpt, underline and translate the words that have been introduced as vocabulary in this book. Circle all words that have the הָ֫ or יהָ֫ or הוּ pronoun endings.

From *Eishet Chayil* (Proverb 31:10–12)

אֵשֶׁת חַיִל מִי יִמְצָא וְרָחֹק מִפְּנִינִים מִכְרָהּ:
בָּטַח בָּהּ לֵב בַּעְלָהּ וְשָׁלָל לֹא יֶחְסָר:
גְּמָלַתְהוּ טוֹב וְלֹא־רָע כֹּל יְמֵי חַיֶּיהָ:

A woman of valor who may find? And far from {above} pearls is her worth.
Trusts in her the heart of her husband {the heart of her husband trusts in her} and gain he does not lack.
She does him good and not evil all the days of her life.

8. Underline and translate the words in the following prayer book excerpt that have been introduced as vocabulary. Circle all words that have the וֹ or יו masculine pronoun endings. Underline twice the words that are derived from the root ה־ל־ל.

From the Torah Service (Psalm 148:13–14)

יְהַלְלוּ אֶת שֵׁם יְיָ, כִּי נִשְׂגָּב שְׁמוֹ לְבַדּוֹ. הוֹדוֹ עַל אֶרֶץ וְשָׁמָיִם:
וַיָּרֶם קֶרֶן לְעַמּוֹ, תְּהִלָּה לְכָל חֲסִידָיו, לִבְנֵי יִשְׂרָאֵל, עַם קְרֹבוֹ,
הַלְלוּיָהּ:

Let them praise the name of the Eternal One, for exalted is God's {His} name alone {by itself}. God's {His} glory is upon earth and heaven. God {He} has exalted [the] horn for {of} God's {His} people, praise for all God's {His} pious ones, for the Children of Israel, a people near God {Him}, praise Yah!

9. Translate the following excerpts from the prayer book and the Bible. Check your translations against the English translations that follow.

a. From the Torah Service

[the one] who gave *(the prefix* שֶׁ *with a form of the root* נ־ת־ן*)* — שֶׁנָּתַן

holiness — קְדֻשָּׁה

בָּרוּךְ שֶׁנָּתַן תּוֹרָה לְעַמּוֹ יִשְׂרָאֵל בִּקְדֻשָּׁתוֹ.

b. II Samuel 8:15

[he] reigned *(from the root* מ־ל־ך*)* — וַיִּמְלֹךְ

David — דָּוִד

and [he] was — וַיְהִי

doing *(participle from the root* ע־שׂ־ה*)* — עֹשֶׂה

justice — מִשְׁפָּט

וַיִּמְלֹךְ דָּוִד עַל־כָּל־יִשְׂרָאֵל וַיְהִי דָוִד עֹשֶׂה מִשְׁפָּט וּצְדָקָה לְכָל־עַמּוֹ:

c. Numbers 12:13

[he] cried out — וַיִּצְעַק

to — אֶל

the Eternal One *(the unpronounceable four-letter name of God)* — יְהֹוָה

saying — לֵאמֹר

please — נָא

heal *(from the root* ר־פ־א*)* — רְפָא לְ־

וַיִּצְעַק מֹשֶׁה אֶל־יְהֹוָה לֵאמֹר אֵל נָא רְפָא נָא לָהּ:

d. From *Yotzer*

who causes light	—	הַמֵּאִיר
those who dwell	—	דָּרִים
goodness	—	טוֹב
renews	—	מְחַדֵּשׁ
continually	—	תָּמִיד

בָּרוּךְ אַתָּה יְיָ ... הַמֵּאִיר לָאָרֶץ וְלַדָּרִים עָלֶיהָ בְּרַחֲמִים,
וּבְטוּבוֹ מְחַדֵּשׁ בְּכָל יוֹם תָּמִיד מַעֲשֵׂה בְרֵאשִׁית.

_____

_____

e. From Psalm 15:1–2

Eternal One *(the unpronounceable four-letter name of God)*	—	יְהֹוָה
may sojourn	—	יָגוּר
tent	—	אֹהֶל
may dwell	—	יִשְׁכֹּן
mountain	—	הַר
the one who walks	—	הוֹלֵךְ
uprightly	—	תָּמִים
and acts	—	וּפֹעֵל

...יְהֹוָה מִי־יָגוּר בְּאָהֳלֶךָ מִי־יִשְׁכֹּן בְּהַר קָדְשֶׁךָ: הוֹלֵךְ תָּמִים
וּפֹעֵל צֶדֶק וְדֹבֵר אֱמֶת בִּלְבָבוֹ:

_____

_____

f. From Exodus 15:26

if	—	אִם
you closely listen *(from the root* שׁ־מ־ע*)*	—	שָׁמוֹעַ תִּשְׁמַע

voice	—	קוֹל
and give ear	—	וְהַאֲזַנְתָּ
and keep *(from the root* שׁ־מ־ר*)*	—	וְשָׁמַרְתָּ
laws	—	חֻקִּים
sickness *(from the same root as* חוֹלָה, חוֹלֶה*)*	—	מַחֲלָה
I placed	—	שַׂמְתִּי
Egypt	—	מִצְרַיִם
I will not place	—	לֹא אָשִׂים
for, because	—	כִּי
I	—	אֲנִי
healer *(participle from the root* ר־פ־א*)*	—	רֹפֵא

...אִם־שָׁמוֹעַ תִּשְׁמַע לְקוֹל יְהוָֹה אֱלֹהֶיךָ ... וְהַאֲזַנְתָּ לְמִצְוֹתָיו וְשָׁמַרְתָּ כָּל־חֻקָּיו, כָּל־הַמַּחֲלָה אֲשֶׁר־שַׂמְתִּי בְמִצְרַיִם לֹא־אָשִׂים עָלֶיךָ כִּי אֲנִי יְהוָֹה רֹפְאֶךָ: _____

_____

_____

Translations:

a. From the Torah service—Blessed is [the One] who gave Torah to God's {His} people Israel in God's {His} holiness.

b. II Samuel 8:15—David reigned over all Israel, and David was doing justice and righteousness for all his people.

c. Numbers 12:13—Moses cried out to the Eternal One saying, "God, please, heal, please, her."

d. From *Yotzer*—Blessed are You, Eternal One,... who causes light for the earth and for those who dwell upon it with compassion, and with God's {His} goodness renews with every day continually the act of Creation.

e. From Psalm 15:1–2—...Eternal One, who may sojourn in Your tent? who may dwell in the mountain of Your Holiness? The one who walks uprightly and acts [with] justice and speaks truth in his heart.

f. From Exodus 15:26—...If you closely listen to the voice of the Eternal One your God ... and give ear to God's {His} commandments and keep all God's {His} laws, all the sickness that I placed in Egypt I will not place upon you, for I, the Eternal One, am your Healer.

EXTRA CREDIT

Psalms and Healing

The Hebrew name for the Book of Psalms is תְּהִלִּים, "praises" (from the root ה-ל-ל introduced in this chapter). While many of the psalms are filled with eloquent praises for God's goodness or compassion or strength or the wonder of God's Creation, praise is not the only theme that finds expression in the Book of Psalms. Some psalms express sorrow, confess guilt, or plea for pardon or relief from suffering. Some have an ethical or instructive character, describing the path of righteous living. In fact, part of the appeal of the Book of Psalms is the wide range of human moods and emotions that find expression there. Throughout the ages, people have turned to the psalms to express their joys, articulate their awe, give voice to their sufferings, and find comfort and solace.

Some but not all of the psalms were originally sung as hymns within the religious service in the ancient Temple in Jerusalem. To this day, there are psalms included within the framework of Jewish daily, Shabbat, and holiday services. There are also psalms included within many other rituals, both joyous and sorrowful, such as the ceremony for חֲנֻכַּת הַבַּיִת, (the dedication of a [new] house), the introduction to בִּרְכַּת הַמָּזוֹן, (the Blessing after Meals), at the bedside of the newly deceased, at a funeral, at the unveiling of a tombstone, and at a house of mourning.

Psalms are also recited at times of fear and anxiety, as a way of seeking strength and solace. There is a long-standing tradition of reciting psalms for both physical and spiritual healing. Some individuals recite psalms on their own behalf; others on behalf of their friends and loved ones. In some communities, when a valued community member is ill, it is a custom for 150 individuals to each undertake the task of reciting one of the 150 psalms daily on behalf of the stricken individual.

The Reading Practice selections of this chapter include both the traditional prayer for healing (*Mi Shebeirach*) as well as Psalm 150. In the eighteenth century, the Chasidic Rabbi Nachman of Bratzlav identified ten psalms in particular as "healing psalms"; the last of these was Psalm 150. The others are Psalms 16, 32, 41, 42, 59, 77, 90, 105, and 137. These psalms vary in mood from quiet faith to expressions of anguish and torment, from deep despair to the overwhelmingly joyous praises of Psalm 150. Taken as a whole, they express the wide range of emotions that can be experienced during times of sickness and healing. (For more information on these ten "healing psalms" as well as suggestions on how to use them, see *Healing of Soul, Healing of Body: Spiritual Leaders Unfold the Strength and Solace in Psalms*, ed. Rabbi Simcha Weintraub [Woodstock, Vt.: Jewish Lights Publishing, 1994].)

Review

In Chapter 9, eight vocabulary words and two Hebrew roots were introduced:

הַלְלוּיָה שׁוֹפָר נְשָׁמָה חוֹלֶה חוֹלָה רַחֲמִים רְפוּאָה דֶּרֶךְ

ה־ל־ל   ר־פ־א

The following Building Blocks were presented:

1. The endings וֹ and יו mean "his" or "its" when attached to a noun. They mean "him" or "it" when attached to a preposition or verb. The ending הוּ can also be attached to a verb to indicate "him" or "it."
2. The endings הָ and יהָ mean "her" or "its" when attached to a noun. They mean "her" or "it" when attached to a preposition or verb.

 ## Reading Practice

Ki Mitziyon (From Isaiah 2:3 and Micah 4:2)

...כִּי מִצִּיּוֹן תֵּצֵא תוֹרָה, וּדְבַר יְיָ מִירוּשָׁלָיִם:

For from Zion will go forth Torah, and the word of the Eternal from Jerusalem.

The First Commandment (Exodus 20:2)

אָנֹכִי יְהֹוָה אֱלֹהֶיךָ אֲשֶׁר הוֹצֵאתִיךָ מֵאֶרֶץ מִצְרַיִם מִבֵּית עֲבָדִים:

I am the Eternal your God who brought out you {who brought you out} from the land of Egypt from [the] house of slaves {the house of bondage}.

אַתָּה גִּבּוֹר לְעוֹלָם, אֲדֹנָי, מְחַיֵּה הַכֹּל אַתָּה, רַב לְהוֹשִׁיעַ.

מְכַלְכֵּל חַיִּים בְּחֶסֶד, מְחַיֵּה הַכֹּל בְּרַחֲמִים רַבִּים. סוֹמֵךְ נוֹפְלִים,

וְרוֹפֵא חוֹלִים, וּמַתִּיר אֲסוּרִים, וּמְקַיֵּם אֱמוּנָתוֹ לִישֵׁנֵי עָפָר.

מִי כָמוֹךָ בַּעַל גְּבוּרוֹת, וּמִי דּוֹמֶה לָּךְ, מֶלֶךְ מֵמִית וּמְחַיֶּה וּמַצְמִיחַ

יְשׁוּעָה? וְנֶאֱמָן אַתָּה לְהַחֲיוֹת הַכֹּל. בָּרוּךְ אַתָּה יְיָ, מְחַיֵּה הַכֹּל.

You are mighty forever, Eternal One, the Life-giver of all {everything} are You, great to save. Sustaining life with kindness, the Life-giver of all with great compassion. Supporting falling ones, and healing sick ones, and freeing captives, and maintaining God's {His} faithfulness to sleepers of dust {those who sleep in the dust}. Who is like You, Possessor of strength, and who resembles You, Sovereign causing death and giving life and making grow salvation! And faithful are You to give life to the all {everything}. Blessed are You, Eternal One, the Life-giver of all.

Prayer Book Translations

G'vurot

Eternal is Your might, O God; all life is Your gift; great is Your power to save!

With love You sustain the living, with great compassion give life to all. You send help to the falling and healing to the sick; You bring freedom to the captive and keep faith with those who sleep in the dust.

Who is like You, Mighty One, Author of life and death, Source of salvation!

We praise You, O God, the Source of life.

GATES OF PRAYER FOR SHABBAT AND WEEKDAYS: A GENDER SENSITIVE PRAYERBOOK, ED. CHAIM STERN. NEW YORK: CCAR PRESS, 1994.

You are forever powerful, ALMIGHTY ONE, abundant in your saving acts.

In summer: You send down the dew.

In winter: You cause the wind to blow and rain to fall.

In loyalty you sustain the living, nurturing the life of every living thing, upholding those who fall, healing the sick, freeing the captive, and remaining faithful to all life held dormant in the earth. Who can compare to you, almighty God, who can resemble you, the source of life and death, who makes salvation grow!

Faithful are you in giving life to every living thing. Blessed are you, THE FOUNT OF LIFE, who gives and renews life.

KOL HANESHAMAH: SHABBAT VEHAGIM. WYNCOTE, PA.: THE RECONSTRUCTIONIST PRESS, 1994.

Your might, Adonai, is boundless. You give life to the dead; great is Your saving power.
From Sh'mini Atzeret until Pesach: You cause the wind to blow and the rain to fall.
Your love sustains the living, Your great mercies give life to the dead. You support the
falling, heal the ailing, free the fettered. You keep Your faith with those who sleep in the
dust. Whose power can compare with Yours! You are the Master of life and death and
deliverance.
Faithful are You in giving life to the dead.
Praised are You, Adonai, Master of life and death.

SIDDUR SIM SHALOM FOR SHABBAT AND FESTIVALS. NEW YORK: THE RABBINICAL
ASSEMBLY, 1998.

Thou, O Lord, art mighty forever; thou revivest the dead; thou are powerful to save.
Between Sukkot and Pesach add: (Thou causest the wind to blow and the rain to fall.)
Thou sustainest the living with kindness, and revivest the dead with great mercy; thou
supportest all who fall, and healest the sick; thou settest the captives free, and keepest
faith with those who sleep in the dust. Who is like thee, Lord of power! Who resembles
thee, O King! Thou bringest death and restorest life, and causest salvation to flourish.
Thou art faithful to revive the dead. Blessed art thou, O Lord, who revivest the dead.

DAILY PRAYER BOOK, TRANS. PHILLIP BIRNBAUM. NEW YORK: HEBREW PUBLISHING
CO., 1949.

Slightly different variations of this prayer exist. The Hebrew version of *G'vurot* included in this chapter's Reading Practice is from the Reform Movement's prayer book *Gates of Prayer for Shabbat and Weekdays: A Gender Sensitive Prayerbook.*

The traditional wording of this prayer, which appears in the Conservative prayer book *Sim Shalom* as well as the Birnbaum *Daily Prayer Book*, contains the phrases מְחַיֵּה מֵתִים, לְהַחֲיוֹת מֵתִים, and מְחַיֵּה הַמֵּתִים ("Life-giver of/gives life to the dead"), which have been changed in the Reform version to מְחַיֵּה הַכֹּל and לְהַחֲיוֹת הַכֹּל ("Life-giver of/gives life to everything"). The Reconstructionist prayer book *Kol Haneshamah* uses the wording כֹּל חַי ("every living thing") instead of הַכֹּל ("everything"), and omits the phrase entirely in the first line of the prayer.

The other three prayer books also contain a seasonal addition regarding wind and rain (and dew, in *Kol Haneshamah*), which is omitted in the Reform prayer book. All of the other variations in the translations above are the result of differing interpretations by the translator, and not due to different Hebrew texts. (See the Extra Credit section at the end of this chapter for a fuller explanation of liturgical changes in *G'vurot*.)

Vocabulary

Try to locate each of these words in the Reading Practice selections (*Ki Mitziyon*, the First Commandment, and *G'vurot*). Some of these words appear with prefixes and/or suffixes attached. Some appear in word pairs.

word, speech *m*	—	דָּבָר
slave, bondsman, servant *m*	—	עֶבֶד
mighty, valiant, courageous *adj*	—	גִּבּוֹר
strength, valor, might *f*	—	גְּבוּרָה
numerous, many, great *adj*	—	רַב
Zion	—	צִיּוֹן
Jerusalem	—	יְרוּשָׁלַיִם
Egypt	—	מִצְרַיִם

Note:

1. In modern Hebrew, the word דָּבָר also can mean "thing," "matter," or "something."
2. As with other adjectives, the words גִּבּוֹר and רַב have four forms:

רַבִּים	*m pl*	רַב	*m sg*	גִּבּוֹרִים	*m pl*	גִּבּוֹר	*m sg*
רַבּוֹת	*f pl*	רַבָּה	*f sg*	גְּבוֹרוֹת	*f pl*	גְּבוּרָה	*f sg*

The word גִּבּוֹר is also used as a noun meaning "hero."

Hebrew Roots

י־צ־א

The root י־צ־א has the basic meaning of "go out" or "come out." In some words derived from this root, the letter י disappears or is replaced by the vowel וֹ. The Hebrew blessing over bread includes a verb form from this root with the meaning "bring out" or "bring forth": הַמּוֹצִיא לֶחֶם מִן הָאָרֶץ, "the [one who] brings forth bread from the earth". A well-known Israeli folk song entitled "Tzeina Tzeina" includes a chorus urging young women צֶאנָה צֶאנָה, "Come out! Come out!" to greet visiting soldiers. Public buildings in Israel have יְצִיאָה, "exit," signs posted over doorways.

The following are words derived from the root י־צ־א. Notice that the root letter י disappears or is replaced by the vowel וֹ in several of these words.

exit, exodus	—	יְצִיאָה
the exodus of {from} Egypt	—	יְצִיאַת מִצְרַיִם
export	—	יְצוּא
exporter	—	יְצוּאָן
bringing out, outgoings, disbursements	—	הוֹצָאָה
publication, publishing {bringing out to light}	—	הוֹצָאָה לְאוֹר
published by...	—	הוֹצָאַת...
outlet, way out, egress	—	מוֹצָא
Saturday night {the outgoing of Shabbat}	—	מוֹצָאֵי שַׁבָּת
the night when a Jewish holiday ends {the outgoing of a holiday}	—	מוֹצָאֵי יוֹם טוֹב
effect	—	תּוֹצָא
result, outcome, consequence	—	תּוֹצָאָה

The root י־צ־א appears twice in the Reading Practice at the beginning of this chapter, once in *Ki Mitziyon* and once in the First Commandment:

will go forth	—	תֵּצֵא
I brought out	—	הוֹצֵאתִי
I brought out you	—	הוֹצֵאתִיךָ

א־מ־ן

The root א־מ־ן has the basic meaning of "firmness" and "support." There are many Hebrew words, both ancient and modern, that are derived from this root. One who provides support for another's child is a אוֹמֶנֶת, "nurse," or "foster-mother"; related words are אוֹמְנוּת, "foster parenthood," and יֶלֶד אָמוֹן, "foster child." One who supports another in the acquisition of a skill is an אוֹמֵן, "trainer" or "educator," or a מְאַמֵן, "trainer," or "coach"; related words are אִמּוּן, "training," מְאֻמָּן, "trained" or "skilled," and אָמוֹן, "apprentice." One who is firm or sure in one's craft is an אָמָן, "artist" or "expert"; related words include אוּמָן, "crafts-man" or "artisan," אוּמָנוּת, "craft" or "craftsmanship," and אָמָנוּת, "art" or "artistry." There is a cluster of words from the root א־מ־ן that have meanings related to "faith" or "faithfulness," "belief" and "trust." Words from the root א־מ־ן with these meanings are most often encountered in the Bible and prayer book. The following are examples of such words, both ancient and modern, derived from the root א־מ־ן:

amen, so be it, surely	—	אָמֵן
confidence, faithfulness	—	אֵמוּן
honesty, fidelity	—	אֱמוּנִים
faith, belief, trust	—	אֱמוּנָה
faithfulness	—	אֹמֶן
trust, faith {also, in modern Hebrew: pact, treaty}	—	אֲמָנָה
in truth, truly	—	אָמְנָה
indeed, truly, surely	—	אָמְנָם
verification	—	הָאֲמָנוּת
believer, [one who] believes	—	מַאֲמִין

The root א־מ־ן appears twice in the *G'vurot* prayer included in the Reading Practice at the beginning of this chapter:

faith, faithfulness	—	אֱמוּנָה
his faithfulness, its faithfulness	—	אֱמוּנָתוֹ
faithful	—	נֶאֱמָן
and faithful are you	—	וְנֶאֱמָן אַתָּה

Building Blocks

The Preposition מ

The Hebrew letter מ is used as a prefix to indicate the preposition "from."

Unlike the prepositions כּ, ל, or בּ, the letter מ does not combine with the prefix ה when it is attached to a word that already has that prefix. Instead, it is attached to the ה:

to the house	—	לְ + הַבַּיִת = לַבַּיִת
in the house	—	בְּ + הַבַּיִת = בַּבַּיִת
from the house	—	מֵ + הַבַּיִת = מֵהַבַּיִת

It also appears as the separate word מִן. Perhaps the best-known example is in the blessing over bread:

בָּרוּךְ אַתָּה יְיָ, אֱלֹהֵינוּ מֶלֶךְ הָעוֹלָם, הַמּוֹצִיא לֶחֶם **מִן** הָאָרֶץ:

*Blessed are You, Eternal our God, Sovereign of the universe, who brings forth bread **from** the earth.*

Participles with the Prefix מ

In Chapter 4, we introduced the participle pattern ◻ֵ◻וֹ◻. Most of the roots included in this book follow that participle pattern. In this chapter, we introduce a different participle pattern, which utilizes the letter מ as a prefix before the root letters:

$$ ◻ֵ◻ַ◻ְמ $$

When the letter מ is used as a participle prefix, it has no connection to the preposition מ. It does not mean "from."

The following roots introduced in this book use the new participle pattern:

sanctifying, making holy, sanctifies, makes holy, sanctifier	—	מְקַדֵּשׁ	ק־ד־שׁ
praising, praises, one who praises	—	מְהַלֵּל	ה־ל־ל
speaking, speaks, one who speaks, speaker	—	מְדַבֵּר	ד־ב־ר
bless, blesses, one who blesses	—	מְבָרֵךְ	ב־ר־ךְ

giving life, gives life, one who gives life, life-giver	—	מְחַיֶּה חי־י־ה
commanding, commands, one who commands, commander	—	מְצַוֶּה צ־ו־ה

The first three participles in the list, opposite, all follow the basic מְ ⬛ ⬛ pattern exactly. The last three participles each have a single vowel variation. Such variations are caused by certain root letters. Unlike the other roots, the root ד־ב־ר forms participles in both patterns: דוֹבֵר and מְדַבֵּר.

Four Forms of the Participle

Every participle pattern, whether it be the ⬛ וֹ ⬛ pattern or the מְ ⬛ ⬛ pattern or one of the others that we have not introduced, has four forms: masculine singular, masculine plural, feminine singular, and feminine plural. The simplest form is always the masculine singular; the others all have additional endings and may have vowel changes. Following are the four forms of the מְ ⬛ ⬛ pattern. Notice that the endings are the same as those in the ⬛ וֹ ⬛ pattern:

	Plural	*Singular*
masculine	מְ ⬛ ⬛ ים	מְ ⬛ ⬛
feminine	מְ ⬛ ⬛ וֹת	מְ ⬛ ⬛ ת

Participle Chart

The following chart uses the root ד־ב־ר to illustrate which participle form is used with each of the Hebrew pronouns introduced in the Grammar Enrichment section of Chapter 1. This material is included for enrichment only. It is not necessary to memorize all these combinations in order to complete this book.

	Plural		*Singular*		
we speak	אֲנַחְנוּ מְדַבְּרִים	I speak	אֲנִי מְדַבֵּר	*first person*	
you speak	אַתֶּם מְדַבְּרִים	you speak	אַתָּה מְדַבֵּר	*second person*	***Masculine***
they speak	הֵם מְדַבְּרִים	he, it speaks	הוּא מְדַבֵּר	*third person*	
we speak	אֲנַחְנוּ מְדַבְּרוֹת	I speak	אֲנִי מְדַבֶּרֶת	*first person*	
you speak	אַתֶּן מְדַבְּרוֹת	you speak	אַתְּ מְדַבֶּרֶת	*second person*	***Feminine***
they speak	הֵן מְדַבְּרוֹת	she, it speaks	הִיא מְדַבֶּרֶת	*third person*	

Reading Practice with Building Blocks

Following are the Reading Practice selections from this chapter with the new Building Blocks highlighted. Reread these selections, noting the use of the letter מ as either a preposition or as part of a participle.

Ki Mitziyon (From Isaiah 2:3 and Micah 4:2)

כִּי **מִצִיּוֹן** תֵּצֵא תוֹרָה, וּדְבַר יְיָ **מִירוּשָׁלָיִם**:...

*For **from** Zion will go forth Torah, and the word of the Eternal **from** Jerusalem.*

The First Commandment (Exodus 20:2)

אָנֹכִי יְהוָֹה אֱלֹהֶיךָ אֲשֶׁר הוֹצֵאתִיךָ **מֵאֶרֶץ** מִצְרַיִם **מִבֵּית** עֲבָדִים:

*I am the Eternal your God who brought out you {who brought you out} **from** the land of Egypt **from** [the] house of slaves {the house of bondage}.*

אַתָּה גִּבּוֹר לְעוֹלָם, אֲדֹנָי, **מְחַיֵּה** הַכֹּל אַתָּה, רַב לְהוֹשִׁיעַ.
מְכַלְכֵּל חַיִּים בְּחֶסֶד, **מְחַיֵּה** הַכֹּל בְּרַחֲמִים רַבִּים. סוֹמֵךְ נוֹפְלִים,
וְרוֹפֵא חוֹלִים, וּמַתִּיר אֲסוּרִים, וּ**מְקַיֵּם** אֱמוּנָתוֹ לִישֵׁנֵי עָפָר.
מִי כָמְוֹךָ בַּעַל גְּבוּרוֹת, וּמִי דְּוֹמֶה לָּךְ, מֶלֶךְ מֵמִית וּ**מְחַיֵּה**
וּמַצְמִיחַ יְשׁוּעָה? וְנֶאֱמָן אַתָּה לְהַחֲיוֹת הַכֹּל. בָּרוּךְ אַתָּה יְיָ,
מְחַיֵּה הַכֹּל.

You are mighty forever, Eternal One, the **Life-giver** of all {everything} are You, great to save. Sustaining life with kindness, the **Life-giver** of all with great compassion. Supporting falling ones, and healing sick ones, and freeing captives, and **maintaining** God's {His} faithfulness to sleepers of dust {those who sleep in the dust}. Who is like You, Possessor of strength, and who resembles You, Sovereign causing death and **giving life** and making grow salvation? And faithful are You to give life to the all {everything}. Blessed are You, Eternal One, the **Life-giver** of all.

FROM OUR TEXTS

The First Commandment

Exodus 20:2

אָנֹכִי יְהֹוָה אֱלֹהֶיךָ אֲשֶׁר הוֹצֵאתִיךָ מֵאֶרֶץ
מִצְרַיִם מִבֵּית עֲבָדִים:

This commandment was given in the singular ("I am the Eternal אֱלֹהֶיךָ your God, אֲשֶׁר הוֹצֵאתִיךָ who brought you out..."—instead of the plurals הוֹצֵאתִיכֶם and אֱלֹהֵיכֶם) because the knowledge of God and the ability to perceive the power and providence of the Creator of the Universe is not given to everyone in equal measure. Each individual understands these things in a manner commensurate with his or her mental and spiritual capacities ... so that every person will have a different conception of the One who has proclaimed "I am the Eternal אֱלֹהֶיךָ your God."

ADAPTED FROM *SIFTHEI KOHEN*, QUOTED IN *WELLSPRINGS OF TORAH: AN ANTHOLOGY OF BIBLICAL COMMENTARIES*, ED. RABBI NISON ALPERT. NEW YORK: JUDAICA PRESS, 1990, PAGE 150.

Exercises

1. Draw a line connecting each Hebrew word to its English translation. For some words, there can be more than one correct translation.

<table>
<tr><td>servant</td><td rowspan="11">

יְרוּשָׁלַיִם

גְּבוּרָה

עֶבֶד

מִצְרַיִם

גִּבּוֹר

דָּבָר

רַב

צִיּוֹן
</td></tr>
<tr><td>mighty</td></tr>
<tr><td>word</td></tr>
<tr><td>strength</td></tr>
<tr><td>slave</td></tr>
<tr><td>Zion</td></tr>
<tr><td>Jerusalem</td></tr>
<tr><td>speech</td></tr>
<tr><td>Egypt</td></tr>
<tr><td>courageous</td></tr>
<tr><td>many</td></tr>
</table>

2. The following are all the nouns and adjectives introduced in this chapter that have singular and plural forms. Draw a line connecting each singular word to its plural form. Translate both into English.

_____	רַבִּים	עֶבֶד	_____
_____	גְּבוּרוֹת	גִּבּוֹר	_____
_____	דְּבָרִים	רַבָּה	_____
_____	גְּבוּרוֹת	דָּבָר	_____
_____	עֲבָדִים	רַב	_____
_____	גִּבּוֹרִים	גְּבוּרָה	_____
_____	רַבּוֹת	גְּבוּרָה	_____

3. Following each noun below are three adjective forms. Circle the adjective that correctly matches the noun. Translate each phrase into English.

a. שָׁלוֹם (רַב, רַבָּה, קְדוֹשִׁים) _____

b. רַחֲמִים (גִּבּוֹר, רַבִּים, טוֹבוֹת) _____

c. מִשְׁפָּחָה (טוֹב, רַבּוֹת, גְּדוֹלָה) _____

d. הָאֵל (הַגְּדוֹלִים, הַגִּבּוֹר, קָדוֹשׁ) _____

e. שְׁמוֹ (רַבִּים, הַגָּדוֹל, טוֹבוֹת) _____

f. נִשְׁמוֹתֵיכֶם (גְּבוּרוֹת, הַטּוֹבָה, הַקְּדוֹשׁוֹת) _____

4. Draw a line connecting the matching singular and plural participle forms. Translate both into English. Hint: This list contains both masculine and feminine participles. When the last letter of the root is ה, the ה is omitted when plural endings are attached.

_____ מְקַדֵּשׁ   מְדַבְּרוֹת _____

_____ דּוֹבְרִים   מְצַוֶּה _____

_____ מְבָרֵךְ   מְקַדְּשִׁים _____

_____ מְהַלְלוֹת   מְחַיָּה _____

_____ מְצַוִּים   מְהַלֶּלֶת _____

_____ מְדַבֶּרֶת   דּוֹבֵר _____

_____ מְחַיִּים   מְבָרְכִים _____

5. Read and translate the following groups of sentences. Masculine and feminine participle forms are used.

a. הַמֶּלֶךְ מְצַוֶּה אֶת הָעֲבָדִים. _____

הַמֶּלֶךְ מְצַוֶּה אֶת עֲבָדָיו. _____

הוּא מְצַוֶּה אֹתָךְ. _____

רַבִּים הַדְּבָרִים אֲשֶׁר הוּא מְצַוֶּךְ. _____

_____

רַבִּים מִצְוֹת הַמֶּלֶךְ וַעֲבָדָיו עוֹשִׂים אֶת מִצְוֹתָיו.

_____

_____

b. אֲנַחְנוּ מְדַבְּרִים מִן הַלֵּב. _____

אַתָּה מְדַבֵּר מִלִּבְּךָ. _____

אָנוּ שׁוֹמְעִים לְדִבְרֵיכֶם. _____

הוּא שׁוֹמֵעַ לִדְבָרִים אֲשֶׁר אֲנַחְנוּ מְדַבְּרוֹת מִלִּבֵּנוּ. _____

_____

c. אֲנַחְנוּ מְבָרְכִים אֶתְכֶם מִצִּיּוֹן. _____

_____

אַתָּה מְבָרֵךְ אֹתָנוּ מִבֵּית אָבִיךְ.

_____

שָׂרָה מְבָרֶכֶת אֶתְכֶם מִבֵּית אִמָּהּ.

_____

אֲנַחְנוּ מְבָרְכִים אֶת בֵּיתְךָ וְאֶת כָּל אֲשֶׁר בּוֹ.

_____

בָּרוּךְ אַתָּה בְּבֵיתְךָ וּבְרוּכָה מִשְׁפַּחְתְּךָ. _____

_____

d. הָרוֹפֵא מְחַיֶּה חוֹלִים. _____

הוּא מְחַיֶּה כָּל חוֹלֵי הָעָם. _____

_____

הָרוֹפֵא מְחַיֶּה אֶת נִשְׁמוֹתֵינוּ.

_____

הוּא מְחַיֶּה אֹתְךָ בְּחֶסֶד וּבְרַחֲמִים רַבִּים. _____

_____

בְּרוּכָה הָרְפוּאָה הַגְּדוֹלָה.

e. אֲנַחְנוּ שׁוֹמְרִים אֶת בְּרִית אֱלֹהֵינוּ. _____

_____

אָנוּ מְקַדְשִׁים אֶת יוֹם הַשַׁבָּת. _____

_____

אָנוּ מְקַדְשִׁים אֹתוֹ מִכָּל הַיָּמִים. _____

_____

קָדוֹשׁ הוּא בִּירוּשָׁלַיִם וּבְכָל הָעוֹלָם. _____

_____

6. Underline and translate the words in the following prayer book excerpt that have been introduced as vocabulary. Underline twice the attached preposition מ. Circle the words that come from the roots ק־ד־שׁ and ז־כ־ר and י־צ־א and ב־ח־ר.

Shabbat Evening *Kiddush*

בָּרוּךְ אַתָּה יְיָ אֱלֹהֵינוּ מֶלֶךְ הָעוֹלָם, אֲשֶׁר קִדְשָׁנוּ בְּמִצְוֹתָיו וְרָצָה
בָנוּ, וְשַׁבַּת קָדְשׁוֹ בְּאַהֲבָה וּבְרָצוֹן הִנְחִילָנוּ, זִכָּרוֹן לְמַעֲשֵׂה
בְרֵאשִׁית. כִּי הוּא יוֹם תְּחִלָּה לְמִקְרָאֵי קֹדֶשׁ, זֵכֶר לִיצִיאַת
מִצְרָיִם. כִּי בָנוּ בָחַרְתָּ וְאוֹתָנוּ קִדַּשְׁתָּ מִכָּל הָעַמִּים, וְשַׁבַּת קָדְשְׁךָ
בְּאַהֲבָה וּבְרָצוֹן הִנְחַלְתָּנוּ. בָּרוּךְ אַתָּה יְיָ, מְקַדֵּשׁ הַשַׁבָּת.

Blessed are You, Eternal our God, Sovereign of the universe, who makes us holy with God's {His} mitzvot and delights in us, and the Sabbath of God's {His} holiness with love and with delight God {He} has bequeathed us, a reminder of the act of Creation. For it is a beginning day for assemblies of holiness {holy assemblies, holy days}, a remembrance for {of} the Exodus of {from} Egypt. For us You chose and us You have sanctified from all the peoples, and the Sabbath of Your holiness with love and with delight You have bequeathed us. Blessed are You, the Sanctifier of Shabbat.

7. Underline and translate the words in the following prayer book excerpt that have been introduced as vocabulary. Underline twice the attached prepositions מ. Circle the words that come from the roots ע־שׂ־ה and ב־ר־א and ק־ד־שׁ and ב־ר־ך.

Vay'chulu (Genesis 2:1–3)

וַיְכֻלּוּ הַשָּׁמַיִם וְהָאָרֶץ וְכָל־צְבָאָם: וַיְכַל אֱלֹהִים בַּיּוֹם הַשְּׁבִיעִי מְלַאכְתּוֹ אֲשֶׁר עָשָׂה וַיִּשְׁבֹּת בַּיּוֹם הַשְּׁבִיעִי מִכָּל־מְלַאכְתּוֹ אֲשֶׁר עָשָׂה: וַיְבָרֶךְ אֱלֹהִים אֶת־יוֹם הַשְּׁבִיעִי וַיְקַדֵּשׁ אֹתוֹ כִּי בוֹ שָׁבַת מִכָּל־מְלַאכְתּוֹ אֲשֶׁר־בָּרָא אֱלֹהִים לַעֲשׂוֹת:

They were completed the heavens and the earth and all their array. And God completed on the seventh day God's {His} work that God {He} had done and God {He} rested on the seventh day from God's {His} work that God {He} had done. And God blessed the seventh day and sanctified it for on it God {He} rested from all God's {His} work that God had created to make.

8. The following is an excerpt from a longer passage in the Passover Haggadah. The lines excerpted are commonly sung at the Passover seder. Underline and translate the words in this excerpt that have been introduced as vocabulary in this book. Underline twice the attached preposition מ. Circle the words that come from the roots י־צ־א and נ־ת־ן.

Dayeinu

אִלּוּ הוֹצִיאָנוּ מִמִּצְרַיִם, דַּיֵּנוּ.
אִלּוּ נָתַן לָנוּ אֶת־הַשַּׁבָּת, דַּיֵּנוּ.
אִלּוּ נָתַן לָנוּ אֶת־הַתּוֹרָה, דַּיֵּנוּ.

If God {He} brought us out from Egypt, [it would have been] enough for us.
If God {He} gave to us the Sabbath, [it would have been] enough for us.
If God {He} gave to us the Torah, [it would have been] enough for us.

9. Translate the following excerpts from the prayer book and the Bible. Check your translations against the English translations that follow.

   a. **Psalm 115:18 (the Last Line of *Ashrei*)**

we	—	אֲנַחְנוּ
[we] will bless (*verb from the root* בּ־ר־ךּ)	—	נְבָרֵךְ
Yah (*the first two letters of the unpronounceable four-letter name of God*)	—	יָהּ
now	—	עַתָּה
until, unto	—	עַד

   וַאֲנַחְנוּ נְבָרֵךְ יָהּ מֵעַתָּה וְעַד־עוֹלָם הַלְלוּיָהּ:

   b. **From Genesis 12:1–2**

and [he, it] said	—	וַיֹּאמֶר
the Eternal One (*the unpronounceable four-letter name of God*)	—	יְהֹוָה
to	—	אֶל
Abram	—	אַבְרָם
go forth (*command*)	—	לֶךְ־לְךָ
birthplace	—	מוֹלֶדֶת
I will show	—	אַרְאֶה
I will make (*verb from the root* ע־שׂ־ה)	—	אֶעֱשֶׂה
I will bless (*verb from the root* בּ־ר־ךּ)	—	אֲבָרֵךְ

   וַיֹּאמֶר יְהֹוָה אֶל־אַבְרָם לֶךְ־לְךָ מֵאַרְצְךָ וּמִמּוֹלַדְתְּךָ וּמִבֵּית אָבִיךָ
   אֶל־הָאָרֶץ אֲשֶׁר אַרְאֶךָּ: וְאֶעֶשְׂךָ לְגוֹי גָּדוֹל וַאֲבָרֶכְךָ...

c. Exodus 6:27

they	—	הֵם
the speakers, the ones speaking *(participle from the root* ד־ב־ר*)* —		הַמְדַבְּרִים
to	—	אֶל
Pharaoh	—	פַּרְעֹה
to bring out *(verb from the root* י־צ־א*)*	—	לְהוֹצִיא
Aaron	—	אַהֲרֹן

הֵם הַמְדַבְּרִים אֶל־פַּרְעֹה מֶלֶךְ־מִצְרַיִם לְהוֹצִיא אֶת־בְּנֵי־יִשְׂרָאֵל מִמִּצְרָיִם, הוּא מֹשֶׁה וְאַהֲרֹן:

_____

_____

d. *Shalom Rav*

may you place	—	תָּשִׂים
for	—	כִּי
eyes	—	עֵינַיִם
to bless *(verb from the root* ב־ר־ך*)* —		לְבָרֵךְ
time	—	עֵת
hour	—	שָׁעָה

שָׁלוֹם רָב עַל יִשְׂרָאֵל עַמְּךָ תָּשִׂים לְעוֹלָם, כִּי אַתָּה הוּא מֶלֶךְ אָדוֹן לְכָל הַשָּׁלוֹם. וְטוֹב בְּעֵינֶיךָ לְבָרֵךְ אֶת עַמְּךָ יִשְׂרָאֵל וְאֶת כָּל הָעַמִּים בְּכָל עֵת וּבְכָל שָׁעָה בִּשְׁלוֹמֶךָ. בָּרוּךְ אַתָּה יְיָ, הַמְבָרֵךְ אֶת עַמּוֹ יִשְׂרָאֵל בַּשָּׁלוֹם.

_____

_____

_____

e. Psalm 148:1–5

praise *(command from the root* ה־ל־ל*)*	—	הַלְלוּ
the Eternal One *(the unpronounceable four-letter name of God)*	—	יְהֹוָה
height	—	מָרוֹם
array	—	צָבָא
sun	—	שֶׁמֶשׁ
moon	—	יָרֵחַ
stars of light	—	כּוֹכְבֵי אוֹר
water	—	מַיִם
let them praise *(verb from the root* ה־ל־ל*)*	—	יְהַלְלוּ
for	—	כִּי
[he, it] commanded *(verb from the root* צ־ו־ה*)*	—	צִוָּה
they were created *(verb from the root* ב־ר־א*)*	—	נִבְרָאוּ

הַלְלוּיָהּ הַלְלוּ אֶת־יְהֹוָה מִן־הַשָּׁמַיִם, הַלְלוּהוּ בַּמְּרוֹמִים:

הַלְלוּהוּ כָל־מַלְאָכָיו, הַלְלוּהוּ כָּל־צְבָאָיו:

הַלְלוּהוּ שֶׁמֶשׁ וְיָרֵחַ, הַלְלוּהוּ כָּל־כּוֹכְבֵי אוֹר:

הַלְלוּהוּ שְׁמֵי הַשָּׁמָיִם וְהַמַּיִם אֲשֶׁר מֵעַל הַשָּׁמָיִם:

יְהַלְלוּ אֶת־שֵׁם יְהֹוָה כִּי הוּא צִוָּה וְנִבְרָאוּ:

_____

_____

_____

_____

Translations:

a. Psalm 115:18 (the last line of *Ashrei*)—And we will bless *Yah* from now and unto eternity. Hallelujah {praise *Yah*}!

b. From Genesis 12:1–2—And the Eternal One said to Abram, "Go forth from your land and from your birthplace and from the house of your father to the land that I will show you. And I will make you to [into] a great nation and I will bless you..."

c. Exodus 6:27—They are the ones speaking to Pharoah the king of Egypt to bring out the Children of Israel from Egypt; it is Moses and Aaron.

d. *Shalom Rav*—Great peace upon Israel Your people may You place forever, for You are Sovereign Ruler for {of} all the peace. And good [it is] in Your eyes to bless Your people Israel and all the peoples at every time and in every hour with Your peace. Blessed are You, Eternal One, the One who blesses God's {his} people Israel with peace.

e. Psalm 148:1–5—Hallelujah {praise *Yah*}! Praise the Eternal One from the heavens; praise God {Him} in the heights.

Praise God {Him} all God's {His} angels; praise God {Him} all God's {His} array.

Praise God {Him} sun and moon; praise God {Him} all stars of light.

Praise God {Him} heavens of the heavens and the water that is from above the heavens.

Let them praise the name of the Eternal One for God {He} commanded and they were created.

EXTRA CREDIT

Reform Liturgical Changes in G'vurot

One of the Reading Practice selections at the beginning of this chapter is *G'vurot*. It is the second blessing of the *Amidah* (the "standing prayer," also known as the *T'fillah*, "the prayer"), the unit of blessings that forms the core of weekday, Shabbat, and holiday services. The theme of this prayer is God's might, demonstrated through compassionate and powerful life-sustaining acts. The core of this blessing is modeled after Psalm 146:7–8:

עֹשֶׂה מִשְׁפָּט לַעֲשׁוּקִים נֹתֵן לֶחֶם לָרְעֵבִים יְהֹוָה מַתִּיר אֲסוּרִים:

יְהֹוָה פֹּקֵחַ עִוְרִים יְהֹוָה זֹקֵף כְּפוּפִים יְהֹוָה אֹהֵב צַדִּיקִים:

[God] does justice for the oppressed, gives bread to the hungry, the Eternal One frees captives. The Eternal One opens eyes of the blind, the Eternal One lifts those bowed over, the Eternal One loves the righteous.

Another name traditionally given to this prayer is תְּחִיַּת הַמֵּתִים, "the resurrection of the dead," for a theme that recurs in the traditional wording of *G'vurot* is the giving of life to the dead. It is these passages that have been altered in the Reform and Reconstructionist versions of *G'vurot* (as noted earlier in this chapter.)

The belief that the dead will be physically resurrected was not always part of Jewish thought. The Bible generally treats death as a final state, though there are a few biblical passages that were later used to provide support for belief in bodily resurrection. During the Second Temple period, belief in bodily resurrection of the dead became a core doctrine of the Pharisees, the progenitors of Rabbinic Judaism. This belief was one of the subjects of dispute between the Pharisees and the opposing Jewish sect of the Sadducees. It is this dispute that underlies the following passage from *Mishnah Sanhedrin* 10:1:

כָּל יִשְׂרָאֵל יֵשׁ לָהֶם חֵלֶק לָעוֹלָם הַבָּא.... וְאֵלּוּ שֶׁאֵין לָהֶם חֵלֶק

לָעוֹלָם הַבָּא, הָאוֹמֵר אֵין תְּחִיַּת הַמֵּתִים מִן הַתּוֹרָה...

All Israel there is for them {they have} a share in the world to come.... But these are [the ones] that there is not for them {they do not have} a share in the world to come: the one who says "there is not the resurrection of the dead from the Torah" {the resurrection of the dead is not from the Torah} ...

Reform Judaism began in nineteenth-century Europe, not as a movement to create a new branch of Judaism, but to reform Jewish liturgy. The Reformers had several concerns, among them the language used for prayer, the length of the service, and the content of some prayers. *G'vurot* was one of the problematic prayers because of its references to the resurrection of the dead, a belief that was no longer shared by the nineteenth-century Reformers.

The various approaches taken with *G'vurot* are illustrative of the larger process of Jewish prayer book reform. One possible approach to problematic content is to retain the original Hebrew wording, but reinterpret the meaning of those words. Over the past 150 years, several such reinterpretations have been offered regarding the resurrection of (or giving of life to) the dead: that this refers to the more abstract notion of immortality of the soul; that it refers to the Divine power to give life to inert matter, demonstrated both in the creation of the universe itself and in the birth of each new creature; or that we have life after death through our children, our accomplishments, or those aspects of ourselves that are preserved here on earth after our departure. Some have also suggested a metaphoric understanding of the phrase מְחַיֵּה מֵתִים, "resurrecting the dead," as referring to the second chance at life granted us after periods of illness or defeat. In almost all Reform prayer books published in Europe in the late nineteenth and early twentieth century, this approach was followed, with the traditional Hebrew wording of *G'vurot* left unchanged, while the translation was altered to include no mention of the resurrection of the dead.

A different approach was taken in America, where the Reformers were much more assertive in their rejection of bodily resurrection. References to the resurrection of the dead were removed from the prayer book or reworded, as noted in this chapter's Prayer Book Translations (e.g., מְחַיֵּה הַכֹּל, "gives life to all," replaced מְחַיֵּה מֵתִים, "gives life to the dead"). The seventh principle in the Reform Movement's Pittsburgh Platform of 1885 includes the following statement: "We reject, as ideas not rooted in Judaism, the beliefs in both bodily resurrection and in Gehenna and Eden (Hell and Paradise) as abodes for everlasting punishment and reward." Later Reform statements of principle make no specific mention of the resurrection of the dead, but include references to some of the more abstract ways in which the notion of life after death has been understood:

Amid the mystery we call life, we affirm that human beings, created in God's image, share in God's eternality despite the mystery we call death."

THE SAN FRANCISCO PLATFORM—CENTENARY PERSPECTIVE OF 1976

We trust in our tradition's promise that, although God created us as finite beings, the spirit within us is eternal.

THE STATEMENT OF PRINCIPLES ADOPTED IN PITTSBURGH 1999

Translations of Hebrew Sentence Exercises

Chapter 1 • Exercise 2: a. Blessed are you. **b.** Blessed is he. *or* Blessed is it. **c.** Blessed is Israel. **d.** Blessed is the name. **e.** Blessed is the world. *or* Blessed is the universe. **f.** He is Israel. *or* It is Israel. **g.** You are Israel. **h.** You are blessed. **i.** It is the name. *or* It/He is *"HaShem"* (i.e., God). **j.** It is the universe. *or* It is the world. **k.** The universe is blessed forever and ever. *or* The world is blessed forever and ever. **l.** Blessed is the name forever and ever. *or* Blessed is *"HaShem"* (i.e., God) forever and ever.

Chapter 2 • Exercise 3: a. You eat. **b.** He eats. *or* It eats. **c.** The king (*or* sovereign *or* ruler) eats. **d.** We eat. **e.** We eat. **f.** The kings (*or* sovereigns *or* rulers) eat leavened food. **g.** The queens (*or* sovereigns *or* rulers) eat leavened food. **h.** You and Israel eat leavened food and unleavened bread (*or* matzah). **i.** We eat unleavened bread (*or* matzah) and bitter herb. **j.** Blessed is the night. **k.** Blessed is the king (*or* sovereign *or* ruler) forever and ever. **l.** We are the kings (*or* sovereigns *or* rulers) forever and ever.

Chapter 3 • Exercise 4: a. You create. **b.** He [God] creates day and night. **c.** The sovereign of the sovereigns creates. *or* The king of the kings creates. **d.** He [God] creates sky (*or* heavens) and earth (*or* land). **e.** You create fruit and bread. **f.** The son eats a fruit. **g.** The Children (*or* Sons) of Israel eat leavened food and unleavened bread (*or* matzah). **h.** We eat bread and bitter herb. ["We" here is a group of females.] **i.** The sovereign (*or* king) is a (*or* the) keeper (*or* guardian) of the Sabbath. **j.** We are keepers (*or* guardians) of Shabbat. **k.** Blessed is the keeper (*or* guardian) of the covenant forever and ever. **l.** We are keepers (*or* guardians) of commandments (*or* mitzvot) forever and ever.

Chapter 4 • Exercise 4: a. The sovereign (*or* king) reigns/is reigning/does reign (*or* rules/is ruling/does rule). **b.** We reign/are reigning/do reign (*or* rule, are ruling, do rule). **c.** The children (*or* sons) of the sovereigns (*or* kings) rule/are ruling/do rule (*or* reign/are reigning/do reign). **d.** God creates/is creating/does create truth and justice (*or* righteousness). *or* God is Creator of truth and justice (*or* righteousness). **e.** The God of Israel cre-ates/is creating/does create day and night. *or* The God of Israel is Creator of day and night. **f.** The God of Israel creates/is creating/does create the world (*or* universe). **g.** The God of Israel creates/is creating/does create the heavens (*or* sky) and the earth (*or* land). **h.** Moses chooses/is choosing/does choose a prophet. **i.** You choose/are choosing/do choose prophets. **j.** Moses chooses/is choosing/does choose [the] prophets of the truth and justice (*or* righteousness). **k.** The name of the prophet is Moses. **l.** The name of the people (*or* nation) is Israel. **m.** God gives/is giving/does give the Torah and the mitzvot (*or* commandments). **n.** Blessed is the giver of the Torah. *or* Blessed is the one who gives/is giving/does give the Torah. **o.** He (*or* It) is the giver of life. **p.** You keep/are keeping/do keep the Sabbath. **q.** The people (*or* nation) of Israel keep/are keeping/do keep mitzvot (*or* commandments). **r.** The people (*or* nation) of Israel keep/are keeping/do keep the covenant. **s.** We are guardians (*or* keepers) of the covenant for-ever and ever. **t.** We eat/are eating/do eat the bitter herb and the matzah (*or* unleavened bread). **u.** We eat/are eating/do eat fruit and bread.

Chapter 5 • Exercise 4: a. He remembers/is remem-bering/does remember the covenant. **b.** We remem-ber/are remembering/do remember the good days. **c.** Isaac and Rebekah remember/are remember-ing/do remember Sarah and Abraham. **d.** The great prophet remembers/is remembering/does remem-ber the commandments of the Torah. **e.** The peo-ple (*or* nation) of Israel chooses/is choosing/does choose a good king (*or* sovereign). **f.** Blessed is the helper of the people (*or* nation). **g.** Jacob chooses/is choosing/does choose the helpers of the people (*or* nation). **h.** Leah and Moses eat/are eating/do eat good bread and good fruit. **i.** The good mothers and the good fathers eat/are eating/do eat matzah (*or* unleavened bread), and the sons (*or* children) eat/are eating/do eat leavened food. **j.** We are good keepers of (*or* good guardians of) Shabbat. **k.** The great God creates/is creating/does create the world (*or* universe *or* eternity) day and night. **l.** God cre-ates/is creating/does create kindness and truth and justice (*or* righteousness).

Chapter 6 • Exercise 4: a. Your big son loves/does love Rebekah. **b.** Rachel loves/does love Moses. **c.** Leah and Sarah love/do love the guards (*or* keepers) of your house. **d.** The king (*or* sovereign) loves/does love the hearers/listeners of (*or* the ones who hear/listen to) the truth and speakers of (*or* the ones who speak) justice (*or* righteousness). **e.** We eat/are eating/do eat fruits and bread on the Sabbath. **f.** We remember/are remembering/do remember your ancestors (*or* fathers) the prophets. **g.** Abraham and Isaac remember/are remembering/do remember your covenant. **h.** Your God remembers/is remembering/does remember the kindnesses of your mothers. **i.** Blessed is the heart remembering (*or* the heart that remembers) the truth forever and ever. **j.** He chooses/is choosing/does choose speakers of justice (*or* righteousness). **k.** The messengers (*or* angels) of peace guard/are guarding/do guard your house on the Sabbath. **l.** He guards/is guarding/does guard the doorposts of the house in the day (*or* by day) and in the night (*or* by night). **m.** Your God creates/is creating/does create the Torah in the heavens and on the earth. **n.** Your souls (*or* minds *or* breaths) and your lives are in the hand of God. **o.** The hand of God is in the world in the heavens and on the earth. **p.** You are the helper of your people (*or* nation) and give/are giving/do give with your heart and your soul.

Chapter 7 • Exercise 3: a. There is no prophet like Moses. *or* There is not a prophet like Moses. **b.** There is no leavened food in our house. *or* There is not leavened food in our house. **c.** Who is the ruler/lord in our land? **d.** Who remembers/is remembering/does remember the house of your holiness {*i.e., your holy house*}? **e.** Who does/is doing kindness and justice/righteousness and good deeds/acts? **f.** We choose/are choosing/do choose you as our savior/deliverer. **g.** Our heart and our soul is in your hand. **h.** You love/do love Rebekah like/as your mother. **i.** We love/do love Moses like/as our father. **j.** We eat/are eating/do eat your bread and you eat/are eating/do eat our unleavened bread. **k.** God guards/is guarding/does guard *or* keeps/is keeping/does keep your lives. **l.** Our mother guards/is guarding/does guard *or* keeps/is keeping/does keep our lives. **m.** The name of our

father is Isaac and he remembers/is remembering/does remember the names of your sons. **n.** There are no guardians/keepers of your commandments and there is no/there is not truth and righteousness/justice. **o.** Blessed is the doer (*or* the one who does/is doing) a holy act/deed. **p.** Blessed is the Creator of our world/universe forever and ever.

Chapter 8 • Exercise 3: a. Isaac hears/is hearing/does hear *or* listens/is listening/does listen to the messengers of the king/sovereign. **b.** He hears/is hearing/does hear *or* listens/is listening/does listen to speakers of the truth. **c.** Abraham and Leah hear/are hearing/do hear *or* listen/are listening/do listen to us and we hear/are hearing/do hear *or* listen/are listening/do listen to you. **d.** Who is our savior/deliverer? There is no helper/one who helps *or* there is not a helper/one who helps for Israel. **e.** The candles and the bread help/are helping/do help the keepers/guardians of the Sabbath. **f.** Blessed is the God who is guarding/who is the guardian over our lives and over our souls. **g.** Blessed is [the] doer/the one who does the act/deed of Creation. **h.** We love all the children of our family. (This could also be translated, idiomatically, as: We love all the members of our family.) **i.** You and Rachel remember/are remembering/do remember the candles/lights/lamps of Chanukah that are in your house. **j.** Rebekah remembers/is remembering/does remember the good earth that you love/do love. **k.** We remember/are remembering/do remember your holy covenant in our heart[s]. **l.** Peace be upon you and upon your house. **m.** Our fathers/ancestors guard/are guarding/do guard over us forever and ever. **n.** There is no mezuzah/doorpost *or* There is not a mezuzah/doorpost in the house of holiness. **o.** The hand of God is in the world like the hand of a mother upon the children. **p.** Who is the nation/people that does/is doing kindness and justice/righteousness and good deeds/acts? **q.** (With) every day and (with) every night God creates/is creating/does create the heavens and the earth. **r.** The lord/ruler of the earth gives/is giving/does give to us fruit and bitter herbs. **s.** Moses the prophet gives/is giving/does give to us the Torah and the commandments of God.

Chapter 9 • Exercise 4: a. He hears/is hearing/does hear *or* listens/is listening/does listen to Jacob. He hears/is hearing/does hear *or* listens/is listening/does listen to him. Isaac hears/is hearing/does hear *or* listens/is listening/does listen to his mother. He hears/is hearing/does hear *or* listens/is listening/does listen to her. We hear/are hearing/do hear *or* listen/are listening/do listen to our mothers. **b.** The sovereign/king rules/is ruling/does rule over his people/nation. The sovereign/king rules/is ruling/does rule over it. The sovereign/king rules/is ruling/does rule over all the land. The sovereign/king rules/is ruling/does rule over it. **c.** He remembers/is remembering/does remember the covenant of the peoples/nations. He remembers/is remembering/does remember it day and night. Rachel remembers/is remembering/does remember him/it every day. The ruler remembers/is remembering/does remember the day of the Sabbath. The ruler remembers/is remembering/does remember it. **d.** The prophet eats/is eating/does eat on the way/in the path. He eats/is eating/does eat his bread and his fruit. All the prophets eat/are eating/do eat on the way/in the path. You eat/are eating/do eat your bread on the way/in the path. **e.** Who is the deliverer/savior for the sick? Who is the deliverer/savior for you and for your families? Who gives/is giving/does give healing to the land? Who gives/is giving/does give healing to all its/her families? There is no healer and there is no healing in our days. *or* There is not a healer and there is not healing in our days. **f.** He makes/is making/does make peace. He does/is doing good deeds. Sarah and Abraham do/are doing good deeds. Sarah and Leah do/are doing for you good deeds. Abraham does/is doing for her good deeds. **g.** He heals/is healing/does heal the sick. He heals/is healing/does heal the hearts of all the lovers/the ones who love. He heals/is healing/does heal your hearts. He heals/is healing/does heal her heart and her soul. **h.** Hallelujah!/Praise *Yah!* Blessed is the name of his/its holiness {his/its holy name} forever and ever. Blessed is he/it and blessed is his/its name. His compassion/mercy is on all his acts and his kindness is forever. Blessed is the world/universe/eternity and all that is in it. **i.** The compassion/mercy in the heart of the mother is upon all her children. Her compassion is upon her sick child/son. He helps/is helping/does help/is a helper to his sick mother. Rebekah helps/is helping/does help/is a helper to her sick children/sons. He helps/is helping/does help/is a helper to his big child/son (note: this could also mean *his oldest child/son*) whom he loves/does love with all his heart.

Chapter 10 • Exercise 5: a. The king/sovereign commands/is commanding/does command the servants/slaves/bondsmen. The king/sovereign commands/is commanding/does command his servants/slaves/bondsmen. He commands/is commanding/does command you. Many are the words that he commands/is commanding/does command you. Many are the commandments of the king/sovereign, and his servants/slaves/bondsmen do/are doing his commandments. **b.** We speak/are speaking/do speak from the heart. You speak/are speaking/do speak from your heart. We hear/are hearing/do hear *or* listen/are listening/do listen to your words. He hears/is hearing/does hear *or* listens/is listening/does listen to the words that we speak/are speaking/do speak from our heart. **c.** We bless/are blessing/do bless you from Zion. You bless/are blessing/do bless us from the house of your father. Sarah blesses/is blessing/does bless you from the house of her mother. We bless/are blessing/do bless your house and all that is in it. Blessed are you in your house and blessed is your family. **d.** The healer gives life/is giving life/does give life to sick ones/those who are sick. He gives life/is giving life/does give life to all the sick ones/those who are sick of the people/nation. The healer gives life/is giving life/does give life to our souls. He gives life/is giving life/does give life to you with kindness and with great compassion/mercy. Blessed is the great healing. **e.** We keep/are keeping/do keep the covenant of our God. We sanctify/are sanctifying/do sanctify the day of the Sabbath. We sanctify/are sanctifying/do sanctify it from [more than] all the days. Holy is it in Jerusalem and in all the world.

Glossary

father, ancestor m (Ch 5) — אָב, אָבוֹת

Abraham (Ch 5) — אַבְרָהָם

lord, ruler m (Ch 7) — אָדוֹן, אֲדוֹנִים

earth, ground, land f (Ch 8) — אֲדָמָה, אֲדָמוֹת

love (Ch 6) — א־ה־ב (אוֹהֵב)

there is/are not, there is/are none (Ch 7) — אֵין

eat, consume (Ch 2) — א־כ־ל (אוֹכֵל)

God m (Ch 5) — אֵל

God m (Ch 4) — אֱלֹהִים

mother f (Ch 5) — אֵם, אִמּוֹת, אִמָּהוֹת

firmness, support, faithfulness, trust (Ch 10) — א־מ־ן

truth f (Ch 4) — אֱמֶת, אֲמִתּוֹת

we (Ch 2) — אֲנַחְנוּ, אָנוּ

earth, land f (Ch 3) — אֶרֶץ, אֲרָצוֹת

who, that, which (Ch 8) — אֲשֶׁר

definite direct object marker (untranslatable) (Ch 4) — אֵת

you m sg (Ch 1) — אַתָּה

ב

with, in (attached preposition) (Ch 6) — בְּ־, בַּ־

choose, select (Ch 4) — ב־ח־ר (בּוֹחֵר)

house m (Ch 6) — בַּיִת, בָּתִּים

son, child m (Ch 3) — בֵּן, בָּנִים

create (Ch 3) — ב־ר־א (בּוֹרֵא)

Creation, in the beginning (Ch 8) — בְּרֵאשִׁית

bless (Ch 1) — ב־ר־ך (מְבָרֵךְ)

blessed (Ch 1) — בָּרוּךְ, בְּרוּכָה, בְּרוּכִים, בְּרוּכוֹת

covenant f (Ch 3) — בְּרִית, בְּרִיתוֹת

ג

mighty, valiant, courageous adj (Ch 10) — גִּבּוֹר, גִּבּוֹרָה, גִּבּוֹרִים, גִּבּוֹרוֹת

strength, valor, might f (Ch 10) — גְּבוּרָה, גְּבוּרוֹת

big, great adj (Ch 5) — גָּדוֹל, גְּדוֹלָה, גְּדוֹלִים, גְּדוֹלוֹת

nation, people m (Ch 8) — גּוֹי, גּוֹיִים

ד

speak, talk (Ch 6) — ד־ב־ר (מְדַבֵּר)

word, speech m (Ch 10) — דָּבָר, דְּבָרִים

way, road, path m and f (Ch 9) — דֶּרֶךְ, דְּרָכִים

ה

the (attached prefix) (Ch 1) — הַ־, הָ־, הֶ־

her, it (attached ending) f sg (Ch 9) — ־הָ

her, its, it (attached ending) f sg (Ch 9) — ־ָה

him, it (attached ending) m sg (Ch 9) — ־הוּ

he, it m (Ch 1) — הוּא

praise (Ch 9) — ה־ל־ל (מְהַלֵּל)

hallelujah, praise Yah! (Ch 9) — הַלְלוּיָה

ו

and (attached prefix) (Ch 2) — וְ־, וּ־, וַ־, וָ־, וֶ־, וִ־

his, him, its, it (attached ending) m sg (Ch 9) — ־וֹ